MICHAEL OAKESHOTT'S SKEPTICISM

PRINCETON MONOGRAPHS
IN PHILOSOPHY

Harry G. Frankfurt, Editor

--------------------•ꟼMP•--------------------

The Princeton Monographs in Philosophy series offers short historical and systematic studies on a wide variety of philosophical topics.

Justice Is Conflict by Stuart Hampshire

Liberty Worth the Name: Locke on Free Agency by Gideon Yaffe

Self-Deception Unmasked by Alfred R. Mele

Public Goods, Private Goods by Raymond Geuss

Welfare and Rational Care by Stephen Darwall

A Defense of Hume on Miracles by Robert J. Fogelin

Kierkegaard's Concept of Despair by Michael Theunissen

Physicalism, or Something Near Enough by Jaegwon Kim

Philosophical Myths of the Fall by Stephen Mulhall

Fixing Frege by John P. Burgess

Kant and Skepticism by Michael N. Forster

Thinking of Others: On the Talent for Metaphor by Ted Cohen

The Apologetics of Evil: The Case of Iago by Richard Raatzsch

Social Conventions: From Language to Law by Andrei Marmor

Taking Wittgenstein at His Word: A Textual Study
by Robert J. Fogelin

The Pathologies of Individual Freedom: Hegel's Social Theory
by Axel Honneth

Michael Oakeshott's Skepticism by Aryeh Botwinick

MICHAEL OAKESHOTT'S SKEPTICISM

Aryeh Botwinick

PRINCETON UNIVERSITY PRESS

PRINCETON AND OXFORD

Copyright © 2011 by Princeton University Press

Published by Princeton University Press,
41 William Street, Princeton, New Jersey 08540

In the United Kingdom: Princeton University Press,
6 Oxford Street, Woodstock, Oxfordshire OX20 1TW

press.princeton.edu

Library of Congress Cataloging-in-Publication Data

Botwinick, Aryeh.
Michael Oakeshott's skepticism / Aryeh Botwinick.
p.   cm. — (Princeton monographs in philosophy)
Includes bibliographical references (p.   ) and index.
ISBN 978-0-691-14717-8 (cloth : alk. paper)
1. Oakeshott, Michael, 1901–1990. 2. Skepticism. I. Title.
B1649.O344B68 2011
192—dc22   2010028375

British Library Cataloging-in-Publication Data is available

This book has been composed in Janson

Printed on acid-free paper. ∞

Printed in the United States of America

1 3 5 7 9 10 8 6 4 2

לזכר נשמת אחותי
האשה הצדקנית
לאה בת הרב אברהם ישעיה׳
זכרונה לברכה
תהי נשמתה צרורה בצרור החיים

A TRUE SKEPTIC WILL BE DIFFIDENT OF HIS PHILOSOPHICAL
DOUBTS, AS WELL AS OF HIS PHILOSOPHICAL CONVICTION;
AND WILL NEVER REFUSE ANY INNOCENT SATISFACTION,
WHICH OFFERS ITSELF, UPON ACCOUNT OF EITHER OF THEM.
——DAVID HUME

Contents

Preface and Acknowledgments

My book constitutes an exploration of the metaphysical-epistemological underside of Michael Oakeshott's skepticism—and it applies its reading of that to all areas of Oakeshott's philosophy. On the surface, it would appear that skepticism is an extremely vulnerable position to sustain. The tenets of skepticism seem so sweeping and inclusive that they engulf skepticism itself—and render it unstatable as a philosophical position. Yet, Oakeshott seems able to mount skepticism as a critique and as a delineator of the path to follow after the critique has been tendered in one area of philosophy after another, without succumbing to the corrosive, self-destructive dynamic of skeptical argument. My book raises the central question: By what strategy—or set of strategies—is he able to do so? What are some of the deep structural features of Oakeshott's many arguments that enable him to keep skepticism afloat?

Another major and surprising feature of Oakeshott's career is the extent to which he remains hospitable to and supportive of religious ideas and practices from its earliest phases until its end. The skeptic, of course, is most often viewed as the arch antagonist of religion. In the course of doing my explorations of Oakeshott's work, I discovered that the most incisive strategies for dealing with both sets of perplexities were mutually implicative: Oakeshott configured religion in such a way as to make it utterly philosophy-friendly—and he theorized skepticism in such a manner that religious categories became integral to comprehending how skepticism works.

My largest debt in the writing of this book is to Oakeshott himself, with whom I studied in my first year as a graduate student in the mid-1960s as a Fulbright Scholar at the London School of Economics. During that year, Oakeshott opened vistas for me concerning rationality and its limits (and how to rationally assess and delineate the nature of those limits) that I have been pursuing until the present day.

Robert Grant (Oakeshott's biographer) has generously shared with me in a number of e-mails his tremendous knowledge of Oakeshott's life and work by clueing me in to the ways in which Oakeshott's "Continental education" in Germany in the early to mid-1920s might have contributed toward shaping and/or reinforcing the larger tendencies and direction of his work. Leslie Marsh has been, since our meeting at the first Oakeshott Conference in 2001, a fruitful conversation partner on Oakeshott.

I have also been the beneficiary of Temple University Summer Fellowships for 2001, 2003, 2004, 2007, 2008, and 2009, which have afforded me the leisure to develop my argument about Oakeshott. I have had during this same period a number of graduate student research assistants who have contributed valuably toward the project: Cathy Bartch, Michael Cesal, John Hykel, and Justin Murphy. I am indebted to Michael Cesal for working up the index. In addition, in this computer age, the computer consultants at Temple's Instructional Support Center have been extremely helpful to me in responding to all of my computer queries and perplexities: Johanna Inman, Rick Moffat, Mike Stabinski, Sean Ta, and their outstanding manager, Peter Hanley. I also wish to thank Wilson Ayerro for serving as an informal computer consultant to me in the early stages of the preparation of this manuscript.

I owe a special debt of gratitude to Professor Harry Frankfurt and to Ian Malcolm of Princeton University Press, whose support, steadfastness, and commitment sustained me throughout the project. I also wish to thank Jill Harris and Anita O'Brien, my production and copy editors, respectively, at Princeton, for their expert assistance in helping me see this manuscript through the production process.

My wife, Sara, was a constant conversation partner with whom I discussed many of the ideas pertaining to the project.

Finally, this book is fittingly dedicated to the memory of my sister, Leah, who died two years ago. Leah was an extraordinarily generous and thoughtful person. During my "Oakeshott year" in London, Leah came to visit me for an extended stay and joined me in sitting in and taking notes on Oakeshott's regular undergraduate lectures in the history of political thought. The special character of that year was reinforced for me by Leah's presence.

MICHAEL OAKESHOTT'S SKEPTICISM

·ҶMP·

I

Introduction: Epistemological Backdrop

MICHAEL OAKESHOTT'S MOST CONSISTENT self-description was that he was a skeptic. Skepticism represents from earliest times the counterassertiveness of human reason against the "givenness" of the world. In response to the age-old question as to why there is something rather than nothing, the skeptic has the audacity to say that there is indeed nothing (nothing irrevocably fixed) about the furniture of the human world or the equipment of the human psyche. The skeptic highlights the role of conceptualization and categorization in yielding the world that we then take for granted. How we linguistically frame a slice of experience is never totally determined by the experience itself. The epistemological slack that accrues from linguistic-symbolic engagements of the world staves off the prospect of certainty indefinitely. The position that I have just described is often called "skeptical idealism" and consigned to the level of the precious and the esoteric because of its patently antirealist bias. Oakeshott was unique in the way that the skeptical idealism of the early part of his career got transmuted into a widespread cultural norm in the form of postmodernism by the later stages of his career. It is even possible to make the case that he was one of the motive forces contributing toward this transformation.

The epochal location at which Oakeshott is situated in the history of skepticism affords us a unique opportunity for reassessing the larger metaphysical import and background postulates of skepticism. What the theoretical trajectory of Oakeshott's career dramatizes for us are the inextricable theoretical fortunes of religious belief and skepticism. There is a very pronounced religious impulse animating skepticism. A world comprehended from start to finish from the perspective of a lack of finality of judgment is a world that negatively recaptures the prospect of wholeness: none of our intellectual schemata have an unreserved claim to truth. The truth (if it exists) is beyond us and elsewhere. The skeptic restores to God the conceptually empty universe that He bequeathed to us at the moment of Creation—indirectly reaffirming by his critical renunciations the space that God occupies.

This book is devoted to making the case that on grounds of reasoned argument skepticism issues forth in mysticism. The skeptic is driven to question everything—except his own deployment of skepticism. To be consistent, he needs to turn the critical engine of skepticism inward in relation to the tenets of skepticism themselves. However, to preserve protocols of consistency, he cannot merely dilute skepticism to the level of a generalized agnosticism—so that what results is a tepid, irresolute maintenance of both skepticism and its critical targets. To be consistently applied, the skeptical questioning of skepticism must encompass a thick, full-blooded rehabilitation of all of the objects of skeptical attack. The theoretical mandate of skepticism extends to making the "yes" of skepticism as resoundingly rich as its "no." Whatever objects are devastated by skepticism need, according to the internal logic of skepticism itself, to be thoroughly rehabilitated by it. This interminable oscillation between rejection and affirmation yields a mystically saturated world where all of the defining markers of human existence simultaneously are and are not. Under the prism of skepticism, the completely familiar world is exposed as a tissue of defamiliarized possibilities—permanently coexisting with and reconfiguring what on one level we believe we are encountering on a regular basis. In the skeptical-mystical universe of our daily habitation, suspended animation becomes a precondition for a recognizable human universe.

The conjunction—or, better still, the confluence—of skepticism and mysticism works to clarify the meaning and status of belief in God as well. The God of all three sets of monotheistic scriptures needs to be conceived as being Absolutely One—utterly transcendent—completely beyond human projection and imagining. If He bore any literal resemblance to things human—if His attributes overlapped with ours in any way—then God would have been situated in a comparative framework with ourselves, and no matter how superlatively superior He was to us in the display of those attributes, His radical and unique Oneness would have been tarnished and undermined. The way to remain faithful to the postulational requirement of God's Unqualified Oneness is to posit Him as subsisting in an infinite dimension, so that all of our descriptions of Him remain irreducibly metaphoric. However, it is precisely at this point that a parallel contradiction and paradox that we noticed emerging with regard to skepticism resurfaces in relation to the biblical teaching concerning God. If God as a matter of definitional and conceptual necessity must be postulated as "occupying" an infinite dimension, then to know that the traditional epithets of monotheistic religion—such as "omnipotent," "omniscient," and "all-merciful"—cannot be applied to Him in a literal sense is already to have pierced through the impassable barrier to infinity in order to know which descriptions need to be ruled out. From a somewhat different angle of vision, we can say that if biblical religion affords us a notion of God only for the sake of parsing away the literal descriptions that religious texts and our own imaginations project unto Him, then in what sense can we be said to be working with an intelligible and sustainable notion of God? If God is only there to be perpetually deliteralized, how can we understand ourselves to be relating to—and speaking about—God at all? Where—and who—is the subject concerning whom these acts of deliteralization occur?

Our logical predicament with regard to God nudges us into a pattern of response that is similar to the one we mobilized in relation to the perplexities surrounding skepticism. The infinity of God debars us from saying both that He is and that He is not—and from coherently assessing how our human vocabularies might impinge upon and reflect His being. The community of believers is forever oscillating between statements and descriptions of Him—and a neutralization and cancellation of those statements and descriptions as being inadequate to or contradictory of the task of reporting who and what He is. Our relationship to God in biblical religion—just as our relationship to the everyday world and to specialized worlds such as science and history invented by human beings over the course of the generations, when viewed from the perspective of skepticism— remains irredeemably, unremittingly mystical. We simultaneously inhabit a "yes" and a "no" without the possibility of permanent release from the one type of response into the other.

Oakeshott was absorbed with questions of religion from his early writings in the 1920s to his later writings in the

1970s. He was also preeminently a philosophical skeptic who analyzed all issues in the domains of practice, morality, politics, science, history, and philosophy from the perspective of skepticism. In this book I endeavor to read his philosophy of religion in the light of his skepticism—and his skepticism in the light of his philosophy of religion, by way of tracing mutual patterns of infiltration and unity that have heretofore not been sufficiently appreciated. To take Oakeshott seriously would involve a dramatic recasting of the traditional ways in which we perceive and practice both philosophy and religion.

Since his death in 1990, there has been a tremendous growth of scholarly interest in and study of Oakeshott's work—and also a more widespread cultural appropriation of him as both an eloquent advocate of political conservatism and a theoretical architect of antifoundationalist, postmodernist sensibility. In order to arrive at a proper historical reconstruction of Oakeshott's antifoundationalism, a number of scholars (following what looks like Oakeshott's own cue) take a historical loop through Hegel and F. H. Bradley.[1] The following sentence and its paraphrases run like an intellectual historical leitmotif throughout a recent book on Oakeshott: "Oakeshott takes Bradley's notion of the 'Absolute' as experience, combines it to Hegel's conception of the 'Absolute' as the totality of thought, and thereby implodes the 'Absolute' into experience itself. This focuses attention upon the modes of thought."[2] While it is true that Oakeshott delved deeply into the thought of Hegel and Bradley and was strongly influenced by them, I think we can say based upon his own theorizing of skepticism and its metaphysical and political import that he did not require more than Plato in order to arrive at what nowadays is usually regarded as an antifoundational position. Even his readings of Hegel and Bradley seem to be cast in a mold that had already been set in the light of his reception of Plato.

In an essay dating from 1948 that has been posthumously published—"The Voice of Conversation in the Education of Mankind"—Oakeshott says that "It was the genius of Plato that first perceived that philosophy is, or should be, conversation, and rescued it for a brief moment from dogmatism."[3] According to Oakeshott, Plato conceived of philosophy as a dialectical discussion rather than an eristic one. In an eristic discussion, the participants view each other as opponents. A person can prevail only at the expense of discrediting or dislodging his or her neighbor. In a dialectical discussion, by contrast, "the impetus of discussion is spent . . . when all simultaneously discover that each has been right all the time."[4] What I think Oakeshott means by imputing to Plato the discovery of dialectical discussion—conversation—in this sense is that the participants in a Platonic dialogue are imbued with (or come to develop) the understanding that the phenomena they are concerned to explore and elucidate are susceptible of multiple, and even contradictory, conceptual encasements. It is the formal skepticism that they share by participating in a conversational form of interaction that enables them to think "that each has been right all the time," even as their substantive understandings of things deeply differ.

From the perspective of this reading of Plato's concept of dialectical discussion or conversation, we can appreciate how one of the most central and enduring substantive components of Plato's thought—his Theory of Ideas—can be seen as a discursive translation of what is already insinuated by Plato's choice of the dialogue-form itself in which to communicate his philosophical teaching. On a straightforward literal level, Plato's Theory of Ideas relegates the facts of the material world to an inferior ontological status, regarding them as mere copies of eternal Forms. However, this formulation can be construed as a metaphoric and picturesque way of stating that so-called facts are theory-dependent, that the world of theory is underdetermined by the universe of fact. When we read Plato's Theory of Ideas in conjunction with his notion of "degrees of reality" (that the Ideas are more "real" than their material embodiments), we can see the two together as compressed, metaphoric statements of the tenets of skeptical idealism. Reading Oakeshott's reading notes on Plato in his Nachlass at the London School of Economics together with his essay on "The Voice of Conversation in the Education of Mankind" reinforces the sense that those scholars who assign equal weight to Hegel and Bradley alongside Plato in helping to shape Oakeshott's philosophical outlook (while it superficially follows Oakeshott's plot line of his own development) are providing us with secondary intellectual history rather than a full-scale reengagement of the steps through which Oakeshott arrived at his own philosophical position. For a reader as theoretically sensitive and nuanced as Oakeshott, all you need in order to have the epistemology of *Experience and Its Modes* and *On Human Conduct* is Plato.

There is a profound connection between Plato's Theory of Ideas and his theory of tacit knowledge (both of which have their counterparts in Oakeshott), which helps to fix for us the most revealing way to make sense of his thought. The underdetermination of theory by fact suggests that diverse—and even contradictory—theoretical formulations can with equal cogency describe and refer to the "same unit(s) of fact." The Theory of Ideas construed in this manner by endlessly staving off contact with an independent universe of facts supports the notion of what we might call "the mysticism of everyday life." The everyday world is not populated by hard, objectively given entities, but by entities conceived as a tissue of possibilities that as a result of certain historical and cultural turns that sometimes endure for very long stretches of time are imputed to have the identities that we consider them to have. Everyday life is therefore lived at one overwhelming, unbridgeable remove from itself. We act as if all of the appurtenances of daily living (all of the objects of our daily interaction) are ready at hand and have known, fixed, and enduring identities. From the perspective of "underdetermination," however, the possibilities are primary, and the conceptual congealments (no matter how lengthy their duration) are contingent.

The unimaginable distance separating God from the world that monotheistic religion posits is traceable within the world itself between each individual human being and all other human beings, and what each one of us conceives to be the furniture of his/her world. The aura of persisting possibility hovers over every move that we take to increase our sense of mastery and at-homeness in the world. Whatever we do to confirm and solidify our sense of reality about the world is unmasked from the perspective of "underdetermination" as further distancing and dislocating it.

The only kind of knowledge that we can have in a mystical universe in which underdetermination prevails is tacit knowledge. According to Plato, it is only by postulating that knowledge (at least of the sort that is useful and is required or searched after by human beings) can proceed in a tacit, unconscious way that we are able to theoretically reconstruct how an infinite regress of interpretation of words can be sealed off and a translation between theory and practice can take place. Since, from the perspective of underdetermination, we can never arrive at a pure, uncontestable, unequivocal determination of what the "things" of the world are, we can only hope to figure out the meanings and references of strings of words by engaging in translations and paraphrases of the original set of words with which we are confronted. Similarly, since the projection of a scene or domain of practice by any theoretical text cannot be shown to intrinsically match what is being suggested by the text (more than one [and sometimes conflicting] theoretical texts can match what is being evoked by any particular scene or domain of practice), we must posit that the gulf or transition between theory and practice is being negotiated in tacit, unconscious ways. On an explicit level in both cases—the interpretation of texts; the movement from theory to practice—Plato argues that we would confront an infinite regress (the sentences doing the interpreting and translating would be as systematically ambiguous as the original set of sentences they were designed to make sense of, given the absence of a fixed and neutral object that the sentences ostensibly relate to) unless we embraced the notion of tacit knowledge. Thus, for Plato (and for anyone sharing a Platonic metaphysics), there is conceptual interdependence between his Theory of Ideas yielding a mystical grasp of ordinary life and his conception of tacit knowledge.[5]

Plato's arguments for postulating the notion of tacit knowledge engender paradoxes of their own that lead to an expanded pedigree for the idea of "the mysticism of everyday life." The infinite regress of interpretation to which theorizing the formation of knowledge and the possibility of communication as subsisting on a purely explicit plane gives rise can be problematically sealed off only by acknowledging or positing the tacit character of knowledge. The tacit medium for processing and building up knowledge comes into being only by being verbally identified through a series of verbally achieved displacements of what might otherwise appear as the explicit components of knowledge. The tacit in multiple ways becomes a function of the verbal. The verbal medium creates space for the tacit—classifies it—and registers its ongoing, heterogeneous impact on the verbal. In addition, the category of the tacit is parasitic upon the contrasting category of the explicit. All of the ways in which we invoke a tacit medium for knowledge presuppose the coexistence of an explicit one. It almost appears as if the tacit were one further specification of the explicit—some phase or moment that explicit knowledge requires in order to be rendered more perspicuous. How can we coherently envision the tacit medium of knowledge as an autonomous overarching category?

It is at this juncture that mysticism comes into play. The tacit, according to Plato, needs to be viewed as a mystical infusion into—or overlay of—the ordinary. It constitutes the pregnant, "vibrating" silence that surrounds discourse and enables discourse to function. The ordinary sense-encounters and acts of verbalization of everyday life are the result of an illusion. It is the accompanying, pulsating presence of the extraordinary (the mystical) that enables the ordinary to happen. Every moment, event, and act of verbalization of everyday life is nudged into existence by what transcends words and rational, logical plotting. The mystical is just the impenetrable obverse side of the real and the everyday. Without the mystical, we would not have our intimate, familiar world(s).

Oakeshott's subscribing to the notion of tacit knowledge in so many different but still overlapping ways—his theorizing of the formation and dynamics of tradition; his political preference for liberalism, the subordination of the more formal and explicit public sphere to the more informal, anonymous, and tacit private sphere; his assigning priority to a morality of habit and custom over a morality grounded in rule selection and compliance—in their own right already bespeak his commitment to the notion of the mysticism of everyday life. These factors are independent of but reinforce the other ways in which Oakeshott's philosophy of religion and his skeptical metaphysics and epistemology open up onto the notion of the mysticism of everyday life.

Some scholars are uncomfortable with and wish "to challenge the 'political' reading of Oakeshott's work and in particular the new orthodoxy (coming largely from North America) that takes the defining characteristic of Oakeshott's work as his liberalism."[6] To get Oakeshott most sharply into focus, I think we need to say that he is a philosophical radical. He is also a practical, ideological conservative and a political philosophical liberal. In his classic depiction of Hobbes in his 1946 introduction to *Leviathan*, Oakeshott becomes one of the major twentieth-century architects of the category of "political philosophical liberal."[7] A political philosophical liberal is someone who calls into question the claims to authority and knowledge advanced by devotees of both Revelation and Reason. After the manner of Hobbes, the political philosophical liberal affirms an unbridgeable conceptual distance between man and God and an equally nonnegotiable distance between the premises of an argument and the background, supporting argumentation needed to vindicate them. With none of our judgments in any sphere of human discourse or experience (from religion to politics to everyday life) conclusively underwritten by sources external to themselves (the Hobbesian sovereign is only a formal

reconstruction of how we bring theoretically limitless con-
testation to an end), the stage is set for acknowledging the
primacy of the values of human freedom and individuality.

There is no logical bridge that links Hobbesian skepticism to the establishment of a state in which freedom and
the pursuit of individuality prevail. The skepticism, in order
to be sustained, has to be mapped in such a way that it incorporates a reflexive gesture that includes skepticism within
its own ambit of skeptical interrogation. This suggests that
there are only rhetorical analogues and affinities (and not
tight logical relations) between philosophical arguments
concerning the limits of reason and theoretical projections
concerning the ideally constituted state. The political philosophical liberal is launched on his or her career in a burst
of recognition of how, in different but related ways, both
the operations and conclusions of human reason and the
most defensible vision of the political state lack foundations.
From this perspective, Oakeshott, following in the footsteps
of the Hobbes he has helped to define for us, was a political
philosophical liberal. To resist this characterization is to be
unfaithful to both Oakeshott's philosophy and his political
theory.

Oakeshott's privileging of practice that some scholars
believe is not adequately accounted for in his canon of writings[8] also has philosophical roots. Without Oakeshott ever
stating this openly, philosophy's continual exposing of the
limited, conditional claims to knowledge of all organized
perspectives on human experience and "reality" (the different "modes" and "voices" in the Oakeshottian philosophical
lexicon) suggests that theorizing itself on one level of analysis constitutes a form of doing, an engagement in a certain
sort of practice. The promise and allure of philosophy is the
possibility of attaining rational consummation—achieving a

total overlap between human thought and whatever stimulates and instigates it into operation. However, what is dramatically evident in Oakeshott in all phases of his career is that the search for unconditionality, which is the hallmark of philosophical reason, can only be manifested negatively in the highlighting of the elisions and gaps that the proponents of different disciplinary approaches to human experience harbor. For Oakeshott, the asymmetry between negative critique and positive restatement (the nontranslatability of the first mode into the second) remains insurmountable. Since philosophy subsists enduringly on the plane of negative critique that over the millennia has not been transcended or transformed, it implicitly has for Oakeshott the character of a form of practice—a type of doing. This for Oakeshott constitutes part of the tacit knowledge of the philosophical endeavor from its origins in Plato. To state this openly would be giving the upper hand again to theory—so that the content of the statement would be in irreconcilable tension with its form. Part of the reason why Oakeshott in his writings assigns centrality to tacit knowledge is that it enables the coherence of his own theorizing to emerge into bolder relief.

What I have just said also helps us make sense of another feature of Oakeshott's thought that has perplexed readers—namely, the fluidity and movement between the different modes of experience that Oakeshott practices and, as his career progresses, increasingly even preaches.[9] What is disconcerting and embarrassing for some of Oakeshott's critics is how philosophical reason theorizes and delineates autonomous regions of human experience such as history, science, and practice, only to have their boundaries continually transgressed not only by Oakeshott himself, in his dual roles of political theorist and historian of political thought,

but by the rest of us as well, in our regular shifting of perspectives in the ways that we approach politics. Given what I
have just said about theorizing being a form of practice, then
the lack of airtight boundaries between the modes and the
constant movement to and fro between them become more
intelligible. The restoration of ontological parity between
theorizing and the objects of theorizing legitimates constant
crisscrossing between these perspectival boundaries.

Some readers have also been disturbed by what they consider to be the insulated and self-referential character of
Oakeshott's writing.[10] Oakeshott always seems to be writing
in relation to himself—with scant reference to the secondary literature surrounding the texts and issues he is writing about, and with abundant allusions to the premises and
points of departure that are found in his own arguments. A
kind of paradox emerges that Oakeshott seems to rely on
closure in order to advance his arguments in favor of liberal
and philosophical openness.

It seems to me that the best way to make sense of this
feature of Oakeshott's writing is to see it as profoundly
implicated in key elements of his philosophy. If the search
for foundational premises in any sphere of human discourse—any region of human experience—only makes us
more thoroughly aware of the partiality and incompleteness
of our starting points (as Oakeshott argues in *Experience and
Its Modes*), then all local arguments that both philosophers
and people situated in everyday contexts make are (despite
the best efforts that the exemplars of these roles make) con-
demned to be circular in character. All of us navigating in
whatever mode (or hybrid mode) of experience we happen to
be immersed in can only proceed to converse by (artificially)
privileging certain premises and moving ahead accordingly.

In argument as well as in conversation (and this is what makes argument like conversation), we are always moving within the charmed circles of our own creation and affirmation.[11] In writing in the manner that irks some readers, Oakeshott is merely dramatizing limits that are enshrined in his philosophy.

One might parenthetically add that Oakeshott's preference for the essay form also results from the same source. The essay, unlike the more fully elaborated and systematically structured treatise, represents on a formal literary level the closest analogue to conversation in the domain of the spoken word. If the counterpart to the treatise is a speech that is fully anchored in some preset beginning and proceeds through measured stages of argument to the conclusions it seeks to endorse and recommend, the literary equivalent to conversation is the essay, which is much more fragmentary in character and less able to camouflage the arbitrariness of its starting point(s) and its subsequent unfolding patterns of argument than the treatise or the speech. Conversation and the essay form embody circularity in a much more open and direct way than the treatise or the speech—and this helps to account for the preferred status that these genres enjoy in Oakeshott's literary production.

Conservative commentators and others have pointed to a moral factor that animates Oakeshott's work that renders it superior to the writings of other philosophers who have contributed importantly toward shaping the philosophical discourse of late modernity.[12] In his theorizing of morality, Oakeshott expresses a clear preference for a morality grounded in custom, habit, and tradition over a morality consisting in compliance with a set of self-consciously selected and affirmed rules. Oakeshott's assigning of priority to customary and traditional morality over rule-based morality is most cogently seen as a direct outgrowth of his philosophical position. Given Oakeshott's skepticism as I have sketched it so far, all systems of thought and the patterns of behavior that they spawn and legitimate have to be viewed as acquiring in the course of time the ontological status of "traditions." Premises in whatever field of human discourse we are considering cannot be authoritatively, non-controversially grounded. The extent to which they become epistemologically and socially salient is largely a function of the inferences and structures of argument they generate, which both buttress and help define perspectives and ways of life that through their very appropriation and integration by human beings become binding upon us.

Explicitly according to the later Oakeshott of "The Voice of Poetry in the Conversation of Mankind" and more implicitly possibly even according to the earlier Oakeshott of *Experience and Its Modes,* the picture does not change even with regard to philosophy. For Oakeshott, philosophizing itself needs to be conceived as constituting (or as devolving into) a series of traditions. How one thinks—how one mentally organizes experience—on the basis of premises that can never be categorized as more than insecure is a function of how a community of thinkers in the course of working out the implications and interconnections of those premises grow accustomed to defining their intellectual horizons in terms of them and thereby in this sense rendering them binding upon themselves.

A critique that has been leveled against Oakeshott is that his philosophizing in general and his political theorizing in particular are so radically individualistic that they leave little room for social, communitarian factors in accounting for the formation and buildup of knowledge claims and the crystallization of value in diverse spheres of human experience.[13] We now have a theoretical corrective to this reading. Oakeshott's thoroughgoing skepticism, which both explicitly and implicitly points to the role of tradition in helping to make sense of how philosophical justification proceeds, becomes the tacit bridge notion that facilitates the recognition and acknowledgment of the role of communitarian factors in the articulation of knowledge and value.

It is very important to recognize that the skeptical idealism that Oakeshott theorizes opens up on both a conservative politics whose watchword is "tradition" and a radical politics governed by the insight that the relationship between human conceptualization and human experience remains enduringly contingent. A leading contemporary political theorist who has capitalized on the radical intimations implicit in Oakeshott's thought is Ernesto Laclau, with his discourse analysis. "Radical democracy would recognize the full play of difference and the constructed character of society."[14] Directly indebted to Wittgenstein and to Derrida for their notions of language-games and difference respectively, Laclau is also indirectly building upon Oakeshott who creates the metaphysical space wherein the notions of "language-games" and "difference" loom as cogent and persuasive. If words are underdetermined by things, then normativity in linguistic usage does not derive from a comparison with the structure and content of things but from patterns of linguistic usage in different regions of discourse that have become entrenched in society (Wittgenstein). By the same token—carrying the Oakeshottian logic one step further— in order to sustain the constructed, contingent character of the worlds that we inhabit, we need to guard against reifying and fetishizing words and thereby transforming them into a surrogate universe of things. We have to make ourselves aware of how the reality conjured up by words will undergo continuing modification in relation to the sets of words that on an ongoing basis we contrast them with. From Laclau's perspective, the Oakeshottian-Wittgensteinian-Derridaean conceptual infrastructure enables us to appreciate how society is constituted as a coexisting series of always precarious "hegemonic articulations," which alerts us to the unceasing relevance and urgency (if we are so inclined) of further pushes toward equality and democracy.

Stuart Isaacs strangely criticizes Laclau from what he takes to be an Oakeshottian perspective for pursuing another version of "rationalism in politics" by cultivating Oakeshottian premises for purposes of promoting political radicalism.[15] To the extent that Oakeshott falls prey to the illusion (which is an open question) that there is a smooth logical circuit that connects his skeptical epistemological and metaphysical premises with his political conservatism, then one could say that Oakeshott, too, falls prey to the snares of rationalism in politics. However, if Oakeshott can be gotten off the hook on this issue, so can Laclau. I am arguing that the way to relieve Oakeshott of this charge is to read him as making a philosophical argument about the limits of reason and the limits of language and then metaphorically extrapolating and projecting a series of analogies and correspondences from it that support political conservatism. One can exonerate Laclau from the charge of rationalism in the same way. The analogies and correspondences that he synthesizes from skepticism are geared to buttressing political radicalism. Part of the glory of Oakeshott as a political philosopher is that in conceiving of philosophy in such a way that philosophy can speak in multiple, contradictory voices to politics, he has in effect dramatized for us that philosophy does not speak to politics at all. On a substantive level—concerning what sort of state to establish, with what constellation of values—philosophy has nothing concrete and decisive to say to politics. In one fell swoop, our responsibility for the political realm that we collectively ordain and nurture (however actively or passively) becomes either nonexistent or infinite.[16]

A number of writers have noted affinities between Oakeshott's and Wittgenstein's thought.[17] One commentator, for example, says that for both Oakeshott and Wittgenstein, "Philosophy describes what we already know and leaves everything as it is."[18] While this is undoubtedly true, I would like to consider how the deep philosophical structure of Wittgenstein's thought might be seen to resonate with that of Oakeshott's thought. To try and show this, I shall outline Oakeshott's thought from its initial premises upward, showing how a mystical Wittgensteinian climax of argument seems appropriate for it as well.

Oakeshott's subscribing to the view of the underdetermination of theory by fact commits him without his overt acknowledgment of this consequence to the pervasiveness and insurmountability of contradiction. If theories are underdetermined by facts, then it is within the realm of possibility that contradictory theoretical formulations will be able to account for the selfsame body of fact. By positing underdetermination, we are bereft of a central censoring mechanism for filtering out contradiction. Once contradictions are allowed to enter into the body of statements that we take to be true, then (as Peano, Bertrand Russell, and Karl Popper have argued[19]) it debars us from blocking the entry of other contradictory statements (beyond the scope of the premises we are considering), so that we have to live with the ineliminability of contradiction.

This awareness yields an internal proof that the version of skepticism to which Oakeshott subscribes is a generalized agnosticism. Given that the opening premises in his skepticism in both *Experience and Its Modes* and *On Human Conduct* state the thesis concerning the underdetermination of theory by fact—that so-called facts themselves are already so theoretically saturated that they qualify as low-level theories—so that there is no body of neutral fact that can be uniquely captured by an objectively appropriate theory or conceptualization—then contradiction is inevitable. We can assume that in the course of time contradictory formulations will be able to account for the selfsame body of "fact." The inescapability of contradiction in which Oakeshott's premise of underdetermination eventuates means that his skepticism will always be lacking a critical apparatus to rule out those conceptual targets of investigation that the skeptic has been traditionally concerned to discredit, namely, God, truth, objective knowledge, justice, happiness, and virtue. At best, the skepticism can only be sustained as a generalized agnosticism—which allows to reenter through the back door (the unconsummable character of the critical apparatus set up by skepticism) whatever has been expelled from the front door (the skeptical interrogation of the entities, concepts, and categories in question).

Translating Oakeshott's skepticism into the vocabulary of a generalized agnosticism on one level appears to resolve the issue of consistency pertaining to skeptical positions in philosophy, but, on another level, it leaves the issue of consistency disquietingly hanging. The level upon which the issue of consistency appears to be resolved is that a generalized agnostic position turns its critical canons inward and interrogates the credentials and viability of skepticism alongside the traditional conceptual targets of skepticism. However, what remains residually inconsistent in a generalized agnostic position is that the everyday, nonskeptical world is affirmed as a continuing possibility—a persistently open question—and does not enjoy the status of assuredness (of givenness) that it possessed before the canons of skepticism (even the canons of skepticism devolved into a generalized agnosticism) were turned against it. A generalized agnosticism is able to register only a certain version of skepticism (one that is more inclusive than the original version), but not nonskepticism or antiskepticism. To know as a result of our translation of the tenets of skepticism into the canons of a generalized agnosticism that our confidence in the perdurability of the everyday world has to be endlessly deferred is already to have crossed an illicit barrier in the direction of skepticism. Knowledge of the need for deferral is a knowledge that epistemologically speaking we have not earned—and we do not have the philosophical credentials to support. A rigorously consistent application of the principles of a generalized agnosticism to the issue of knowledge of the everyday world therefore would require us to leave all of our verbal and logico-metaphysical registers behind and approach it mystically—which is to say, in a way that cannot be defined either by what our theoretical and logical approaches, pursued to their outermost limits, tell us about its existence or its nonexistence.

We need to analytically distinguish between what a generalized agnosticism alludes to in terms of historical process—what the relationships of the explorations, investigations, and findings of one generation are to those of the next and ensuing generations—and what a generalized agnosticism signifies in relation to a theory of truth. With regard to the historical process, a generalized agnosticism suggests a continuing openness concerning the issues that human beings have dealt with—including the issue of skepticism. When it comes to the translation of the import of a generalized agnosticism for the notion of truth, I am arguing that a generalized agnosticism rehabilitates in their pristine ontological force all alternatives under consideration, and thereby its perpetual oscillation between conflicting possibilities engenders a mystical approach to reality. Invoking for heuristic purposes the artificial distinction between what human beings do and how we make sense of what we do, we willynilly endlessly defer the completion of our inquiries—but each stage of our inquiries properly interpreted and understood signifies a mystical embrace of reality.

It is negative gestures that launch skepticism upon its career in philosophy and work to define its character once it has taken off. One can have the things—the furniture—of the world both by positing an overlap between words and things and by assuming a freedom of application of different (and even contradictory) strings of words to designate and make sense of a delimited body of things. The pursuit of this latter option is a function of engaging in a negative gesture—raising the question, "Why not?" Why not make sense of things through a lesser ontological commitment, rather than a more grandiose and inflated ontological commitment that posits a univocal relation between words and things?

When one follows through on the inspiration of this negative gesture, one realizes that one can sustain a mapping of what is on the basis of an even more dramatic negative gesture. One can preserve a delineation of what is not just on the basis of uncertainty, but on the basis of paradox and

genuine (even if false) thought. If not, then the utterance is shown to be a piece of nonsense and thus not a thought at all."[21] The problem that Wittgenstein confronts toward the end of the *Tractatus* is that the philosophical statements that compose the metaphysics of logical atomism and articulate the picture theory of the proposition cannot themselves be validated in accordance with that metaphysics and that theory. This means that even the delineation of a narrow class of empirically verifiable statements is jeopardized. Issues of consistency and coherence have hobbled the identification of even this class of statement. The upshot of these probings is that no statement whatsoever can be conclusively empirically verified. It is these considerations that approximate to Oakeshott's understanding of the relationship of underdetermination that subsists between words and things that point Wittgenstein in the direction of the mystical. If our skeptical rejection of a secure correlation existing between words and things were sustainable, Wittgenstein would not have to have recourse to mysticism. He simply would have clinched the argument in favor of skepticism. It is the fact that skepticism itself faces issues of consistency of the sort we have discussed that reorients Wittgenstein's whole discussion in the direction of mysticism. All of our concepts and categories—and the material entities that are implicated by them—Wittgenstein seems to suggest at the end of the *Tractatus* remain in an ongoing state of suspended animation between belief and disbelief. We can neither confirm nor disconfirm them. We can neither accord them credence nor discredit them. Our multiple everyday and specialized vocabularies constitute a vast, impenetrable veil, whose status as "veil" remains in question because we are bereft of words to describe what the veil might or might not be covering.

Not-knowledge of the whole does not translate into denial (even permanent deferral) of the whole. To circumvent this treacherous line separating not-knowing from denial, it becomes compelling to opt for a mystical reading of the whole. The whole is only sustainable as either belief in God as the ultimate explanatory factor accounting for everything or as skepticism—a denial of the possibility of secure knowledge altogether. The structures of argument—and the blockages—are parallel in both spheres. What drives belief in God as well as skepticism is a craving for ultimate explanation. What undermines both sets of arguments is that ultimacy defeats the prospect of intelligibility. God can serve as the final explanation of things only if He is located in an infinite dimension, which thereby only resituates our problem of being able to account for how He can be the ultimate factor responsible for events and phenomena encountered in finite space-time. The very comprehensiveness of the God-factor (which drives us to conceive of Him as infinite) defeats our efforts to insert Him into an explanatory framework. Analogously, it is the very broad scope of skepticism that prevents us from satisfactorily connecting it to the phenomena it was invoked to rebut. If skepticism is all-inclusive, then it must encompass a gesture of recoil that leads to the skeptical disruption of skepticism itself—and its consequent neutralization as an organizing perspective from which to account for the radical insecurity of all of our knowledge-statements and claims. A mystical relationship to reality (including God) is evocative of an awareness of the parallel structures of both belief and skepticism—and their attendant blockages.

We remain impervious to any set of ultimate factors validating our understanding of nature and the cosmos. Whether that factor or factors are taken to be immanent to the natural order (i.e., skepticism) or transcendent to it (i.e., God) remains immaterial. We can say from a mystical perspective that our inability to penetrate to this level of analysis is what is connoted by the idea of God. From this angle of vision, pantheism and negative theology (resting upon the claim that we can only say what God literally is not but not what He is) become categories or notions that posit the equivalent unknowability of ultimate immanentist and transcendental factors. At the level of unknowability upon which ultimacy operates, the distinction between immanent and transcendent becomes blurred.

One can either speak about the supremely transcendent biblical God in contradictory accents (as existing on a theological plane of analysis that we cannot decipher and [necessarily] not existing on a sheerly human level of discourse[22]) or relate to Him exclusively in silence. All of the traditions and appurtenances of the religious life (including prayer) are part of the contradictory speech—projecting Him as existing even while logically speaking, given His lofty, transcendent, infinite status, He cannot exist in any terms that we can understand. What takes over after these appurtenances and traditions cease (if we are aware of their incompleteness) is silence. The everyday world for Wittgenstein and Oakeshott is sustained in the same way as the mystical God by the community of believers.

The reflections on skepticism and its limits that have been the crux of this introduction yield an unusual and unexpected thesis about Oakeshott that I will develop in the remainder of this book. In a letter to Patrick Riley, Oakeshott lamented in the last decade of his life that his greatest unfulfilled desire was to return to religion (his fellowship dissertation at Cambridge, which has been recently published and which I will discuss at length later on, was about the inescapable merging of philosophy into mysticism[23]) and to write an essay on theology:

> During the last couple of years since I came to live here [in Dorset], spending much of my time re-reading all the books which I first read 50 or 60 years ago, I have gone back to "theology"—or rather, to reflection upon religion. And I would like, more than anything else, to extend those brief pages in *On Human Conduct* into an essay (you know how I admire and value this literary form) on religion, and particularly on the Christian religion. This ambition came to me, partly, from the re-reading of all that St. Augustine wrote—St. Augustine and Montaigne, the two most remarkable men who have ever lived. What I would like to write is a new version of Anselm's, *Cur Deus Homo*—in which (amongst much else) "salvation," being "saved," is recognized as [having] nothing whatever to do with the *future*. Oh, but I know I can never do it now; I have left it too late.[24]

If my reading of Oakeshott is on the right track, then we can say that Oakeshott had actually written what he felt he did not have enough time to write. His existing oeuvre utilizes the texts and arguments of philosophy to offer us a theological reading of some of the most persistent and defiant conundrums of philosophical reasoning. Oakeshott unmasks the familiar worlds of science, history, politics, and everyday life as tissues of never fully actualized possibilities teetering on the brink between existence and nonexistence. From the vantage point of critical reason, all regions of human experience have been—and are not-yet. What is salvageable from religion—just like what is salvageable from all other areas of human experience—is the now of uncertainty and possibility. Religion, in a sense that blurs the ideological line separating the religious from the secular, gives us the key for unlocking the rest of the universe. From that metaphysically resplendent future described in the great monotheistic texts, all that remains is this analytically carved-out now pointing to ignorance and impenetrability. This is our most coherent vision of both eternity and the now.

2

Metaphysics

THERE IS A STYLISTIC PARADOX about Oakeshott that matches a key substantive paradox of his thought. Though he wrote primarily in the essay form—even his longer works often read like ensembles of self-contained essays—he addressed questions of the deepest and broadest significance. His authentic precursors and models were such epic theorists as Plato, Hobbes, and Hegel—the last two of which at least were fond of systematic treatises as the appropriate vehicles for expressing their labyrinthinely interconnected philosophical ideas. Oakeshott was as devoted to systematic exploration and explication as these illustrious predecessors, yet his literary medium of choice was the short compass of the essay rather than the more elaborately mapped out and executed treatise.

Corresponding to this paradox on a stylistic level is a systematic paradox on a substantive level. In some of his most famous essays, such as "Rationalism in Politics" and "The Tower of Babel," Oakeshott favors a morality grounded in habit and custom rather than one fashioned out of rules.[1] The Tower of Babel symbolizes for Oakeshott how a too heightened self-consciousness is ruinous for human beings.

The paradox implicit in this substantive position is that Oakeshott is arriving at it in the course of philosophizing about the human condition. The question immediately presents itself: Isn't Oakeshott in his role as philosopher acting in violation of his own descriptive-normative principles? In pursuing philosophy—what he famously called in *Experience and Its Modes* "experience without arrest"[2]—is he not manifesting the highest degree of self-consciousness? How does one reconcile the meta-theory implicit in Oakeshott's practice as philosopher with his official theory concerning the desirability of a lowered stage of self-consciousness? The substantive paradox runs parallel to the stylistic paradox: there Oakeshott does systematic philosophy in the compressed essay form; here Oakeshott theorizes diminished self-consciousness in the form of allegiance to habit and custom while himself exercising the highest degree of self-consciousness in theorizing this conception.

I would like to state my resolution of this paradox first shortly by way of reaffirming an analytical frame of reference for this book and then in a longer, more leisurely fashion that will explore the ramifications of this analytical framework in a number of different spheres of Oakeshott's philosophy. In the end, I would also like to recontextualize the paradox on the stylistic level, so that the tension between systematic philosophy and the choice of the essay form in which to communicate it gets ameliorated.

I believe that the most persuasive resolution to the substantive paradox I have depicted concerning an apparent simultaneous embrace and rejection of a diminished self-consciousness has to do with the deliverances that the pursuit of philosophical reason—the engagement in "experience without arrest"—vouchsafes. What this pursuit discloses for Oakeshott is how even so-called facts constitute low-level theories—how naming has ontological priority over that which it names. As Oakeshott states it in *On Human Conduct*: "There can be no absolute distinction between 'fact' and 'theorem.' A fact has no finality and no authority over further adventures of understanding: it is a first and conditionally acceptable understanding of a 'going-on.'"[3] Or, as Oakeshott states it even more succinctly: "*Facts* and *things* are not another world from the world of opinions; they are merely relatively unshakable opinions."[4] The unbounded skepticism that this philosophical understanding gives rise to is sustainable only as a generalized agnosticism—a skepticism that incorporates within its own doctrinal formulation a skepticism of itself. A generalized agnosticism, in turn, restores (to the extent possible) on a discursive level the morality of habit and tradition and the indefinitely diminished self-consciousness that Oakeshott affirms on an experiential level. A generalized agnosticism (when appropriately debugged) opens a window upon a diffused mystical approach to everyday reality and everyday life and also carries important implications for how one construes scientific theories and historical reconstructions of events.

To begin to make this case more expansively of Oakeshott as the proponent of a generalized agnosticism, I would like to counterpose to the essay "Rationalism in Politics" and Oakeshott's diagnosis of the categorical backdrop to the pathology of Rationalism the implicit corrective category that emerges from the "Tower of Babel" essays[5] (and, more acutely, the first one). Oakeshott's condemnation of modern politics in "Rationalism in Politics" is extremely broad-ranging:

> Rationalism has come to color the ideas, not merely of one, but of all political persuasions, and to flow over

every party line. By one road or another, by conviction, by its supposed inevitability, by its alleged success, or even quite unreflectively, almost all politics today have become Rationalist or near-Rationalist.

He [the Rationalist] has no sense of the cumulation of experience, only of the readiness of experience when it has been converted into a formula: the past is significant to him only as an encumbrance. He has none of that *negative capability* (which Keats attributed to Shakespeare), the power of accepting the mysteries and uncertainties of experience without any irritable search for order and distinctness, only the capability of subjugating experience; he has no aptitude for that close and detailed appreciation of what actually presents itself which Lichtenberg called negative enthusiasm, but only the power of recognizing the large outline which a general theory imposes upon events. His cast of mind is Gnostic.

Intellectually, his ambition is not so much to share the experience of the race as to be demonstrably a self-made man. And this gives to his intellectual and practical activities an almost preternatural deliberateness and self-consciousness, depriving them of any element of passivity, removing from them all sense of rhythm and continuity and dissolving them into a succession of climacterics, each to be surmounted by a *tour de raison*.

With an almost poetic fancy, he strives to live each day as if it were his first, and he believes that to form a habit is to fail. And if, with as yet no thought of analysis, we glance below the surface, we may, perhaps, see in the temperament, if not in the character, of the Rationalist, a deep distrust of time, an impatient hunger for eternity and an irritable nervousness in the face of everything topical and transitory.

He does not recognize change unless it is a self-consciously induced change, and consequently he falls easily into the error of identifying the customary and the traditional with the changeless. This is aptly illustrated by the rationalist attitude towards a tradition of ideas. There is, of course, no question either of retaining or improving such a tradition, for both these involve an attitude of submission. It must be destroyed. And to fill its place the Rationalist puts something of his own making—an ideology, the formalized abridgment of the supposed substratum of rational truth contained in the tradition.

The heart of the matter is the preoccupation of the Rationalist with certainty.[6]

The key words in the series of quotations I have assembled are "gnosticism," "ideology," and "certainty." What typifies modern Rationalism are the ways in which the tendencies and momentum of all three concepts converge. As Oakeshott might well have asked if he were conducting a seminar rather than writing an essay, to what is "gnosticism" opposed? What does it signify? As we will see shortly reinforced from our analysis of Oakeshott's philosophy of religion derivable from the first "Tower of Babel" essay, the appropriate contrasting term to "gnosticism" appears to be something like "negative theology." (Notice the structural affinity between this term and the terms "negative capability" and "negative enthusiasm," which Oakeshott directly employs in his essay.) Negative theology emphasizes that with regard to God we cannot pierce beyond the Name— that we can never be even conceptually in contact on a literal

level with what the Name names. All we can ever do in relation to God is to discount the literal import of the constituent terms in our definitions and the realistic signification
of our terms of reference. Negative theology both requires
and presupposes our being able to sustain an abiding tension
between our regular deployment of the God vocabulary and
our inability to cash in any of its metaphors.

The whole model of skeptical idealist argument practiced
by Oakeshott is already encapsulated in the position of negative theology. In negative theology, you have potentially an
infinite string of names to pin down an entity, namely, God,
that can never be literally conceptually delimited. Analogously, skeptical idealism maintains that all of the words in
our regular vocabularies can never be taken to certainly pin
down the things or events to which they ostensibly refer.
Those "things" or "events" could theoretically be captured
by still other verbal constellations without end. Both negative theology and skeptical idealism posit an unbridgeable
conceptual distance between words and the One Absolute
Being or the things they ostensibly refer to.

Early in the development of Western religion in the writings of Marcion and others, it seemed jarring to certain
intellectuals and ordinary believers that the Creator God
who fashioned what turns out to be a defective and imperfect
universe should also be the author of redemption.[7] Gnosticism (in contrast to negative theology) seeks to resolve the
tension between the creative and redemptive moments of
religious faith by assigning the creative and redemptive
vocations of Divinity to two different gods—thereby irrevocably breaching the absolute distance that negative theology posits between God and human beings. Gnosticism thus
originates as a remodeling of God to make Him answerable
to a human intellectual need (of reconciling God's power

with His goodness). The converse of Oakeshott's previously cited statement seems equally true: gnosticism is Rationalism in religion (instead of Rationalism is gnosticism in politics).

The other elements of gnosticism that have been historically significant are linked with this irrevocable breaching of distance between God and human beings. Gnosticism emphasizes that emancipation and salvation come from cultivation of esoteric knowledge of spiritual truth whose content has the effect of rendering God answerable to human rational needs. The secret knowledge that is attained by gnostic initiates has to do with being privy to God's design for the world—of being able to reconcile through the abrogation of metaphysical distance between God and ourselves conflicting strands in the cosmic apparatus. Penetrating this secret knowledge often leads to assigning a God-like role to those who have attained gnosis and serves as the basis for establishing a rigid demarcation between an initiated elite and the uninitiated masses.

Profound political implications follow from my delineation of the contrast between gnosticism and negative theology. Negative theology leads to the toleration of metaphor and to a recognition of the unrelievedly metaphoric nature of language. The verbal currency of human life is approximations. We never get to "the real thing." From a negative theological perspective, ordinary linguistic usage accomplishes a tremendously important socializing function by normalizing our lack of closure in the concepts and descriptions that we apply to experience. Gnosticism has the opposite effect. It induces a festering impatience with the compromises and limitations encapsulated in ordinary linguistic usage. To resort to language is already to be surrendering to the sleazy, second-rate character of human life that is experienced now only in mediated form through a series of words that can only distort and deflect from (and in a whole host of other ways can only imperfectly reflect) the urgencies of immediate experience. The gnostic wants "wind, earthquake, and fire."[8] He (or she) wants to be overwhelmingly riveted by the actuality of his or her experience. The distancing and mediating mechanisms of human life taint it for the gnostic beyond recall.

In his edited volume on *The Social and Political Doctrines of Contemporary Europe*, which appeared in the late 1930s, Oakeshott very pointedly stated that Nazism's "opposition to Representative Democracy is fundamental, and not based merely upon the alleged defects of democratic political arrangements. Its doctrines of Race and Blood and of Leadership separate it firmly from every other current doctrine."[9] In the light of our elaboration upon Oakeshott's description of modern politics as being heavily gnostic in character, we could say that Nazi Germany was the epitome of a society that had a radical revulsion against metaphor. In other societies (and in Germany at other times) if you call someone vermin, or a louse, or a leech, it is perceived by the other and also often by the person saying it as an expression of extreme annoyance or impatience. These words often constitute ways of "letting off steam" that then prod both the person expressing annoyance and the target of the person's annoyance to realign their behavior as a prelude to restoration of normal relations. In the gnostic atmosphere that pervaded Germany during the Nazi era, if Jews were vermin they needed to be exterminated. The safety valves of language that normally protect the rest of us from the extremes of our own behavior had been obliterated through the gnostic purging of metaphor.

One could raise the question at this point: why do not Oakeshott's strictures against rationalism in politics engulf and devastate his own skepticism? If he knows that skepticism is true—and he applies it as an unquestioned doctrine in establishing and assessing political institutions—then he appears vulnerable to the same charge that he levels against so many other "theorists" and practitioners of modern politics. We would then have to say that Oakeshott's critique of rationalism is so sweeping that it undermines his own skepticism.

To get Oakeshott off the hook, perhaps the fairest and most pertinent thing to say (as we have already discussed in other contexts) is that the version of skepticism he subscribes to includes skepticism itself within its orbit of critical interrogation. A generalized agnosticism, therefore, serves as the foil and contrast to the rationalism he condemns.

From this perspective, a prime vulnerability of rationalists in politics is their insensitivity to requirements of consistency. Whatever organizing outlook for the structuring and governance of political affairs they favor, they do not question whether their preferred criterion is able to meet its own critical canon. For example, is the promotion of the value of efficiency efficient? Does not a too rampant pursuit of efficiency lead to a sacrifice of other values, such as nurturing a sense of personal satisfaction, which in the end leads to a downgrading of efficiency itself? Or—to take another example—does not an emphasis on social and economic redistribution presuppose a series of distributional schemes in the name of which each pattern of redistribution is tacitly justified, so that redistribution is really a misnomer for a series of differentially—and even contradictorily—motivated distributional schemes?

It is this scrupulosity concerning issues of reflexivity that constitutes the authentic litmus test (given Oakeshott's philosophical practice) for distinguishing between ideology and theory. As we have seen, Oakeshott links rationalism in politics with ideology. Ideology dispenses with scruples concerning reflexivity—and theory does not.

In accordance with this reading, the case for Oakeshott's adherence to liberalism is already fixed by the time of the publication of the essay "Rationalism in Politics" in the late 1940s and does not have to await the drawing of the distinction between *societas* and *universitas* in *On Human Conduct* published in the mid-1970s. Only a liberal society institutionalizes the antirationalist ideal of self-interrogation—of harboring the infrastructure to call liberalism itself into question alongside its alternatives. A liberal society constitutes the institutional analogue to Oakeshott's animus against rationalism. Before one gets to issues of minimal governmental intervention in the life of society, there is the factor of colossal self-restraint and potential self-abnegation that makes a liberal ordering of governmental institutions immensely attractive to Oakeshott.

Reading Oakeshott in this light places him in the company of some leading Continental philosophers of the middle to late twentieth century—each of whom went out of his way to reconcile the metaphysical or political understandings they adhered to with the requirements of consistency. It was the reconstructed version of their philosophical teaching that then became the pivot of their argument. These writers—just like Oakeshott—dramatize the ascent from ideology into theory.

Emmanuel Levinas, Gilles Deleuze, and Michel Foucault were arch-exemplars of an antirationalist impulse in politics. Levinas in the priority that he assigns to ethics over all other branches of philosophizing invokes skeptical argument as an internal support for his thesis. Levinas says that "It is as if the correlation of the Saying and the Said were a diachrony of the unassemblable."[10] As I read him, Levinas's argument seems to go something like this: The best internal (by "internal" I mean internal to philosophical argument and exploration itself) support for the ideas of God and the Other comes from the breakdown of what Levinas calls synchrony—and the triumph of diachrony. What the history of philosophy shows to be one of the most dramatic expressions of the urge toward synchrony—encompassing all of the moves that it is dialectically inviting and metaphysically compelling to make in one concentrated philosophical vision—are formulations of skepticism. However, it is precisely here that the urge toward synchrony trails off into incoherence, as the skeptic, in order to remain consistent, needs to skeptically question the tenets of skepticism, which aborts his attempt at synchronous formulation of skepticism as a vision of the whole. Only some move in the direction of diachrony—of in a barely intelligible sense separating out the "saying" from the "said" (the urge to say something, which when it is outfitted with words proves to be inert)—can salvage skepticism.

The breakdown of synchrony as manifested most glaringly in the case of skepticism creates metaphysical space for the notions of the Other and of God. Since formulations of skepticism give rise to dilemmas of consistency that are best resolved by imagining logical grids that enable us to dissociate the "saying" of skepticism from the "said" of skepticism—logical grids that offer us an alternative to the binary constraints of the traditional Aristotelian logic, so that contradiction is normalized —then indirect support is received for a generalized agnosticism that engenders receptivity to such logics. A generalized agnosticism leaves the door open to an endlessly unfolding future, which might be the most cogent way to construe Levinas's notion of infinity[11]—and its attendant openness to the ideas of the Other and of God.

Foucault's summarizing of Deleuze's philosophy in *Difference and Repetition* and *The Logic of Sense* gives us an illuminating analog to Levinas's notion of dissociating the saying from the said of skepticism.[12] In order to formulate a coherent theory of difference—of plurality in all of its manifold cultural, personal, and metaphysical senses—one confronts the paradox that the categorical notion of "difference" already introduces a homogenizing element—an expression of the impulse toward Sameness—into the very delineation of difference. How would it be possible to formulate an understanding of difference that was reflexively uncontaminated? This is the way Foucault (paraphrasing Deleuze) formulates the dilemma—and resolves it:

> What if it conceived of difference differentially, instead of searching out the common elements underlying difference? Then difference would disappear as a general feature that leads to the generality of the concept, and it would become—a different thought, the thought of difference—a pure event. As for repetition, it would cease to function as the dreary succession of the identical, and would become displaced difference.[13]

Apropos of our previous discussion, Foucault states very pointedly that the problem of conceiving "difference differentially"

> cannot be approached through the logic of the excluded third because it is a dispersed multiplicity. . . . The freeing of difference requires thought without contradiction,

without dialectics, without negation; thought that accepts divergence; affirmative thought whose instrument is disjunction; thought of the multiple—of the nomadic and dispersed multiplicity that is not limited or confined by the constraints of similarity; thought that does not conform to a pedagogical model (the fakery of prepared answers), but that attacks insoluble problems—that is, a thought that addresses a multiplicity of exceptional points, which are displaced as we distinguish their conditions and which insist and subsist in the play of repetitions.[14]

What methodological principle is at work in Deleuze's and Foucault's resolutions of the problem of conceiving of difference differentially? Foucault states it very sharply and succinctly: "What is the answer to the question? The problem. How is the problem resolved? By displacing the question."[15] In their discerning of this methodological principle, Deleuze and Foucault are prefigured by a great rabbinic sage of the late nineteenth/early twentieth centuries—Rav Simcha Zissel of Kelm—who said that "Every question that is especially strong and does not have a solution, then the question is (becomes) the solution."[16] Deleuze's and Foucault's resolution of the problem of delineating difference differentially which involves "the suppression of categories, the affirmation of the univocity of being, and the repetitive revolution of being around difference"[17] consists in a reinsertion of the constitutive features of the problem in the infrastructure of its solution. The solution as it were stabilizes and institutionalizes the problem—thereby transforming it from problem to solution.

Oakeshott's statement that "Almost all politics today have become Rationalist or near-Rationalist"[18]—and his identifying of a rationalist temper with gnosticism—give rise to a number of questions: First, historically and descriptively, why did only some European societies succumb to fascism while the rest did not? Second, what is the background metaphysical model that inspires Oakeshott's own theoretical vision of a rule-centered *societas* in contrast to the enterprise-association that he also calls *universitas*[19] as the preferred type of human social and political organization? I believe that Oakeshott's "Tower of Babel" essays offer us an implicit answer to these two interrelated questions. These essays suggest that the inspiration for the form of state Oakeshott most admires comes from the metaphysical emptiness that the builders of the Tower were not able to live with, and that motivated them to build the Tower. The proceduralist, rule-governed liberal state encodes the emptiness of negative theology better than more authoritarian structurings of the state. Those European and North American states that were historically liberal therefore had the best defenses theoretically and institutionally against the allures of fascism. The extent to which modern liberal states themselves can be classified as being Rationalist in character is at least partially a function of the overweening self-confidence with which some of them have turned to a reformist politics, thinking that they have at last moved decisively to resolving some of the perennial conundrums and challenges of politics.

In the first "Tower of Babel" essay, Oakeshott distinguishes (as we have seen) between two forms of the moral life: the moral life as "a habit of affection and behavior; not a habit of reflective thought, but a habit of affection and conduct,"[20] and the moral life as "determined, not by a habit of behavior, but by the reflective application of a moral criterion. It appears in two common varieties: as the self-conscious pursuit of moral ideals, and as the reflective observance of moral rules."[21] In both essays on "The Tower of Babel," Oakeshott favors a morality grounded in tradition rather than a morality founded on rules. The Tower of Babel symbolizes for him how a too acute self-consciousness is the bane of human existence. Since this theoretical understanding is elaborated upon in relation to a distinct biblical text,[22] I think that it is fair to say that according to Oakeshott the God of the Bible is in crucial ways denied by an excessive self-consciousness. The paradox emerges that God who vouchsafes to us ultimate coherence is available to us only if we renounce the quest for ultimate coherence. It is only in the series of never-ending emotional and intellectual displacements that constitute tradition (tradition as a tissue of endlessly receding displacements) that human life finds its highest level of repose and stability.

In reality there is something that might appropriately be labeled as a third "Tower of Babel" essay in Oakeshott's writings. It constitutes a partially self-contained discussion in his longer essay, "Political Philosophy," which is included in the posthumously published *Religion, Politics and the Moral Life*.[23] In this essay, Oakeshott speaks very forthrightly in his own voice and invokes the symbol of the tower to explicate the nature of philosophical thinking, no longer providing exegeses of the biblical text. For him, the tower symbolizes "the enterprise in reflection," which "may be likened to ascending a tower liberally supplied with windows at every level. The world seen from the ground floor is the world with which all reflection begins."[24] What distinguishes philosophy as a mode of thought from all other modes is its willingness to reconceive both what is given and what is interpreted at each level of ascent: "The important distinction is between the thinker for whom the different levels of observation provide different views of 'things' already known, and the

thinker who, as it were, uninfluenced by memory and carrying nothing with him as he climbs, knows at each level only
the scene presented to his vision and the mediation by which
it came into view."[25] What stamps someone as a philosopher
is just "the predisposition" to preserve the ascent. Oakeshott
very pointedly says, "There is no top to this tower."[26] This
phrase encapsulates a negative theological mapping of the
intellectual universe. The mind restlessly reconfigures its
previous ensembles of givens and interpretations without
approaching any final reading of the data or how to make
sense of them. In Oakeshott, as we will see most dramatically in discussing his philosophy of law, the data just are
how we make sense of them. They have no more enduring
substratum than that.

In a crucial sense one could say that for Oakeshott there
is a convergence between the religious and the philosophical vocations. The biblical God becomes God as it were in a
moment of supreme recoil when He withdraws into Himself
to make room for what is other than Himself—namely, the
world. Creation is paradoxically but very compellingly bound
up with withdrawal—with the impossibility of vouchsafing
final disclosure. Creation is coextensive with the fixing of
an unbridgeable distance—with a hiding of the end or ends
and an indefinite prolongation of the middle or means. The
optimal human life for Oakeshott—the philosophical—consists in an ongoing reenactment of the Divine role. A person
is to be identified as a philosopher, Oakeshott says, "not in
respect to something he achieves at the end, but in respect
of his predisposition towards the ascent. Indeed, it might be
said that his only tangible achievement is the maintenance
of this predisposition."[27] From this perspective, the pivotal
transgression of the builders of the original Tower of Babel
was to try and translate into substance what can remain only

process. On the basis of "The Tower of Babel" essays, I think it makes sense to characterize Oakeshott's own philosophy of religion as agnosticism rather than as atheism. The atheist is primly self-conscious in his denial of God. The agnostic, by preserving fidelity to the question of God's existence and withholding a final answer, is able to assimilate God as it were on a consistent basis to a not-fully-heightened self-consciousness. The doctrinal (philosophical) counterpart to a not-fully-developed self-consciousness on a psychological plane is agnosticism in religion and a generalized agnosticism outside of the sphere of religion. Agnosticism and a generalized agnosticism, in turn, receive their most coherent expression (as I have argued) in the form of mysticism.

Our emotional makeup is as uncertain as our claims to reason. Oakeshott is devastating in his analysis of the moral flaw of the builders of the Tower of Babel. He says, "But whether the identity [of the builders] was that of Heaven-Seekers, or merely of Tower-Builders, remained obscure."[28] This captures in one sentence the problem of seeking Heaven. One can never conclusively verify or validate even for oneself that that is what one is really seeking. The builders' ultimate sin from Oakeshott's perspective was that "In the undertaking to subjugate God and Nature to human ambitions they had stumbled upon a life-work and had become the slaves of an ideal."[29] They had become, in other words, Rationalists in morality:

> The morality of the Rationalist is the morality of the self-conscious pursuit of moral ideals, and the appropriate form of moral education is by precept, by the presentation and explanation of moral principles. This is presented as a higher morality (the morality of the free man: there is no end to the clap-trap) than that of habit, the unself-

conscious following of a tradition of moral behavior; but, in fact, it is merely morality reduced to a technique, to be acquired by training in an ideology rather than an education in behavior.[30]

Given the fascination that St. Augustine exerted upon Oakeshott throughout his career (he is supposed to have written an early book about him which he never published), regarding negative theology as the tacit countervailing doctrine to the gnosticism animating the builders of the Tower of Babel makes even more sense. St. Augustine combated Marcionite gnosticism (and triumphed over his own early allegiance to gnosticism) by formulating a doctrine of radical human freedom. The evil and suffering in the world were the result of faulty investments of human will and did not reflect in any direct way on God so as to require a gnostic resolution of the contradiction. The emergence and theological legitimation of the institutionalized Church superintending an in-between time whose termination point could not be plotted even by the Church was a direct result of St. Augustine's theorizing.[31]

In my reading, then, the "Tower of Babel" essays tacitly invoke negative theology as a foil for the overweening pretensions of the builders of the Tower of Babel. If the builders of the Tower of Babel were proto-Rationalists in religion, morality, and politics, then the implicit biblical contrasting model to them is that of adherence to negative theology. The logical structure of negative theological argument parallels the logical structure of skeptical argument, and they both arrestingly converge upon agnosticism (in the strict sense of lack of knowledge). As we have seen, skepticism and monotheism (construed negatively theologically) confront common dilemmas of consistency, of self-referentialism. In order to emerge as properly consistent, skeptical doctrine must encompass a reflexive maneuver whereby skeptical critical canons are turned against the tenets of skepticism themselves—forcing them into a movement of recoil and thereby inhibiting their adequate formulation. Analogously, the utter conceptual removal of the monotheistic God (posited by the negative theological reading of monotheism), which renders Him unlike anything human, requires some kind of grammatical subject concerning whom the continual divestiture of predicates can take place. Skepticism is a doctrine of radical critique that both presupposes and denies a stable subject (in a grammatical sense)—the tenets of skepticism. Monotheism (in negative theological perspective) is also a doctrine of radical critique (of idolatrously inclined popular religion) that simultaneously presupposes and denies a stable grammatical subject, namely, God.[32]

The self-referentialist dilemmas that stand poised to dismantle both skepticism and monotheism suggest that the most coherent reading of both doctrines takes the form of a generalized agnosticism. A generalized agnosticism implicitly points to the continued vitality of the questions it is unable to resolve. If skepticism must accommodate a moment of self-questioning of its own doctrine, then the most defensible version of skepticism emerges as the one that includes skepticism within its own ambit of skeptical interrogation—that is, a generalized agnosticism. Analogously, if under the impact of negative theology monotheism can no longer literally affirm its utterly transcendent version of God, in order to remain properly consistent it has to acknowledge that it cannot conclusively invalidate God's existence either. Negative theology is restricted to the more limited claim that monotheistic argument cannot work to establish the veracity of God's existence. Its writ does not

dominant modes through which we apprehend, relate to, and translate experience. "Practice is, in general, the assertion of reality by means of action, and in particular it is the attempt to make coherent the given world of practical existence by qualifying it by 'what ought to be'; and religion I take to be the form of practical activity in which this attempt is carried furthest." "Religion is, itself, the conduct of life" in the light of the "oughts" stipulated by the particular religion one is following. "All religions are ways of living" and "a way of living is (and not merely implies) a way of thinking; and consequently religion is at once a way of thinking and a way of living."[2]

If religion is the maximal manifestation of the mode of experience called "practice," how is this mode itself validated? If "mode" refers to one of the primary forms through which experience gets assimilated and articulated, how could the medium through which something gets expressed be validated without simultaneously implicating itself (without already taking for granted its own presence or existence)— and thereby endlessly deferring the prospect of validation? Perhaps the most fruitful move to make at this point is to reallocate the conceptual work previously assigned to the category of "mode" conceived in a strict sense to the sociologically more realistic category of "tradition." In fact as we move from *Experience and Its Modes* to *Rationalism in Politics*, the category of "tradition" increasingly takes over the analytical and hermeneutical roles previously occupied by the term "mode." Apparently Oakeshott came to the realization that in order to confer maximal coherence on his earlier notion of "mode," it might make sense for the sake of diminishing the aura of necessity surrounding "mode" to interpret it more loosely as being analogous to "tradition," which conjures up sheer contingency. The circular nature of Oakeshott's argument thereby becomes more prominent. The contingencies associated with practical experience are now understood contingently—through an investigation of the traditions to which they give rise. The ineliminability of circularity, in turn, suggests that our categorical divisions of experience are underdetermined by experience itself, which thereby renders intelligible our recourse to circularity. As I shall shortly more fully elaborate, adherence to a radical principle of underdetermination in turn introduces the possibility of contradiction: there is no way to effectively logically block the invocation of contradictory categories to make sense of experience. Once the possibility of contradiction is acknowledged, the rules of inference of Aristotelian logic give us no resources for ruling out any possibilities whatsoever—including the possibility of God, for which Oakeshott has already created the theoretical infrastructure for mystically appropriating.

From the perspective of this analysis, Oakeshott emerges either as an agnostic or mystic in religion and a generalized agnostic or a generalized mystic in other areas of his thought, based upon the implications of the structure of his arguments, despite any alternative or contrary descriptions he might have applied to himself.

In addition, Oakeshott (in a certain sense like Hobbes[3]) has a very Judaized reading of religion (even when he is ostensibly referring to Christianity): for him religion is virtually all action and no dogma. He says that "There is no exact point in the conduct of life at which religion can be said to begin."[4] In other words, it is coextensive with all of our practical activities. From this perspective, one could argue that Oakeshott believes that even cooking can be considered religious—that is, we begin it even though our explicit knowledge of how to execute it is always necessarily less than is required.[5] This lack of knowledge does not keep us from doing it; we practice it.[6] As with religion, we can run the gamut from initiating it to going through all of the steps associated with its practice without ever confronting the theoretical objects of our practice (knowledge of God; knowledge of what it means to be a successful cook)—or, indeed, even experiencing the lack of knowledge as a deficit in our practice. Religion is a matter of what we do and is in no way restricted to what we merely think or believe. The emphasis on doing would appear to follow from a negative theological understanding of the nature of God. Because all of the attributes that we ascribe to God can only be understood figuratively and metaphorically—but not literally (we can only imitate His external manifestations, as it were, not his internal beliefs or understandings)—the premier way to relate to God is through assertions of will that approximate to actions ascribed to Him.

Many of the enthralling ways in which Oakeshott describes a religious way of life in contrast to a worldly one in his 1929 essay "Religion and the World" conform to this model. According to Oakeshott, the following are some of the postulates of a religious (in contrast to a worldly) way of life: "The whole value of life" is "found in the actual living of it."[7] "Ambition and the world's greed for visible results, in which each stage is a mere approach to the goal, would be superseded [in religion] by a life which carried in each of its moments its whole meaning and value."[8] "The religious man will inherit nothing he cannot possess by actual insight."[9] "Religion, then, is not as some would persuade us, an interest attached to life, a subsidiary activity; nor is it a power which governs life from the outside with a, no doubt divine but certainly incomprehensible, sanction for its authority. It is simply life itself, life dominated by the belief that its value is in the present, not merely in the past or the future, that if we lose ourselves we lose all."[10] Not being able to penetrate the mind of God and see His attributes for what they truly are, we are left with the biblical projection of Him as an Instantaneous Doer for whom none of the hiatuses that characterize a traditional human life—e.g., between intention and action and action and the results or consequences of action—applies. God represents a present that is so compelling and self-sufficient that, according to the official biblical imagery and vocabulary, He does not experience Himself nor is He experienced by us as inhabiting merely the present. God's present symbolizes an enactment and fulfillment that are so complete (that are indeed barely distinguishable from each other) that they serve as a dramatic contrast to all those spaces that open up in the course of a typical human life between desire, thought, and action (and their accompanying engenderings of self-consciousness) that vex and ultimately defeat our project of inhabiting the present. For every eruption of heightened self-consciousness, according to Oakeshott, we need to countermaneuver by reoccupying our present.

For Oakeshott, living life in a religious dimension means pushing the limits of our present to the furthest extent possible: "A generation that would be religious must be courageous enough to achieve a life that is really contemporary. And then, in our age, as in all great ages, we might find more men living their lives and fewer merely hoping for life in some vague, ill-imagined future."[11] "In the extemporary life he [the religious man] deserves to live, nothing is of final worth except present insight, a grasp of the thing itself."[12] "*Memento vivere* is the sole precept of religion."[13] "The only immortality which fascinates him [the religious man] is a present immortality; 'so far as is possible he lives as an immortal.'"[14] In "religious faith," "the fugitive adventures of human conduct [are] recognized neither as merely evanescent adventures nor as emblems of better things to come, but as *aventures*, themselves encounters with eternity."[15] "This, then, is the religious man, who sees all things in the light of his own mind, and desires to possess nothing save by present insight. For him the voices of the world have not drowned the voices of youth and life. Firm in the possession of himself, he lacks nothing. Fear has no meaning, safety no charm, anxiety no occasion, and success is bound up with no dim and problematical future."[16]

For Oakeshott, "living the present" becomes the organizing image or metaphor of the biblical narrative of God. Being negatively theologically debarred from access to what God is like in and for Himself, we only have the action-descriptions strewn throughout the biblical text to go by, which for Oakeshott suggest an Entity that so furiously and pervasively occupies its present that nothing subsists beside the present.

There is a motif of "weak messianism"[17]—of theological redemption in a special sense that is compatible with negative theology—that can be teased out of Oakeshott's skepticism and can serve as a basis for linking his philosophy of religion with the other branches of his philosophy. A more minimally generalized agnostic and more maximally mystical reading of Oakeshott's skepticism grounded in the logical and metaphysical impossibility of closing the gap between word and thing (and between meaning and text) suggests that there is no reliable, objectively ascertainable order of givenness attached to any sector of the world. Descriptive statements of all sorts always harbor disguised normative elements. The primary constitution of the world by things and texts thus remains continually fluid and open—and irresolvable. In a crucial sense, the world with its series of events and sectors of experience has not yet happened (come into being). The possible readings and constructions have not yet congealed into entities with fixed shapes, features, and configurations.

In a negative, indirect way, skepticism can be understood as a gigantic placeholder for a transfigurative redemption of the world. A world that is not in a solid ontological sense in the first go-around can be/become the redeemed world of the monotheistic theological imagination on the second go-around (which might, for all we know, be the first go-around, since in accordance with our "secularly trained" critical faculties, the first go-around remains incomplete and imperfectly realized). In its exposure and finding-wanting the claims to final definition and identity of virtually all human phenomena, skepticism evinces a commitment to wholeness. Its standards of intelligibility are stark and exacting to be better able to sustain and nurture a vision of the possibility of the whole (which, in monotheistic theological terms, translates into a vision of the cosmos spanning Creation through Redemption). As Hölderlin astutely realized, the skeptic "is secretly feasting at the table of the gods"[18] and restores to the range of rational accessibility and relative plausibility the whole panoply of monotheistic theological categories and understandings that are now conceived as being no more *and* no less bizarre and fantastic—no more *and* no less "representative of reality"—than more conventional scientific and commonsensical inventories of the real.[19]

The role of philosophical argument is to point to the ineffability of human experience—to pave the way for a reception of the idea of the mysticism of everyday life. The skepticism embedded in the modal analysis of experience suggests than an everyday, "realist" conception of the different sectors of experience can be resurrected—not under the auspices of realism itself but under the aegis of "tradition" as the temporally generated and provisionally legitimate series of rubrics in accordance with which we generally group experience (labels such as "history," "practice," "common sense," and "science," and their various cognates and subdivisions). The idea of "tradition" leaves it as an open question whether the different sectors of human experience with their accompanying names and categories and subcategories will ever receive unreserved validation as autonomous zones of human experience—or will everlastingly retain their character as instrumental posits or wagers that most economically and efficiently organize experience for us, without being able to offer us the assurance that they transparently reflect the order of reality. In this feature, the notion of "tradition" becomes the correlative of the idea of God in religion: God on a rational level registers a limit to human thought reflected in the doctrine of a generalized agnosticism—and, on a mystical level, can be projected as subsisting in a "realistic" sense within a set of parameters that defy our comprehension.

A negative theological understanding of God which (as I have argued) can be translated more minimally as agnosticism and more maximally as mysticism is also evinced in the following passage: "I shall be content here with the assertion that religion is practical experience (which is not seriously denied), and that, prima facie, there is no reason to assume the identity of what is true for practice and what is true ultimately."[20] Religion, which is the highest form of practical experience, leaves it as an open question whether what is true for it "is true ultimately." In other words, religion for Oakeshott is predicated either upon agnosticism or upon mysticism, a symbolically uncalibrated encounter with the hidden, unknown God, in vain search for ultimate confirmation of our beliefs and practices. Oakeshott goes further and steadfastly asserts that he wants to keep the two truths (practical and ultimate) distinct: "Practical truth is not ultimate truth; and what is real, or what is asserted of the real in practice is not ultimately real. What contributes to the coherence of the world of practical experience is, of course, true for practice; and from that standpoint there is nothing more to be said. Every truth is true in its own place."[21] Oakeshott does not despise—but ranks very highly—the truth associated with practice: "Practical truth is the truth that we can live by and act upon; it is the truth which can give freedom."[22] But Oakeshott is very persevering and systematic in his embrace of a "two truths" doctrine: the truth of practice and ultimate truth.

> Yet religion, in the persons both of its defenders and those who have attacked it, has claimed more. It has claimed that its truths are not merely practical, but belong to the world of concrete truth. But, were this so, their practical value would at once disappear. And the business of establishing both the practical and the ultimate truth of religious ideas is a task which any one who is aware of the conflict involved is not likely to undertake. If religion has anything to do with the conduct of life, then the ideas of religion—ideas such as deity, of salvation and of immortality—are practical ideas and belong to the world of practice. And an idea which serves this world can serve no other. So far from it being the case that nothing less than

ultimate concrete truth will serve the purpose of religion, those who have any conception of what they mean by such truth know well enough that where it is not irrelevant to religion it must be inimical.[23]

"Practical experience, to gain the whole world, must lose its own soul."[24]

If "ultimate truth" turned out to be something substantive, then there would indeed be some other kind of truth that superseded the truth of practice—including religious truth. However, given Oakeshott's conception of philosophy, I think we need to see "ultimate truth" as an ongoing process—as "the totality of experience" come into "self-consciousness"[25] and experienced "without modification or arrest"[26]—which is to say that all of our beliefs and assertions, whether in history, science, or practice with its multiple domains of everyday judgments, morality, and religion, are ontologically insecure, without foundation. "Experience without arrest" discloses to us the underdetermined character of all of our more partial, abstract, and modified worlds of experience. In relation to the endless possibilities and inventiveness of thought, our modes of categorizing experience and the specific judgments rendered under each of their rubrics remain in the end underdetermined. They could have been other than what they are. "Experience without arrest" serves as a critique in my view not only of how our abstract worlds originate and therefore taint the solidity of the judgments rendered under their purview, but also of what becomes the fate of those judgments once they have been inserted in place in their respective abstract worlds. They are subject to endless questioning and revision—and each generation's formulations become more perspicuous (without achieving permanence) only with the passage of time.

In rejecting the claims of religion to ultimate truth, Oakeshott says that "Since the world of practical experience is abstract and defective, a modification of experience, it cannot be considered a necessary form of experience."[27] Given our discussion of Oakeshott's conception of philosophy as "experience without arrest," I think that what he means here in condemning practical experience and religion as its most heightened and coherent form as "abstract" and not being "a necessary form of experience" is that practice in general and religion in particular, by abridging out of the endless flux and movement of experience in order to achieve their specific identities, are unfaithful to the principle of "underdetermination." They are unfaithful at the level of origins in terms of their original grouping into distinct categorical rubrics. They are also unfaithful at the level of continuations. Once judgments have been rendered under these rubrics, they are again vulnerable to the charge of being underdetermined. Both in relation to available classificatory rubrics and to potential ones that have not been articulated under the current categorical dispensation, current judgments remain underdetermined. The "necessary form of experience" that Oakeshott refers to, then, needs to be construed as the insurmountability of contingency. In the furthest reaches of his metaphysics, it would appear that Oakeshott is pointing to a convergence between the necessary and the contingent.

One can also view Oakeshott's agnosticism in religion as being constrained by the generalized agnosticism flowing from his overall skepticism (his subscribing to the principle of the underdetermination of theory by fact). The most consistent version of skepticism is the one that includes skepticism itself within its own skeptical orbit. One can look upon this facet of Oakeshott's religious identity as a movement of thought from the general (a generalized agnosticism) to the particular (agnosticism in the sphere of religion). As we have already seen and shall elaborate upon more fully below, the factors that lead one to classify Oakeshott as both an agnostic and a generalized agnostic can also be more coherently channeled in the direction of mysticism.

In this context, it is worth noting that the negative theological metaphoric projection of God as being totally immersed in the present implicitly provides Oakeshott with a model for resolving the contradiction that I pointed out at the start of this essay. On the one hand, Oakeshott sees a not-fully-developed-self-consciousness as being conducive to optimal human living, and, on the other hand, he arrives at this conception through the application of a highly refined philosophical self-consciousness. Oakeshott's image of God provides us with a model of how these two extremes can be reconciled. God represents a self-consciousness that is so complete (so concentrated and intense) that it is experienced and expressed as unself-consciousness. At the level of intensity at which the negative-theological God occupies His present, the experience of the Self is lost. For Oakeshott, that becomes the ultimate goal for human emulation.

Eastern texts for Oakeshott most fittingly capture the mysticism of everyday life into which we are catapulted by both religion and philosophy. With regard to religion, we can neither say that God is nor that He is not. Concerning the objectively durable identity of the multiple objects that go to constitute our world, philosophy counsels us that we can neither affirm nor deny their durable identity. Our statements, whether abstract or concrete—speculative or practical—

constitute distortions or abridgements out of a complex discourse of possibility that is unable to tender unreserved claims about anything. An intractable and irresolvable silence becomes the deep metaphysical accompaniment of the human condition. Speech—which can only unravel one distortion at the cost of introducing another—is both after the fact and beside the point. Our lives are pitched against a background of unmitigated and unredeemed silence in relation to which our verbal discourse shapes up as a merely ironic counterpoint.

The practical (in contrast to the merely technical) knowledge that the wheelwright of the *Chuang Tzu* in Oakeshott's essay "Rationalism in Politics" exemplifies becomes emblematic of the most grandiose and comprehensive of philosophical gestures characteristic of skeptical idealism, whereby the uncompletability and unstatability of theory transform the theoretical enterprise itself into a gigantic holding operation for practice—sustaining it into the indefinite future—or (as we shall see shortly) as itself a form of practice:

> "Speaking as a wheelwright," he replied, "I look at the matter in this way; when I am making a wheel, if my stroke is too slow, then it bites deep but is not steady; if my stroke is too fast, then it is steady, but it does not go deep. The right pace, neither slow nor fast, cannot get into the hand unless it comes from the heart. It is a thing that cannot be put into words [rules]; there is an art in it that I cannot explain to my son. That is why it is impossible for me to let him take over my work, and here I am at the age of seventy still making wheels. In my opinion it must have been the same with the men of old. All that was worth handing on died with them; the rest, they put in their books. That

is why I said that what you were reading was the lees and scum of bygone men."[28]

The nonnegotiability that prevails between practice and theory—with theorizing being most appropriately conceived in the end either as a holding operation for practice or as itself just another mode of practice[29]—suggests that the optimal stance for the secular/religious person is enjoyment of the moment, the sweet relishing of the fleeting and the transient. Here is Oakeshott on the activity of fishing—followed by a passage from the *Chuang Tzu* devoted to the same subject—addressing what we might call the ethical import of the mystical:

> Consider fishing. If your project is merely to catch fish it would be foolish to be unduly conservative. You will seek out the best tackle, you will discard practices which prove unsuccessful, you will not be bound by unprofitable attachments to particular localities, pieties will be fleeting, loyalties evanescent; you may even be wise to try anything once in the hope of improvement. But fishing is an activity that may be engaged in, not for the profit of a catch, but for its own sake; and the fisherman may return home in the evening not less content for being empty-handed. Where this is so, the activity has become a ritual and a conservative disposition is appropriate. Why worry about the best gear if you do not care whether or not you make a catch? What matters is the enjoyment of exercising skill (or, perhaps, merely passing the time), and this is to be had with any tackle, so long as it is familiar and is not grotesquely inappropriate.[30]

> When Prince Wen Wang was on a tour of inspection in Tsang, he saw an old man fishing. But his fishing was not real fishing, for he did not fish in order to catch fish, but

to amuse himself. So Wen Wang wished to employ him in the administration of government, but he feared his own ministers, uncles and brothers might object. On the other hand, if he let the old man go, he could not bear to think of the people being deprived of his influence.[31]

A negative theological, agnostic, or mystical reading of Oakeshott's philosophy of religion also receives support from the way that he conceives that the implicit critiques of history and science are irrelevant to the claims of religion. With regard to history, Oakeshott says that "Whenever the past is regarded . . . as the authority for a body of religious beliefs . . . wherever the past is seen in specific relation to the present, that past is not the past in history."[32] Analogously, with regard to science, Oakeshott says that "Practical moral and religious beliefs must submit themselves, not to the criticism of science, but to that of life. And a science which ventured to take a hand in organizing the world of religious beliefs would be a science which had ceased to be scientific without becoming anything else."[33] The negative theological God is thus not affected by the latest findings of either history or science. As we have seen, what looks like the autonomy of religion is really a function of its incompleteness (its occupying and "colonizing" the world from a particular point of view)—and this "autonomy" and incompleteness it shares with the domains of history and of science. None of these domains is in an ontologically superior position to any of the others. From the perspective of "experience without arrest," they are all equally underdetermined and they all equally await further specification and elaboration of their contents during the course of an indefinitely unfolding future. To allow history and science to furnish critical vantage points from which to impugn the claims of religion would be another example of what Oakeshott in *Experience and Its Modes* regularly refers to as an *ignoratio elenchi*—the logical fallacy of supposing a point proved or disproved by an argument proving or disproving something not at issue. Since history and science are abstractions and modifications of "experience without arrest" no more and no less than practical experience as a whole and religion in particular, critiques of religion generated from historical or scientific premises only prove that history and science differ from religion, not that they are superior to it. The negative case for religion (that no other organizing perspective on experience is intrinsically superior to it) is as powerful or limited as the negative case for history and science.

Based upon our discussion so far, we can say that Oakeshott is an adherent of underdetermination of theory by fact, of words by things—the hard conceptual core of skepticism—in both local and global senses. Underdetermination of theory by fact is a central motif in Oakeshott's thought in a straightforward epistemological sense as a result of his emphasizing throughout his philosophical career, from *Experience and Its Modes* to *On Human Conduct*, how both theories and facts are mutable in the same way and serve in a comparable vein as invitations for further exertions of human understanding. As Oakeshott formulates it in *On Human Conduct*: "A theorem is not an unconditional terminus; it, also, is an understanding waiting to be understood. What distinguishes a theorist is his undistracted concern with the unconditional, critical engagement of understanding in which every understanding (be it 'fact' or 'theorem') is recognized as a not-yet-understood and therefore as an invitation to understand."[34]

For Oakeshott, facts are low-level theories and theories are magnified and expanded facts. Neither so-called facts nor theories place us in secure contact with any reality outside of themselves, that is, their linguistic formulations. "Facts" represent an effort to understand a going-on—that is to say, circumscribing the going-on within some conceptual framework that enables us to make sense of what is taking place or what lies in front of us. For example, to refer to something as an apple or a pencil already presupposes multiple preunderstandings and commitments that orient us in the direction of atomistic individuation of objects rather than more sensually agglomerated designations of them. Atomism is a presupposition of our specification of objects—not something that we could say is directly inferable from them without our theories of perception becoming viciously circular.

It appears that Oakeshott would agree with Nietzsche that "Even in the concept of 'immediate knowledge,' which theoreticians permit themselves, I sensed a *contradictio in adjecto*."[35] The ascent from "immediate" to "knowledge" destroys the immediacy of the subject matter and therefore renders vulnerable from a sheerly objective standpoint the claim to knowledge. Nietzsche and Oakeshott apparently reject the view that our theories or names totally correlate with and exhaust the content of reality and suggest instead that there are infinite possibilities for our theories and names to make sense of and refer to reality. Invoking Emmanuel Levinas's central distinction between totality and infinity, we could say that skeptical idealism as practiced by Nietzsche and Oakeshott militates against totality and underwrites infinity—infinity of interpretation, infinity of theoretical movement toward a mystical unknown.

Oakeshott's adherence to negative theology that is only sustainable as a form of agnosticism or mysticism suggests that he subscribes to a principle of "underdetermination" in a global sense as well. Everything that we encounter in the world (in our experience) is compatible with both an affirmation of God and a denial of Him. Underdetermination of theory by fact is thus woven into the fabric of our ontologies—of how we understand being.

Karl Popper, in his essay "What Is Dialectic?," has argued that according to the rules of inference enshrined in the traditional Aristotelian logic, a toleration of contradiction (such as that encapsulated in the principle of "underdetermination") means that no possibilities can be ruled out, so that a generalized agnosticism (which officially, theoretically leaves the door open to all possibilities) becomes one of the major corollaries of adherence to a principle of "underdetermination." As Popper succinctly states his thesis: "If two contradictory statements are admitted, any statement whatever must be admitted; for from a couple of contradictory statements any statement whatever can be validly inferred."[36]

Oakeshott directly emphasizes that philosophical thinking—what he also calls reflection—is dialectical in character: "The process of reflection is *dialectical*, a process of considering something recognized as knowledge and supposed to be true, yet considering it with the assumption that it is not true—an assumption which we sometimes improperly interpret as 'not wholly true' or 'not the whole truth.' "[37] The ceaseless self-questioning and expansion of the horizons of inquiry that are constitutive of philosophy and which attest to its dialectical character are partially the result of its grappling with issues of reflexivity. If philosophy is conceived as perpetually opening up presuppositions of argument to further scrutiny and investigation (which is a dominant connotation of the phrase that philosophy consists in "experience without arrest"), then it is not allowed to be about something, to have any kind of stable substantive content: "For if we call it [philosophy] 'the continuous and relentless criticism of all the assumptions of human knowledge,' we must somehow avoid the suggestion that 'human knowledge' is something fixed, *about* which the philosopher is anxious to learn something *more* than he already knows."[38] To circumvent this paradox of reflexivity, Oakeshott categorizes philosophy as "dialectical"—as being committed simultaneously to the truth and the untruth of all of the propositions that it entertains.

The logical symbolic notation that Popper uses to make his point applies directly to the way skeptical idealists have traditionally conceived the relationship between theory and fact. For them, it was never the case that only "p." There are always theoretical alternatives to conceptually circumscribe any given set of facts. There is thus always the contradictory possibility of "not-p" as well as "p." According to the traditional rules of inference that Popper applies, this entails the affirmation of any premise whatsoever. According to the basic framework for analyzing the rules of inference that Popper adduces out of Aristotelian logic, the idea of a generalized agnosticism (the impossibility of foreclosing any premise) is derivable from the structure of inference of the traditional logic once the possibility of contradictory premises is affirmed and does not have to await confirmation from the presuppositions and postulates of multivalued logics.

There is an important metaphysical issue at stake in the controversy between Popper and Oakeshott concerning the acceptability of dialectical modes of argument. Popper wants to limit the scope of contingency for the sake of being able to do science as he conceives it. Oakeshott wants to keep the scope of contingency as broad as possible. This is the way Popper sees the crux of the issue: "We must tell the dialectician that he cannot have it both ways. Either he is interested in contradictions because of their fertility: then he must not accept them. Or he is prepared to accept them: then they will be barren, and rational criticism, discussion, and intellectual progress will be impossible."[39] From Popper's perspective, in order to do science in a fruitful way we need to circumscribe the scope of contradiction to the furthest extent possible. Then our results harbor the prospect of being cumulative, linear, and progressive.[40]

Oakeshott's implicit response to this approach, which one can glean from his remarkably prescient chapter on "Scientific Experience" in *Experience and Its Modes*, is to argue in defense of a skeptical idealist philosophy of science. Science has very little to do with reality in any kind of direct, head-on way and a great deal more to do with science itself—how to structure and organize it. For Oakeshott, highlighting the role of circularity in scientific argument is irrepressibly driven by the desire to sustain the primacy of contingency as a dominant mode for apprehending the world. If science is primarily about its own vocabulary and the relationships that subsist between its own statements, then the world slips out of range of full scientific accountability. The following are two examples of Oakeshott's approach: "The primary generalizations of science are analytic generalizations, derived from the analysis of the structural concepts of the world of scientific knowledge, and they express the relations between these concepts which are inherent in the concepts themselves. The integration of the world of science is, first, in terms of the relations which can be deduced directly from the structural concepts of that world." "Without the categories and the method, there is no matter; without the instruments of measurement, nothing to measure."[41] With a remarkably steadfast commitment to the primacy of contingency, Oakeshott manages with the selfsame set of arguments to safeguard the sanctity of contingency as a categorical mode for apprehending the world and to restore contingency to a central role as an organizing category for making sense of the activity of doing science. In Oakeshott's universe—just as in Kandinsky's—we are forever moving in "circles in a circle."[42]

From a slightly different angle of vision we can also say that Oakeshott's skepticism lies at the heart of his philosophy of science. No scientific experiment in the world can fully address the initial acts of conceptualization that yielded the hypothesis that is being hauled before the bar of science. Science (experimentation) can only adjudicate a claim that has been defined. But if defining a claim in a hypothesis is a function of closing theoretical indeterminacies that allow us to pinpoint what is being tested, then those tests cannot speak to or resolve those indeterminacies. If those indeterminacies exist prior to the inauguration of the scientific enterprise and are not resolvable by it—and if they serve as a precondition for there being science altogether—then science understood in a crude, positivist sense is either after the fact or beside the point.

Oakeshott's early work—"An Essay on the Relations of Philosophy, Poetry, and Reality" (probably the dissertation that Oakeshott wrote between September 1924 and July 1925 in support of his successful application for a fellowship at Gonville and Caius College, Cambridge[43])—helps to situate in sharp focus how Oakeshott's awareness of the pervasiveness of circularity in argument leads him to be especially receptive to the claims and priority of mysticism (denominated in the essay by the term "poetry") for apprehending Reality conceived in manifold senses. If my reading of Oakeshott is on target, then virtually the whole corpus of his later philosophy beginning with *Experience and Its Modes*

(1933) onward can be read as being extraordinarily faithful to and consistent with the insights and categories developed in this early essay.[44]

Oakeshott starts the essay with three epigraphs—the first comes from Spinoza, the second derives from Plotinus, and the third is a citation from Pascal. At the conclusion of the essay, Oakeshott refers to the graduated, comprehensive character of the three quotations: "The three passages quoted in the front of the essay are intended to sum up the whole position. The first defines Reality. The second describes the only true way in which Reality may be expressed. The third gives the true use of the intellect in search after the Reality. As will be seen, they logically follow one another."[45]

The first epigraph, from Spinoza, reads: "I understand Reality (*substantia*) to be that which is in itself and is conceived through itself: I mean that, the conception of which does not depend on the conception of another thing from which it must be formed."[46] Spinoza thus understands Reality to be that which is not variable or theory-dependent, but rather "that which is in itself and is conceived through itself." "Reality" requires no extraneous conceptualization but is rather something that as a matter of internal necessity has to be what it is.

The second epigraph, from Plotinus's *Enneads*, says: "The principal cause of our uncertainty is that the only comprehension we may have of Reality (The One) comes neither by scientific observation, nor by the strivings of the mind—as comes our understanding of other things—but by an immediate Presence, which far transcends all learning. . . . This is why Plato says that Reality is ineffable and indescribable. Yet we speak and write of it; but only in order to arouse our souls and to start ourselves on the way to that Divine Vision: like as when one showeth a pilgrim on his way to some shrine that he would visit: for our words may only show us the way and guide us thereon, the Vision itself is the sole work of him who hungers to see."[47]

According to Plotinus, Reality can only be comprehended "by an immediate Presence, which far transcends all learning." It "comes neither by scientific observation, nor by the strivings of the mind." Apparently, what is apprehended in these ways can be skeptically called into question. Plausible counterarguments and well-grounded suspicions can be mobilized to attempt to invalidate virtually all claims to knowledge and to certainty. "Our understanding of other things" (aside from "Reality" or "The One") can be achieved through "scientific observation" and "the strivings of the mind." Presumably, this is because to intellectually engage and to practically control these "other things" does not require certainty or the attainment of truth. Our skeptical questioning of our scientific grasp or commonsensical approach to these other things does not yield the certainty that they do not exist or that they have not been properly understood. For the sake of consistency (if for no other reason), our skeptical questioning can be skeptically interrogated in turn, and we are thus licensed to confer upon our "scientific observation[s]" and "regular strivings of the mind" a provisional legitimacy, awaiting what further scientific observations and further interactions with the world and reflections upon them by the mind might yield.

Our deferral of reality is occasioned not only by the lack of finality that attends any series of "scientific observation[s]" and any set of intellectual exertions by human minds, but also by the fact that the vocabularies that we invoke to register those observations and encode our reflections upon particular sectors of experience can never be conclusively, authoritatively shown to be the only relevant vocabularies for the subject matters at hand. What we are observing and thinking can be translated into other vocabularies than those we are currently employing without disrupting the continuity and coherence of our worlds of observation and thought as long as we make the appropriate adjustments elsewhere along the line in the bodies of observational and reflective statements that we take to be true.

What emerges from the quotation from Plotinus is that the relationship between language and reality can be conceived as being one of radical underdetermination—with language and reality hardly ever unself-consciously (with overwhelming certainty) overlapping or intersecting. The problem of their relationship is further deepened by its systematic character. It is not only the case that in individual instances of scientific observation or reflection different strings of words can be summoned up to capture what we are "seeing" or thinking. On a higher level of abstraction, when we consider the relationship between words and things generally, we confront conflicting possibilities of words being taken to immediately capture things or theorizing words as bearing a "softer" relationship to things, so that things can enter into our stream of experience under variable conceptual and verbal auspices and our experience as a whole can still be sustained as coherent. At a third level still, we have to acknowledge the inevitability and irremovability of contradiction in terms of how language shapes up vis-à-vis reality. Given the ontological gap that surrounds the relationship between words and things, we can never rule out the possibility that contradictory verbal formulations will be able to intelligibly circumscribe the same body of things (on at least some kind of formal level of sameness). Once this occurs— and we have allowed contradiction to enter into the stream of statements that we take to be true—then we have no way of confining contradiction to just that one instance but must be prepared for the proliferation of contradictions, and the ultimate legitimation of the category of contradiction itself for encoding our experience of the world.

At this juncture in our movement toward coming to grips with Reality, words lose their efficacy and become overtaken by silence and by the sense that "Reality is ineffable and indescribable." In the vocabulary of Plotinus, "being" must now supervene upon "knowing."[48] When "knowing" exhausts itself by exposing the inevitability and insurmountability of contradiction, "being" takes over. "Being" is sensed as an "immediate Presence" that redeems and transcends the irresolvability and unexitability of thought. "Being" conjures up some kind of merging (if only through our inability to proceed any further) with those contradictory entities such as God that thinking is incapable of either ratifying or excluding.

Art (with "Poetry" serving as the stand-in for all artistic genres in Oakeshott's essay) illuminates for us the unstructured character of human existence—susceptible to infinite reformations. Realism is only one mask among a multitude of unimaginably many masks for shaping the material of art. Art is humanity's ongoing testimonial to the mysticism of everyday life.

In his theorizing both of metaphysics and of religion, Oakeshott seems to be pursuing a via negativa. He says that "We may distinguish two main approaches to Reality of which man has made constant use. The one we may call the approach of the *Intellect*, recorded in the history of Philosophy; the other, the approach of *Intuition*, set down for the most part in the history of Mysticism."[49] Oakeshott identifies philosophy with a process of reasoned argument. As we have seen embedded in the quotation from Plotinus, the process recoils in upon itself and is not capable of negotiating a substantive outcome or conclusion—by way of either affirmation or negation. For Oakeshott, "The claim of the intellect to know Reality has no foundation. Apparently there is no alternative to the adoption of a skeptical, or at least agnostic, position. From the point of view of the intellect there is indeed no alternative, but we have yet to consult the claims of poetry. Poetry claims to be able to join itself to Reality."[50]

The method of philosophy is description.[51] Philosophy tries (unsuccessfully) to plot or negotiate a point of entry into Reality by privileging a particular starting point—and inaugurating its process of description from that artificial beginning. The philosopher must assiduously dissociate himself from his object of study and deliberately, systematically cultivate doubt in order to nudge the process of philosophical description along.[52]

"To my mind," Oakeshott says, "there are certain axiomatic qualities which we must apply to Reality by definition before we start our enquiry. Indeed, if this were not so all enquiry would be vain; for how can we search for something which we shall not recognize when we see it?"[53] Expanding upon Plato's defense of tacit knowledge in the *Meno*, Oakeshott regards some version of circularity in argument as unavoidable—and salutary. For the skeptical philosopher (as we have seen), his circular starting point consists in descriptively exploring how opting for the most nominalist and minimalist assumptions that one can come up with—such as "underdetermination of theory by fact" instead of "correspondence between word and thing"; the ontological priority of language over extralinguistic entities; and the pervasiveness and salvageability of contradiction—is still sufficient for theorizing the intersubjective, everyday world as well as the specialized disciplinary explorations that take place under the rubrics of science and history.

In contrast to philosophy, "poetry [and its closest metaphysical analogue, mysticism[54]] knows Reality all at once; process is foreign to its method."[55] "Philosophy possesses, poetry [and by implication, mysticism] is possessed by its knowledge."[56] For Oakeshott, religion, intuition, and mysticism come into their own only after the pursuit of philosophy has led to the devaluation of reasoned argument in one's discourse. This takes place upon the heels of an awareness that philosophical analysis is doomed to retrace its theoretical options and alternatives forever, without being able to resolve discussion in favor of any one of them as against any or all of the others. However, just as philosophy is circular, so, too, are religion and mysticism. Oakeshott quotes approvingly the statement of T. H. Green that "In its true nature, faith can be justified by nothing but itself."[57] There is nothing intrinsic to the experiences of irresolvability and ineffability that overhang philosophy through all of its movements that compel us to translate them in a religious or mystical direction. Religion and mysticism are the starting points that we provide for rendering humanly intelligible and usable the inchoate and loose-hanging texture of experience that the pursuit of philosophy both makes us aware of and engenders. In the intuitive approach to Reality endemic to poetry, religion, and mysticism, the process character of human thought reflected in philosophy is suspended.[58] In poetry and mysticism, "the first thing" that is seen "is the last thing." "It knows Reality (that is, claims to know Reality) at a bound by an immediate intuitive contact with the thing."[59] The first/last thing that it knows is, of course, what it has situated and designated as a worthy successor to the infinitely extending irresolvabilities of philosophical reason.

For Oakeshott, mysticism and logic do not mix. "Intuitive knowledge . . . cannot justify its claim by a logical argument: to do so would be a negation of its first assertion."[60] Mystical belief can be grounded in nothing else but mystical belief. It is tautologies that define the outer limits of human existence. "Arguments so far from being added reasons for belief are an absolute and final condemnation."[61] Poetry and mysticism, in contrast to philosophy, do "not describe but create."[62] They rely on the infectiousness of a tautology that fills in the space cleared by the self-nullifying operations of reason to inspire and validate the lurches toward the ineffable and the beyond of poets and mystics.

In "An Essay on the Relations of Philosophy, Poetry and Reality," Oakeshott seems to have self-consciously adopted the approach to religion and mysticism of negative theology. He quotes Spinoza with approval: "As Spinoza says, 'Intellect, finite or infinite, in actuality, must comprehend the attributes of God and the modifications of God and nothing else.' God Himself, Reality, is beyond its grasp or knowledge."[63] Again: "If intellect and will appertain to the eternal essence of God, something far else must be understood by these attributes than what is commonly understood by men."[64] The role of the human intellect in relation to God is to engage in radical disassociation. The human mind must be continually focused on prying loose the attributes of God from God. These attributes must be relentlessly deliteralized so that only unintelligible verbal shells are left of them, without discernible sense or reference. Since denuding God's attributes of literal import cannot be taken to imply that He does not have them because then we would be claiming to know what God's utter transcendence debars us from knowing, then the "withholding" of attributes from God needs to be construed not as a "description" of God but as a metaphor for how we should conceive the relationship between words and things on a sheerly human level. Just as the word "God" remains endlessly open in relation to the entity that it names—we have no conception of what any of His officially imputed attributes signify, nor how they relate to Him—so, too, do the words in the human vocabulary remain endlessly open in relation to the reality (the things) that they conjure up. Words are underdetermined by things, so that how and where they hook up to the furniture of the world cannot be fixed on an a priori or enduring basis. New enlargements and constrictions and revisions of words in relation to things can take place all of the time, without any of them necessarily issuing forth in a precise fit between a word and a thing. Negative theology thus encodes skepticism and the paradoxes to which it gives rise as part of its pristine cognitive content.

At the second plateau when the paradoxes surrounding negative theology and skepticism propel us toward a mystical translation and transfiguration of theological and philosophical argument, negative theology is palpably animating Oakeshott's argument when he reminds us that the practice of mysticism cannot be validated by the logical conundrums that led up to it, but only in relation to itself. In circular fashion, it is our intellects and imaginations that fix the object of our intuitive grasp—and it is that circle (and nothing outside it) that can be invoked to justify our intuitive insights and raptures.

In the third epigraph, from Pascal, that Oakeshott places at the beginning of his essay—which he says "gives the true use of the intellect in the search after Reality"[65]—the thematics of negative theology are again stressed: "It is good to be tired and wearied in the vain search after the Ethical Reality (*le vrai bien*), that we may stretch out our arms to the Redeemer."[66] Oakeshott (and perhaps also Pascal) clearly identifies the "vain search after the Ethical Reality" with philosophy—which in its inability to deliver the real thing induces fatigue and weariness. The vocation of philosophy is to highlight ignorance and incoherence—and to make us dramatically aware of our limitations. I have also suggested that, for Oakeshott, the theory of mysticism as compensating for the deficiencies of philosophy is also comparably limited and tainted. The circular character of mysticism will (just like philosophy itself) deny the superrational cravings of human beings their hoped-for repose. Mysticism only works out of the depths of Wittgenstein's "silence" and Plotinus's "being," where we leave that which we claim to know (if only to know that we do not know it), and that which we acknowledge that we do not know but are able to specify on some rhetorical level as the target that we are seeking, far behind.

One of Oakeshott's great precursors in reshaping otherworldly discourse into a series of this-worldly analogues (including the humanly developed and articulated category of "mysticism" itself) is St. Augustine. By disenchanting his former captivation by the gnostic heresy and theorizing an unbridgeable metaphysical distance between the *civitas terrena* and the *civitas dei*, St. Augustine sets the stage for the reinsertion of Christian eschatology within a worldly setting and time frame. He conjures up the prospect of the limits to human rational penetration both required and presupposed by faith overlapping with philosophical reason's insights into its own limitations, which becomes Oakeshott's life theme. Out of Augustinian theological resources and inspirations, Oakeshott is able to envision a meeting ground between the believer and the nonbeliever: The most the believer can hope to know—and to show—is that God is not on a literal level all those things that human beings attribute to Him. He is inscrutably above and beyond all of those things. The most the nonbeliever can hope to know and to show is that we can never know for sure that God is. He does not and cannot claim to know for sure that God is not. Neither the believer nor the nonbeliever can move beyond the same tissue of possibilities. Oakeshott's thought contributes importantly toward theorizing and legitimating this whole discourse of possibility. Therefore, the arena for the encountering and the unfolding of both the religious and the secular dimensions of human life is the common world of the now.

I have been arguing that a major strategy to invoke for grappling with the contradictions to which both negative theology and skepticism give rise is to reallocate God and truth from the domain of discursive speech to the realm of the ineffable—the mystical. Both negative theology and skepticism attempt to do what appears to be logically impossible. Negative theology wants to conceptualize God by paring down the literal significations of His attributes— apparently oblivious of the fact that if this is the only way we approach Him, we can legitimately raise the question, whose attributes are we paring down? If God subsists only as a subject for the sake of having the literal import of His attributes be torn away, we are bereft of a viable subject concerning whom negative theology can do its critical work. Skepticism gives rise to a parallel dilemma and contradiction. The skeptic who asserts the epistemological right to question everything leaves skepticism out of his purview of questioning. Staying within the discursive domain wherein the traditional constraints of logic and language prevail, the dilemmas and contradictions I have described seem insuperable. Shifting the domain of communication from regular verbal discourse to mysticism seems like a propitious move to make to revive and sustain the theological and theoretical quests.

The fifteenth-century German cardinal of the Roman Catholic Church, Nicholas of Cusa, who was also a philosopher, jurist, mathematician, and astronomer, theorizes in an especially cogent way the stages through which one passes from theologically and theoretically registered ignorance to mysticism:

> O Lord my God, the Helper of them that seek Thee, I behold Thee in the entrance of Paradise, and I know not what I see, for I see naught visible. This alone I know, that I know not what I see, and never can know. And I know not how to name Thee because I know not what Thou art, and did anyone say unto me that Thou wert called by this name or that, by the very fact that he named it, I should know that it was not Thy name. For the wall beyond which I see Thee is the end of all manner of signification in names. If anyone should set forth any concept by which Thou couldst be conceived, I know that that concept is not a concept of Thee, for every concept is ended in the wall of Paradise. And if anyone should set forth any likeness, and say that Thou wert to be imagined as resembling it, I know in like manner that that is no likeness of Thee. So too, if any were to tell of the understanding of Thee, wishing to supply a means whereby Thou mightest be understood, this man is yet far from Thee. For Thou art separated by an exceeding high wall from all these. The

high wall separates Thee from all that can possibly be said or thought of Thee, forasmuch as Thou art Absolute above all the concepts which any man can frame.[67]

In this extraordinary passage, Nicholas's whole enterprise seems to be shot through with contradiction. Nicholas is writing about—which is to say, he is trying to make sense of—a subject matter, namely, God, about whom he *says*, "It behoveth, then, the intellect to become ignorant and to abide in darkness if it would fain see Thee."[68] The performative contradiction could not be any starker than it is in this moment of Nicholas's mapping of his (our) descent (ascent) into ineffability. Apparently, from Nicholas's perspective, our inability to make sense of God-talk—to rationally grasp what it would mean to have an experience of Divinity—does not mean that such talk or experience are unavailable to us. To get the Radically One, biblical, monotheistic God into focus, we continually have to pare down the literal applicability of the terms that we are traditionally motivated to apply to Him. We incessantly have to declare that we are incapable of grasping the significance of such terms as "knowledge," "power," and "compassion" in relation to Him. He is so inconceivably elevated above all things human that we are unable to fathom what these terms signify concerning Him. However, if unremitting disowning of the literal meanings of words is the only point of conceptual access to God, then we are thrust into an intensely paradoxical and even contradictory position. What is the nature of the entity whose attributes we are continually literally disowning? If we only have God through the mobilization of the apparatus of conceptual disowning, then do we have God at all? If we have no independent way of identifying Him, whom or what are we disowning of literal descriptions? Does not the

Subject disappear in the inclusiveness of the critical apparatus aimed at clarifying His identity?

So the concept of God is contradictory in the sense that
I have just described. However, superimposing a paradox
upon a paradox, if we are willing to admit this contradiction, then (as we have seen in our discussion of Popper)
contradiction in general will have been legitimated in our
discourse—and thus the basis for wanting to exclude God-
talk in the first place will have been dismantled. Once we
go through the stages of argument I have summarized, we
can appropriately classify the region of God-talk and God-
experience as mystical, since although we have no way of
rationally mapping it, we also do not have a way of rationally
discrediting it. "God" just refers to a separate mystical zone
of human experience.

The same phases of argument—with the same acknowledgment of a distinctively mystical dimension to human
experience—can be charted in relation to how we map the
furniture and contours of the everyday world. By view-
ing our everyday experience of the world from the organized perspective of the underdetermination of theory by
fact, we immediately open ourselves up to the possibility of
contradiction. If facts are to any important extent theory-
dependent, then it is possible that contradictory theoretical formulations will be able to make sense of (appropriately conceptually encompass) the formally self-same body
of fact. Once contradiction is admitted, we have no way of
further blocking it or keeping it at bay and preventing its
future proliferation. We are willy-nilly thrust into a mystical
stance in relation to the everyday world. A skeptical idealist
approach for making sense of "ordinary reality" dislocates,
and even uproots, our commonsense understanding of the
world, but also, given the requirements of consistency so

that the skeptic must include skepticism within the ambit of his skeptical interrogation, restores to us the "old world" as a limit, now in an exotic and "deracinated" form. Pursuing a skeptical idealist approach to reality recasts the everyday world in a mystical frame. God and the world subsist on the same mystical level.

One can spin a variation on the argument I have just made concerning the transition between skepticism and mysticism. Instead of a propulsion to a new dimension of experience (namely, mysticism) being provided by the need to resolve paradoxes of reflexivity attendant to formulations of negative theology and skepticism, one can say that skepticism (and negative theology, which represents the breakdown of reason in relation to conceptualizations of God, can be labeled as a form of skepticism) by itself already constitutes a version of mysticism. With its notion of the underdetermination of words by things, skepticism traces nothingness (amorphousness, emptiness, intractability) in the world. What cannot be securely charted through words, concepts, and categories remains a vast nothingness, now located within the world of experience instead of outside it. Where firm conceptualization has not entered, wholeness prevails. From this perspective, skepticism is mysticism without the rapture.

By the same token, one can conceive of negative theology as already a mystical religious practice. If one defines mysticism (which is such an elastic and inclusive term) negatively as the breakdown of reason, then negative theology can be viewed as an instrumentality for embracing and practicing mysticism. Negative theology is adopted in the world to deal with the other of reason—what is not permeable to the light of reason. The object of negative theology can then be redefined as being not-reason (a continuing inventorying with

regard to the question of God of the limitations and recalci-
trance of reason), instead of its original object—God—that
reason was originally preoccupied with in its search for a
ground for itself.

One of the prime practitioners of negative theology in this
sense in the history of Christianity was St. Anselm of Can-
terbury in the eleventh century. In his prologue to *Proslogion*
("which means a speech made to another"[69]), St. Anselm says
that "I began to wonder . . . whether it might be possible to
find a single argument that needed nothing but itself alone
for proof, that would by itself be enough to show that God
really exists; that he is the supreme good, who depends on
nothing else, but on whom all things depend for their being
and for their well-being; and whatever we believe about the
divine nature."[70] As St. Anselm defines his project, it consists
of two main goals: (1) to adduce an argument that would
show that God is the source "on whom all things depend
for their being"; and (2) to fashion an argument that would
be "single" and need "nothing but itself alone for proof." St.
Anselm is seeking to terminate the theological and philosophical quest concerning God by coming up with an argument that would be utterly self-contained and self-sufficient:
it would neither require nor invite extension, elaboration, or
proof by the development of further arguments, nor would
it be vulnerable to the onslaught of counterarguments. In
other words, St. Anselm is searching for the philosophical Rosetta stone that would render all further arguments
on his chosen topic—the existence of God—superfluous.
In the body of the *Proslogion* proper, one can discern two
strands of argument that respond to these two stated goals
of the prologue. In engaging his first aim, St. Anselm says,
"Indeed, everything that exists, except for you [God] alone,

can be thought not to exist. So you alone among all things have existence most truly, and therefore most greatly; for whatever else exists has existence less truly, and therefore less greatly."[71] Everything else that exists in the world (aside from God) is contingent. It is always possible for us to imagine that it does not exist, and its existence occasions further probing as to what lies behind it to enable it to exist. Only God in His utter and complete transcendence of things human can be envisioned as the Necessary Being or the Necessarily Existent behind whom it is by definition impossible to probe. He is the Necessary Entity that legitimates our recourse to contingency in diagnosing intermediate ranges of occurrences in the world.

But now the true challenge for St. Anselm—and for us as his interpreters—begins. How can the metaphysical and logical necessity for the postulation of God as the Necessary Being be transformed into an irrefutable argument validating His existence? God can only bring the quest for explanation and understanding to a halt because He subsists in a dimension above and beyond the human. It is because He is infinite that we cannot probe beyond Him. By the same token, His being infinite dislodges any explanatory efficacy that we might be tempted to attach to the notion of His being the Necessarily Existent. St. Anselm has only answered the question as to why we are driven to attribute necessary existence to God. But his very answer to this question seems to have burned all bridges for adducing a proof for God's existence. For that, we would need a primary level of explanation that stayed within a finite human framework that would be intelligible to us.

I believe that what takes place at this point is a remarkable alchemical transformation that contributes to resituating how we view the Western past. Steeping himself in his Augustinian credo of "seeking to understand what he believes"[72]—that belief precedes understanding in all domains of human thought and practice, that this priority is not a special "obfuscation" introduced by and restricted to religion but affects all areas of human experience—St. Anselm turns to words and concepts and how human beings use them to generate the "single argument" that "by itself" would "be enough to show that God really exists." He states his proof very elegantly and succinctly: "This [being] exists so truly that it cannot even be thought not to exist. For it is possible to think that something exists that cannot be thought not to exist, and such a being is greater than one that can be thought not to exist. . . . For God is that than which a greater cannot be thought. Whoever understands this properly, understands that this being exists in such a way that he cannot, even in thought, fail to exist. So whoever understands that God exists in this way cannot think that he does not exist."[73]

If my reading of St. Anselm is correct, he is using his very inability to trace and affirm God through the labyrinth of logic and language—evinced by how His ultimacy as an explanatory factor (His infinity) defeats the possibility of propounding a rational defense of His existence—as a new basis for validating His existence. God, as it were, is not situated in a privileged position vis-à-vis all other linguistic entities. Just as all the objects of the world have to be believed-in before they can be known, so, too, with God. The delineation and specification of objects has to go through the loop of language before their validation can occur. Language has to endlessly fold in upon itself first to give us a world of objects—and then to give us a world of proven, existent objects. There is no point at which we can opt out of the ebb and flow of language and its role in the identification and confirmation of objects to obtain an independent assessment of their identity and validity. Only by moving through the circle of our language do we have the world. The most secure validation of God's existence is the one that extends the insecurities institutionalized in language to encompass God. The move from monotheism to skepticism and back again—the flagging of an enduring stationary metaphysical moment in Western consciousness—occurs in St. Anselm as he tries to come up with the "single argument" that needs "nothing but itself alone for proof" to clinch the case for God's existence. He then moves into the built-in limitations of language and its relationship to the world to establish an "irrefutable" case for the reality of God-talk.

To be maximally charitable to St. Anselm, the point to emphasize is that he believes that you end up with a tautology no matter how you proceed. If you invoke God subsisting in an infinite dimension to bring your explanatory quest to a halt, you have achieved ultimacy but sacrificed intelligibility. To restore intelligibility, you are reduced to stating a tautology: God is God. In that case, St. Anselm appears to be telling us, there is no need to directly invoke the infinite at all. We can stay on the level of our regularly deployed language and concepts and simply point to the conceptual import of our everyday use of the term "God." According to St. Anselm, existence is implied in that everyday use. If one then becomes resistant and says, "You have only shown me that in our traditional linguistic usage, we regularly make use of the term 'God,' harboring implications of ultimacy and infinity. You have not shown me that this God exists," the best rebuttal to make to this argument is a negative one. "If I straightforwardly try to validate God's existence, I end up with a tautology. I am not able to theorize the point of intersection between the finite and the infinite. When I stay on the level of ordinary linguistic usage, I confront the same tautology sooner, without having expended grandiose efforts to transcend it."

During 1095–1098, St. Anselm wrote *Cur Deus Homo*, which is the one work in Christian theology that Oakeshott lamented he would not live long enough to write a modern version of. *Cur Deus Homo* consists in an arresting reading of the Incarnation that can be said to implicitly build upon the central role St. Anselm assigns in the *Proslogion* to conceptual investigation conducted within the parameters posted by language.[74] There were two main factors in the immediate historical context that prodded St. Anselm to embark upon the composition of the *Cur Deus Homo*. The first was the influence and increasing historical visibility of the Jews who argued against excessively allegorical readings of the "Old Testament" as just consisting in tendentious and anachronistic interpolations into the "Old Testament" of what had emerged only later and could only authentically be found in the "New." Another line of attack being put forward by Jewish scholars at this time was the extent to which the blood and gore of the Crucifixion and Incarnation flagrantly subverted and undermined God's dignity, majesty, and transcendence. God had become too melodramatically human to justify retaining his identity as God.[75]

Simultaneous with the emergence of a Jewish challenge on the left to a traditional reading of the Incarnation, there also emerged a Christian challenge on the right. From the newly prominent secular (as opposed to monastic) school in Laon, there circulated an understanding of the Incarnation as a move in a game to outwit the Devil in his dominion over humankind. With the Fall, the Devil had a rightful claim to establish his sovereignty over human beings. The only way to reclaim Divine sovereignty over the human scene was to ensnare the Devil to transgress the bounds of his legitimate assertiveness by attacking a totally innocent human being, and thereby forfeiting his right to rule over the human race. The innocent victim who became the decoy enticing the Devil to overstep the limits of his legitimate authority was, of course, Christ. Hence, the Incarnation.[76]

St. Anselm found it theologically offensive to impute to the Devil the idea of "rights." That the Devil who was himself the embodiment of "fallenness" and sinfulness should have rights seemed to him utterly bizarre. There was an eerie confluence in the provocations that the Jewish critique of the Incarnation and the School of Laon's rendering of it induced in St. Anselm. The Jewish scholars highlighted for St. Anselm how a literal reading of the Incarnation constituted a source of acute theological embarrassment by degrading God. The School of Laon, by thrusting a literally conceived Devil into the very center of the plotline of the Incarnation, only heightened St. Anselm's sense of the inappropriateness of a literal reading of the Incarnation. It might have sent him scurrying back to the framework of the ontological argument developed some twenty years earlier in the *Proslogion* to see how he could apply its methodology and structure to unraveling the mysteries and depths of the Incarnation.

Pursuing this line of approach, we might say that for St. Anselm, the Creation story is not complete without implicating God in the drama of Redemption. Our craving for higher and more inclusive patterns of explanation leads us to postulate God as the Necessarily Existent, who out of an infinite dimension that human beings cannot negotiate created and governs the universe. The universe (after an acknowledgment of the role of God in its Creation) can now be conceived as harboring symmetry, order, beauty, and balance that seem to have been sullied once and for all by the eruption of human sinfulness. Human beings ought to be mobilizing huge and unremitting efforts toward atonement in the form of total subservience and obedience to God. However, any group of human beings' rechanneling their lives fully in the direction of God cannot make up for the totality of disobedience and wrongdoing committed by human beings in the course of the generations. Only God can (has the capacity to) make up, to compensate, for the wrongdoing, but He is the sinned-against and not the sinner. The only plausible (necessary) solution is to synthesize a human "ought" with a Divine "can" in the form of a God-Man who restores the beauty and symmetry of original Creation by achieving universal Redemption and atonement. The Incarnation as an infinite symbol that we can never fully decode restores coherence to Creation.[77]

It is important to gauge the weight and scope—the metaphysical trajectory—of St. Anselm's argument. His strictures concerning the Divine vocabulary apply to his deciphering of the Incarnation. The first theological exploration sets the context for the second. St. Anselm gets rid of the Devil from the theological transactions leading to the formulation of the doctrine of the Incarnation in order to render the Christian theological vocabulary less realistic in accordance with the standards of his contemporaries, and to highlight the extent to which our words feed off the meanings and connotations of other words and hardly ever confront a more obdurate and substantial reality than that. God having a Son is the case of a metaphor begetting another metaphor, so that the metaphysical equations surrounding the first metaphor should come out right. One could also say that the Incarnation serves as a negative theological metaphor for how Christianity differs from Judaism. God is a word that we have in our languages as a means of expressing the source of all things. God-Man as symbolized in the Incarnation is a term that is nurtured in the Christian religious vocabulary as an expression of the superseding of law by love—of bifurcation and division by wholeness and healing—that constitutes the Christian monotheistic stance in the world. Waiting for our worlds of words to disclose a universe of redeemed objects is transformed under Christian auspices into an anticipation that assigns priority to wholeness and healing in our metaphysical state of endless waiting. The Incarnation in St. Anselm's hands becomes a Christian supplement to the idea of God: both terms serve as symbols of how the chafing against the limits of language conjures up in thought and imagery the realm of the postlinguistic.

In my reading of St. Anselm, he appears much closer to his contemporary Peter Abelard's position on the Incarnation than a surface reading of both thinkers might suggest. Abelard says that "We are justified in the blood of Christ and reconciled to God by this singular grace shown to us, in that his Son received our nature, and in this nature left us an example by word and deed of enduring until death."[78] In Abelard's reading, the Incarnation models optimal human behavior. It encodes for us the lengths that we need to go in sustaining love and devotion. To a superficial reader it might appear that while St. Anselm is still preoccupied with applying and refining theological reason so that reconciliation is achieved between God and man, Abelard is predicating his construal of the Incarnation on a critique of theological reason, so that all that is left of the Incarnation is a magnified image of human potential. I think that painting such a contrast would be mistaken. I believe that St. Anselm in his interpretation of the Incarnation pushes theological reason to its limits. In his discussion of the Incarnation—just as in his exposition of the ontological argument—he explores the meaning and significance of words and concepts, and what they disclose also relates only to words and concepts, which now endlessly feed off each other in what we might characterize as a disquisition on the limits of the human. St. Anselm's application of theological reason therefore sets the stage for using our discussions of Divinity as a guide to human behavior. St. Anselm dramatizes for us how, on theological grounds, the human sphere becomes the supreme arena for actualization of our conceptualizations of the Divine.

Very paradoxically, St. Anselm theorizes the Incarnation as an expression of a radical monotheistic impulse:

> Do you not understand that human beings would be rightly judged to be subservient to any other person whatsoever who redeemed them from eternal death? And if that were the case, they would by no means be restored to that dignity that they were going to have if they had not sinned, since they who were not going to be subservient to anyone but God and were going to be in every respect equal to the good angels would instead be subservient to someone who was not God, someone to whom the angels would not be subservient.[79]

This passage manifests the profound Augustinian influence on St. Anselm. From this perspective, the Incarnation represents a further strategic theological move to keep the gnostic bifurcation of Divinity (that the God of Creation and the God of Redemption are primordially distinct) at bay. Creation and Redemption both emanate from the one God. The Redeemer could only be God Himself because otherwise human beings would be plagued by divided loyalties between God the Creator and man the redeemer. Paradoxically, to maintain God's wholeness—and the integrity of human loyalty and obedience to Him—the Redeemer could only be God (the God-Man of Christianity).

The surge toward unity becomes overwhelming. From the perspective of St. Anselm's reconfiguration of the Incarnation, Creation and Redemption are one. Other paraphrases of the same idea encapsulated in the Incarnation might be the following: doing and redoing are one; sinfulness and atonement are one; commander and commanded are one; Creator and created are one. In the interstices of St. Anselm's reenvisioning of the Incarnation, one can discern a movement toward pantheism. The pantheism correlates with what I have been arguing is the negative theological backdrop to St. Anselm's argument. The endless displacement of God in monotheism means that on theological grounds we can no longer speak theologically but only pantheistically: wherever we as monotheistic believers are tempted to say "God," monotheistic theology warns us that that we can only say "the world," a further exemplification of a natural manifestation or a human fabrication. According to the ontology of negative theology, there is an enduring, negatively reinforced equivalence between the world and God.[80] From this analytical perspective, Christianity in insisting on the idea of an inscrutable God-Man can be decoded as an expression of an extreme negative theological impulse.

In accordance with the reading of St. Anselm on the Incarnation that I am proposing, the strict conditions of service that St. Anselm imposed upon the monks in his charge (and, by extension, upon all worthy and righteous Christians[81]) was not grounded upon any literal, direct, or personal relationship with God. The Incarnation is just an embellishment, an elaboration, of the original God-metaphor. In no way does it personalize or literalize the relationship with God. In the end, tautology on the human level matches tautology on the Divine level. We obey because we obey—just as God is God for no apparent reason that we can fathom. (In the realm of the infinite, our words are nothing more than metaphors—which is to say they are just words.) We cannot get to Him, and, by the same token, we cannot get to the wellsprings of our sources of obedience. We obey because we obey—just as God commands because He commands.

How negative theology already bespeaks a mystical relationship to God is also sharply delineated by Nicholas of Cusa in the following passage:

> I exist in that measure in which Thou art with me, and, since Thy look is Thy being, I am because Thou dost look at me, and if Thou didst turn Thy glance from me I should cease to be.
>
> But I know that Thy glance is that supreme Goodness which cannot fail to communicate itself to all able to receive it. Thou, therefore, canst never let me go so long as I am able to receive Thee. Wherefore it behoveth me to make myself, in so far as I can, ever more able to receive Thee. But I know that the capacity which maketh union possible is naught else save likeness. And incapacity springeth from lack of likeness. If, therefore, I have rendered myself by all possible means like unto Thy goodness, then, according to the degree of that likeness, I shall be capable of the truth.
>
> Lord, Thou hast given me my being, of such a nature that it can make itself continuously more able to receive Thy grace and goodness. And this power, which I have of Thee, wherein I possess a living image of Thine almighty power, is free will. By this I can either enlarge or restrict

my capacity for Thy grace. The enlarging is by conformity with Thee, when I strive to be good because Thou
art good, to be just because Thou art just, to be merciful because Thou art merciful; when all my endeavor is
turned toward Thee because all Thy endeavor is turned
toward me; when I look unto Thee alone with all my
attention, nor ever turn aside the eyes of my mind, because
Thou dost enfold me with Thy constant regard; when I
direct my love toward Thee alone because Thou, who art
Love's self, hast turned Thee toward me alone. And what,
Lord, is my life, save that embrace wherein Thy delight-
some sweetness doth so lovingly enfold me? I love my life
supremely because Thou art my life's sweetness.[82]

God who sees us in a way that we cannot grasp—and in
relation to whom *our* capacity to see is not even an approxi-
mation—can only be approached by us through our "free
will." We cannot apprehend God's thoughts or the nature of
His abilities. We can only strive to emulate the actions that
the Bible on a literal level ascribes to Him—which Nicholas
groups together under the rubric of "goodness." Just as God
is "good," "just," and "merciful," so, too, can we strive to cultivate and exhibit all three traits.[83]

The logical-conceptual barrier separating us from God
is impenetrable. The primacy that Nicholas assigns to "free
will" in terms of how human beings "navigate" their relationship to God is suggestive of how the whole idea of
God is sustained from Nicholas's perspective. God, apparently, cannot be ruled out—just like skepticism cannot be
precluded. The affirmation of God is just as much a vol-
untary act as raising the question concerning His existence.
The affirmation is not more fully grounded than the question. All of our beginnings (and all of our actions constitute

nothing more than beginnings) are interchangeable and lead nowhere. Mysticism begins with a clearing of space for a beginning that is not human—a Divine beginning, what Nicholas refers to as "Thy look" or "Thy glance." The irresolvable threads that emerge from the assertion of human free will culminating in negative theology and skepticism release or prod our imagination to project the notion of a beginning that emanates from God in the form of His gaze that serves as the precondition of all faltering human beginnings. Since the rational bridges between conceptualization and reality have all been burnt from the human side, in a mystical universe we are free to invert relationships beyond how they were conceived under auspices of sheerly human logical and argumentative constraints. Human uncertainties concerning the reliability and stability of beginnings can become mystical certainties without having to be discounted by the force of the transition. The exposure of a tissue of possibilities in the human world concerning God and truth can simply be succeeded or replaced by the unveiling and embrace of these very possibilities in the realm of Divinity, now mystically registered as certainties.

This mystical image of the Divine gaze in conjunction with human nonpenetration of the Divine has its human counterparts in Wittgenstein's and Oakeshott's mysticism of everyday life. Wittgenstein and Oakeshott both emphasize how we cannot see or know the external world for what it truly, unconditionally is. We only know it in relation to categories and presuppositions encoded in and sanctioned by our particular vocabularies. These vocabularies are contingent—and could have evolved in ways other than those we are accustomed to. Nevertheless, as metaphysically ungrounded as our worlds are, they still beckon us and we are able to achieve our required satisfactions within them.

Our worlds are there for us to inhabit and cultivate—despite the fact that we cannot figure out what they ultimately, irrevocably are (if anything). We move in their orbits of meaning and orientation coextensively with our not being able to fathom the depths of their possibilities or the reliability of their foundations. In the idiom of Nicholas of Cusa, which is unconsciously reflected in the writings of Wittgenstein and Oakeshott, the worlds of theory and practice that we engage, as it were, "see" us—they polarize and grip us—even as we cannot "see" them.

The same kind of asymmetry between seeing and being seen affects Oakeshott's notion of a morality of habit and custom—and his understanding of tradition. According to Oakeshott, we are not able to pierce through to the governing factors as to why the customs, habits, and traditions that we adhere to have the structures and contents that they do (how and why we dignify their contingencies as some versions of necessities)—and what is the source of their binding power over us. Customs, habits, and traditions rivet us and confer meaning and direction upon our lives—and we can deconstruct them back to their constituent elements (what historical and conceptual materials they are being fashioned out of)—but we are not able to penetrate to the source of their mesmerizing and disciplining effects upon us. They "see" us—they infiltrate, shape, and reshape our lives—but we are not able to "see" them. "Tradition" on one definitional level serves as a surrogate for Revelation. It is what Revelation gets deflated into once the logical conundrums surrounding the idea of God are confronted—and protocols of consistency debar us from simply denying God. Tradition itself, however, partakes of the inscrutability of its mysterious source in exactly the way that Nicholas projects: it irradiates us—but we cannot unmask it as long as we continue to relate to it as tradition.

Nicholas of Cusa audaciously goes on to say that "life
eternal" coexists with this world: "Now I behold as in a mirror, in an icon, in a riddle, life eternal, for that is naught
other than that blessed regard wherein Thou never ceaseth
most lovingly to behold me, yea, even the secret places of
my soul."[84] For Nicholas, "that blessed regard wherewith"
God "never ceaseth most lovingly to behold me [us]" just *is*
"life eternal." "Life eternal" is a continuing, extended now—
under the perpetual gaze of the Divine. It would seem that
for Nicholas, the naturalization of the category of the mystical—locating the supreme manifestation of *Imitatio Dei* in
the human capacity of "free will," with its attendant confrontation with the paradoxes and conundrums of reason,
thereby exposing and exploring the roots of the mystical
in ordinary human nature and regular human reason, with
their vicissitudes and limitations—enables us, as it were, to
"supernaturalize" the natural, to see traces of "life eternal"
in the ordinary postures and interactions that human beings
assume and undertake in the world.

Nicholas conceives of mysticism as "the absolute maximum of every rational desire, than which a greater cannot
be."[85] Mysticism is the maximum expression, fulfillment, and
embodiment of rational desire. Reason pushed to its outermost limits—attempting to engage all of the conundrums
that are generated through the normal operations of reason—results in mysticism.

In an authentic mystical transvaluation of value, Nicholas says that our actions here on Earth have an immediate
correlative in the way that God is positioned toward us. It
is almost as if the same set of events, actions, attitudes, and
outcomes were being described from two different angles:
the Divine and the human. Nothing is added by interweav-
ing God into the picture beyond what is already contained

in a strictly human narrative of the same events: "He, then, who looketh on Thee with loving face will find Thy face looking on Himself with love, and the more he shall study to look on Thee with greater love, by so much shall he find Thy face more loving. He who looketh on Thee in wrath shall in like manner find Thy face wrathful. He who looketh on Thee with joy shall find Thy face joyful, after the same sort as is his own who looketh on Thee."[86] Mysticism, from this perspective, enables us to leave everything human as it is (with the human penchant for a Divine Realist vocabulary intact) even after we mystically invoke Divine involvement and judgment. Mysticism (at least along one dimension of its meaning) becomes the reified expression of the ostensibly irresolvable character of negative theology and skepticism, so that all of our imputations to Divinity—as well as all of our this-worldly moves and affirmations—can stand as they were.

Nicholas says that the Divine Face does not become visible until "above all faces a man enter into a certain secret and mystic silence where there is no knowledge or concept of a face."[87] That "secret and mystic silence" in which words (discursive argument) are no longer crystallizable or formulable enables the Divine Face to emerge. It is our inability to proceed that registers for us that we are where we want to (have to) be.

In this context, we are able to more fully appreciate the force of Hölderlin's observation that "the skeptic finds contradiction and imperfection in all that is thought, because he knows the harmony of perfect beauty, which is never thought. The dry bread that human reason well-meaningly offers him, he disdains only because he is secretly feasting at the table of the gods."[88] Hölderlin as a latter-day spiritual descendent of Nicholas of Cusa and as a precursor of

Wittgenstein and Oakeshott helps us to see that in an inverse, negative way, the skeptic remains faithful to the mandate of the One by interrogating and discrediting all would-be earthly claimants to that category. The skeptic by practicing skepticism is already a practicing mystic. Or, in Nicholas's version of this notion: "That which sateth the intellect, or that is the end thereof, is not that which it understandeth; neither can that sate it which it no whit understandeth, but that alone which it understandeth by not understanding."[89]

In the light of Hölderlin's and Nicholas of Cusa's observations, we might say that another point of congruence between the skeptic and the mystic is that the primary focus of both falls on the unmediated, untheorized, point-instant of the present. As Emmanuel Levinas points out in *Otherwise than Being*, one needs to be able to dissociate the "saying" from the "said" of skepticism in order to be able to preserve it as a viable doctrine. The "said" of skepticism—its cognitive content—self-destructs. The impulse to wholesale questioning that skepticism represents cannot be manifested consistently without skepticism engulfing itself. Once the protocols of skepticism are directed against the tenets of skepticism themselves, skepticism as a concerted linguistic statement gets aborted. It is only by configuring skepticism as a "saying"—the bare point-instant of intentionality, of wanting to utter a sentence that encapsulates the ethic of questioning without reserve—that the impulse that it registers is sustainable.[90] In parallel fashion, the mystic is concerned to be in contact and to saturate himself with the unplummeted and unfragmented depths of the moment, before human conceptual grids have been applied that divide and eviscerate.

Perhaps the most straightforward link between skepticism and mysticism is the one theorized by Ludwig Wittgenstein in the last sentence of the *Tractatus Logico-Philosophicus*: "7. What we cannot speak about we must pass over in silence." In a general vein, one can say that the formulation of skepticism confronts daunting issues of reflexivity—the statement of skepticism undermines and defeats itself before it can achieve coherent expression—and therefore one is willy-nilly thrust into a domain of mysticism and silence. The images and metaphors that one deploys as a philosopher (or as a theologian) now all conjure up ineffability (inexpressibility).

In a more specific sense, the last sentence of the *Tractatus* evokes Wittgenstein's letter to Bertrand Russell written in 1919: "Now I'm afraid you haven't really got hold of my main contention to which the whole business of logical propositions is only corollary. The main point is the theory of what can be expressed (*gesagt*) by propositions, i.e., by language (and, which comes to the same thing, what can be thought) and what cannot be expressed by propositions, but only shown (*gezeigt*); which I believe is the cardinal problem of philosophy."[91] In the *Tractatus*, Wittgenstein advances a notion of "elementary propositions" to which he believes it is possible to decompose more complex sentences—and also the "picture theory of the proposition," which would account for the hookup between the words and names that constitute elementary propositions and components in the world beyond themselves. Our more complex sentences, in order to be validated, would then have to be reconstructed as truth functions out of more elementary propositions. The need for showing beyond overtly stating in Wittgenstein— the recourse to mysticism—is a result of the fact that the philosophical statements that speak about elementary propositions and the picture theory of the proposition cannot themselves be analyzed into elementary propositions and shown to link up with reality in the direct way required by the picture theory.

The self-acknowledged failure of Wittgenstein's empiricist project in the *Tractatus* evokes the failure of his illustrious predecessors Hobbes and Hume in meeting the demands of an empiricist philosophical program. For both Hobbes and Hume, the necessary recourse to nominalism even for an empiricist corrodes the empiricist project.[92] The data (external and internal stimuli) that are received and processed by the senses have to be grouped and categorized through the application of names and labels before they become usable even as the experiential building blocks of knowledge. These names and labels have a prospective reach as tools for classifying currently unavailable and possibly unimagined streams of experience and do not have only a contemporary and retrospective frame of reference. This suggests that there is always a margin of wagering—of uncertainty—hovering over the body of statements that we take to be true at any given point in our lives.

The nominalistic factor also works to destabilize Wittgenstein's empiricist program. Even before the reflexive issue emerges that the theory of elementary propositions and the picture theory of the proposition cannot be validated in terms of the criteria that they encode, there is the problem that the names and labels highlighted by elementary propositions do not straightforwardly intersect with objects in the world. In Peter Winch's words, "the lines of projection" between words and things envisioned by Wittgenstein's theory "only function in the context of a method of projection."[93] Only through the generation and application of some antecedent conceptual-verbal framework (a nominalistic set of understandings about how words work to individuate and delimit things) do the "lines of projection" between words and things symbolically protruding out of elementary propositions have what to hook on to. But, as Winch and Wittgenstein suggest, once the role of "methods of projection" is acknowledged in facilitating both our discourse about the world and communication in the world, then the postulation of physical objects to which the "lines of projection" might attach themselves becomes sheerly otiose—a needless duplication of the verbal frameworks that are already in place for identifying and interacting with "objects" in the world.

The breakdown of the empiricist project that Wittgenstein's *Tractatus* both summarizes and dramatizes with special poignancy provides us with a handle for diagnosing what I have called "the mysticism of everyday life." In the empiricist self-critique extending in the reading I am proposing here from Hobbes to Wittgenstein, words are amulets—magical charms—relating only opaquely and obliquely to what might lie beyond them. The very need for a theory of nominalism to be conjoined to that of empiricism in the classical empiricists suggests the primacy of context over text—of naming over the objects named. Because names are not securely engendered and certified by things, there are often multiple (and sometimes even contradictory ways) for denominating things. Words and names fix the contours of worlds—and shape the configurations of meaning—in a manner that resonates and reverberates with other words and names, staving off indefinitely contact with the extralinguistic. The real world is unmasked by the classical empiricists and Wittgenstein as an enchanted, mystical kingdom—with words endlessly bouncing off other words in a continually protracted confrontation with and deferral of our metaphysical isolation and our unfathomable depths.

One might want to object that my invocation of a mystical vocabulary to deal with the larger import of Oakeshott's epistemology and metaphysics is vulnerable because the whole theory and practice of mysticism seems to be predicated upon a performative contradiction. To demarcate and designate a realm of the unsayable already seems to be breaching it and rendering it accessible if not transparent to human discourse. If you know what you cannot say and comprehend, then you have already to some extent said it and comprehended it. From this perspective, the mystic is a rationalist *malgre lui* (despite his best efforts and intentions), testifying by his rigid bifurcation of human experience between the mystical and the normal to the endurance of those paradoxes that his very delineation of the two realms was intended to neutralize.

On the basis of what I have just said, we are afforded a new gloss upon Max Kaddushin's previously cited phrase concerning "the normal mysticism of the Rabbis." If one theorizes the monotheistic God through the pursuit of the normal—as a function of the regular human urge to situate the events and occurrences of our lives in relation to antecedent reasons and causes, which eventuates in the course of time in the postulation of the most far-reaching and ultimate reason and cause we can arrive at, namely, God—then the paradoxes attendant to the formulation of God (that ultimacy is purchased at the price of intelligibility, which therefore mocks the very idea of ultimacy) seem to propel us to shift ground from the normal to the mystical. The notion of Divinity conjures up the special realm of the mystical, which is precisely defined by the suspension of the protocols of rationality and of discursive speech, which are the hallmarks of the normal. However, if the mystical subsists in a state of contrast with the normal, then it has already been infiltrated and (de)formed by the normal, so that it is subverted even before it can be adequately grasped and nurtured. A resolution of this contradictory awareness is to conceive of monotheism in general and Judaism in particular as normal mysticism—with normality converging upon mysticism and mysticism being tainted (if not saturated) by normality. "The mysticism of everyday life" of Wittgenstein and Oakeshott can also correspondingly be viewed as registering the interpenetration of the mystical and the diurnal, so that the identification of a new unitary entity mitigates to some extent the paradoxes associated with painting a contrast between the two.

In his classic introduction to *Leviathan*, Oakeshott points to the formative role of medieval Jewish and Islamic philosophy and theology in shaping the consciousness that renders the modern, skeptical liberal state possible. He says that "the master-conceptions of Will and Artifice" drew their inspiration "from many sources, not least from Israel and Islam."[94] Modern skepticism, which dramatizes the limitations of reason and by implication, at least, magnifies the importance of the will as the representative of the irrational in our human makeup, has an important part of its pedigree lodged in the works of the great Islamic and Jewish philosophers and theologians—Avicenna and Maimonides. In order for their skepticism not to unravel, the thought of these philosophers needs to be turned in a generalized agnostic direction or a mystical one—with mysticism being the more coherent resolution of the two. Turning first to Avicenna, we notice that in contrast to "the normal mysticism of the Rabbis" and "the mysticism of everyday life" of Wittgenstein and Oakeshott, he espouses philosophical mysticism in a more overt and systematic way as authorizing a special regimen of bodily discipline and deprivation all the better to facilitate the cultivation and magnification of one's intellectual powers. This strand of philosophical mysticism is captured in a passage such as the following:

> The work of the human rational soul is the noblest of tasks, since it is the noblest of spirits. Thus its office is to contemplate reflectively on the marvels of God's art, its face turned toward the higher world. For it does not love this lower realm and meaner station. As the guardian of higher things, preserving the thought of the Primal Realities, it has no interest in food or drink and no need for kissing or coupling. Rather its task is to await the unveiling of realities and focus its perfect intuition and unsullied consciousness on the apprehension of the subtlest of principles and read with the inner eye of insight the tablet of God's mysteries, combating with every device at its command the pretensions of vain fancy. It is distinguished from all other spirits by its perfect rationality, its comprehensive and articulate intellectuality; and its object, throughout life, is to purge the sensory and grasp the conceptual. God gave it a power specific to it, the like of which no other spirit shares: the power of reason. Reason is the tongue of the angels, which have no voice or verbal language but through this gift apprehend without sensation and impart understanding without words. It is reason that orders man's relation to the supernal world, and speech itself merely follows after. For one who does not know how to reason is powerless to set forth the truth. . . . The activity most distinctive to the human soul is knowing, consciousness.[95]

Two ideal types of mysticism thus emerge from our analysis. There is the normal mysticism of the Rabbis and the normal mysticism of everyday life of Wittgenstein and

Oakeshott—and there is the extraordinary mysticism of those who fast and oppress/repress their bodies in order to achieve communion with the numinous source of inwardness as it connects with or in some way reflects the numinous source of what might lie outside the self and the world (God or some other Force or Higher Power). Avicenna in his formal mystical writings clearly pursues this second variety of mysticism. His theological and philosophical writings with their negative theology and skepticism insinuate the first form of mysticism.[96] As a strategy of reconciliation of the copresence of both types of mysticism in Avicenna's writings—and for purposes of theorizing the continuity that subsists between these two leading types of mysticism—I propose the following.

The mystical regimens that Avicenna practices—the fasting and the other means employed for containing and disciplining the body—paradoxically have the effect of reminding him (and other philosophical mystics of his persuasion) of the impossibility of transcending beyond a certain extent the limits imposed by the body. One can purify oneself through fasting and other regimens of physical withdrawal and hardship that one imposes upon oneself. The ascetic rites of self-purification will induce in the mystic a sense of achieving spiritual elevation by sundering to the extent possible his bodily needs and appetites from his spiritual yearnings and intellectual explorations.

But this can proceed only up to a point. Pressing oneself too hard, the body reclaims its sovereignty over the self by alerting one to prospects of physical failure and breakdown (which overwhelm the mind and spirit as well as the body), even as bodily and somatic experiences are felt more keenly initially as one seeks to impose an ascetic regimen on the body. The skeptic and the negative theologian

(ordinary mystics) through a pursuit of mind—pushing reason as far as it will take them in discerning the basis (bases)
of knowledge and apprehending God—confront the limitations of reason. Both skepticism and negative theology fail
to negotiate their intellectual targets. The consistent skeptic
cannot even adhere to skepticism, and the negative theologian cannot logically sustain the God concerning whom
the ongoing denuding of literal attributes takes place. The
extraordinary mystic, by contrast, enacts and dramatizes the
limitations of reason in an existentially more urgent way.
By sequestering his bodily impulses to enable his mind and
spirit more auspiciously to take off, he confronts again and
again his bodily infrastructure, which resists being treated
so heroically and cavalierly. On a somatic level—as well as
on a theoretical level—he realizes without letup how limited
human beings are—or, rather, how our built-in limitations
contribute to drastically redefining our conception of the
human. The extraordinary mystic enacts on a bodily level
what his mind has already perceived on an intellectual level:
that our limitations are not a stumbling block to but are
integral to human self-realization. The extraordinary mystic's intellectual gropings and explorations and his austere
bodily regimens are all of a piece—expressions of the human
self's romance (its dialectical shifts of enchantment and dis-
enchantment) with its limitations.

Avicenna as a negative theologian is passionately aware
of—and passionately committed to—his non-Divinity.
Paradoxically, it is our deep awareness of our non-Divinity
(that we are not God) that serves as the basis for our most
rapturous evocations of God. It is our lacks—what we are
not—that serve as the most potent and urgent reminder of
(the possibility of) God. The self-disciplinary regimens of
the extraordinary mystic that stimulate and trigger constant

reencroachments of the physical upon the intellectual and spiritual just intensify this negative route toward God.

The enactment in one's own life of the Divine attributes and imponderabilities (including the subordinating and sequestering of the physical elements of our being) constitutes, for the extraordinary mystic, the point of mystical contact with God. What he ends up doing at the desperate edge of his thirst for communion with God (following the circuitous route of all of the logical constraints and deflections that we have discussed) is the closest (at any given point in time) that he gets to God. The hunger—the question—the search become their own responses (since no unambiguous response is forthcoming outside of them—or beyond them).

Looked at under the prism of mysticism (both normal or ordinary mysticism—and extraordinary mysticism), the distance between the faith of skepticism and the skepticism of faith is much closer than the proponents on either side of the official Great Divide would have us believe.

Oakeshott's argument in his book *The Politics of Faith and the Politics of Scepticism* suggests that he affirmed the view of the metaphysical continuity between Western religion and Western skepticism. He says that "There are versions of the politics of skepticism which antedate any of the politics of faith in the modern world."[97] On the surface, this is an extremely puzzling statement. Does not the history of the West consist in a movement from dominance by a religious outlook to primacy being assigned to secular understandings of the world? First there is Christianity and then there is Enlightenment, with their accompanying politics. In what sense can "the politics of skepticism . . . antedate . . . the politics of faith"?

I think that what Oakeshott is alluding to is how in the course of Western theoretical and institutional development

the analytically irresolvable character of monotheism is succeeded by the equally analytically irresolvable character of
skepticism. Monotheism and skepticism represent two diametrically opposed engagements in self-transcendence that
become unraveled by a common set of conundrums. In
Oakeshott's understanding of the politics of skepticism—
where skepticism is associated with "human imperfection"
and "governing is not a matter of establishing the 'truth' of
a proposition and of translating the proposition into conduct"[98]—both monotheistic religion and secular culture can
be acknowledged as skeptical. Oakeshott conceives of the
politics of faith—riveted on perfection, salvation, the unlimited and omnicompetent character of government, antino-
mianism, and government as a godlike adventure[99]—as a
traditionalistic response to the inability of the modern to
supersede the dilemmas posed by monotheistic religion and
his consequent reinscribing of them in his own rebellious
doctrines of skepticism. Only a modern person—but not an
unself-conscious member of medieval society—could be an
exponent of the politics of faith. When faith genuinely pre-
vailed, the believer did not need more than the particular
variety of skepticism packaged by his faith.

The patterns of argument and informal logical connections that I have traced in Oakeshott, Wittgenstein, and Avicenna have their analogs in the writings of the great Jewish legal codifier and philosopher, Moses Maimonides. The
very first paragraph of Maimonides's "Laws Concerning
the Foundations of the Torah" (with which his Code, called
Mishneh Torah, begins) confronts Maimonides and his readers with a paradox that he nowhere directly addresses. The
paragraph reads as follows: "The foundation of the foundations and the pillar of the sciences is to know that there is
a first existent, and it is he who brings into existence every-

thing that exists. All existent things of heaven and earth and whatever is in between them would not exist but for the true reality of His existence."[100]

The bald statement of this principle of the primacy of God in the scheme of existence thrusts Maimonides and his readers into an immediate quandary. If God is merely the first in a numerical series, then it would make sense to probe further and ask what lies behind Him—what precedes or antedates the series. To disarm this challenge, "firstness" has to be consigned to the level of metaphor and cannot be understood literally. God's firstness has to be deliteralized and transposed to the level of infinity rather than being construed on a literal level as being the first in a finite series. As a result, the explanatory quest to which the postulation of the existence of God is supposed to constitute a solution has merely been deferred—without being resolved. One would still need to explicate how the Infinite can interact with the finite—and paragraph 1 of Maimonides's Code has not resolved the challenge it set out to tame.

Maimonides indirectly concedes the force of this critique when he says toward the end of chapter 1 of the "Laws Concerning the Foundations of the Torah" that the expressions referring to God "in the Torah and in the sayings of the prophets are all of them figurative and metaphoric."[101] Presumably, the reason why biblical and prophetic references to God have to be viewed as irredeemably metaphoric is that a consistent logical constraint operates upon them which is epitomized and dramatized by the quandary that Maimonides finds himself in after his declaration of principle in paragraph 1. In order for the explanatory quest to be brought to a satisfactory halt—and for us to have a coherent and intelligible grasp of the proliferation of beings in the world—we need to postulate the existence of a First Being, or First Existent, who is the unimpeachable and logically necessary source of the other beings. To seal off God's ultimacy as an explanatory factor, Maimonides appears to be telling us, we need to consign all of the attributes surrounding Him (and thereby also, willy-nilly, Him) to the domain of metaphor, where His insulation from literalism allows Him to safely rebuff all attempts to attain a more primary explanation than Himself.

Maimonides's wholehearted embrace of the Divine vocabulary as metaphoric renders the first paragraph of his Code intensely problematic. If the point of invoking God is to find a satisfactory resting place in our search for reasons and causes, then we have no recourse but to posit God as metaphoric. By the same token, we have placed God so far out of reach of our original explanatory design that we have achieved ultimacy only by sacrificing intelligibility. We are back where we started from when we inaugurated the quest. Once we take stock of the moves we were driven to make in our search for explanatory comprehensiveness and ultimacy, we realize that a universe with God is ontologically equivalent to (interchangeable with) a universe without God. In neither case do we have God as a necessary rational resolution to a rational quandary. With regard to Maimonides, God ends up being resituated outside of the scope of the rational quest altogether.

Maimonides's relentless discounting of the literal import of the attributes and descriptions applied to God throughout the Hebrew Scriptures—his thoroughly consistent pursuit of negative theology—seems to lay the groundwork for approaching the issue of God from the organizing perspective of a generalized agnosticism. As we have seen, this framework of analysis also generates and supports more than one approach—and the second of the two approaches I shall be sketching leaves the idea of God thoroughly intact and might therefore constitute the most charitable approach to take in reading Maimonides. The logical conundrums in which the rational search for God eventuates might be seen as highlighting agnosticism—preserving God as an open question—as the furthest the human mind can travel in moving toward God. Maimonides dramatizes how the search appears to be incoherent—in destructive conflict with itself—but that is only if we thoroughly discountenance and reject contradiction. However, if we expand and rearticulate our agnosticism as a generalized agnosticism— acknowledging that the returns are not yet in with regard to the whole menu of large questions that the human mind from earliest times has raised about itself and its relationship to the world—then we would have contributed toward shaping a metaphysico-logical context in which to make sense of negative theology. A generalized agnosticism could then be seen as a metaphysical placeholder that sustains an open door toward an indefinitely unfolding future that might in the course of time support and render more widespread the development of multivalued logics that encode, and thereby indirectly legitimate, contradiction.

However, Maimonides's dramatization of the principles of negative theology in the first chapter of the "Laws Concerning the Foundations of the Torah" posts an implicit methodological warning about how this second usage of agnosticism needs to be conceived. If what propels Maimonides in his postulation of the unbreachably metaphoric nature of the Divine vocabulary is the prospect of an unending spiral of ever higher and higher ascents in bringing the causal and explanatory quests to a final repose that in the end logically necessitates a shift to the level of metaphor in our designation of an ultimate explanandum, then we have to translate and make sense of even our most coherent version of skepticism as a generalized agnosticism in such a way that it does not reflect in any manner whatsoever upon the possibility of God. Even the deferral of the question has to be reflexively related back to us and should not in any way be taken to illuminate the notion of God. To know on the basis of the application of a generalized agnosticism that our grasp of God has to be continually deferred is already to have illicitly crossed the boundary between literalism and metaphor that Maimonides so strikingly posts in the first chapter of his Code. To know that "God" has to be deferred is already to know more than we are entitled to know.

In keeping with the Maimonidean strategy of Divine exploration as developed in the first chapter of his Code, we need to view the generalized agnosticism that we come up with as our approach for engaging God as a metaphor that is instructive for and illuminating of the human condition, without in any way reflecting back or delimiting the nature of God. The negative theology that Maimonides implicitly practices in the first chapter of the *Mishneh Torah* has to be understood in the general mold of how the Rabbis interpret the biblical imperative of V'Halachta B'Drachav—"And you should walk in the ways of God."[102] The Rabbis ask how it is possible for human beings to walk in the ways of God, who is described as an all-consuming fire.[103] So the verse must refer to human imitation of Divine attributes: just as God is merciful so you, too, should be merciful; just as He is compassionate so you, too, must be compassionate. In the light of Maimonides's theological practice in the first chapter of the *Mishneh Torah*, we now need to extend the imperative of V'Halachta B'Drachav to encompass the injunction: "And you should walk in the ways implicitly stipulated by your limited understanding of the nature of God." That is to say, cultivate an attitude of open-endedness with regard to all of your pursuits of knowledge and of truth in the world. In relation to God, however, you have to leave all of your verbal and logico-metaphysical registers behind and approach Him mystically—which is to say, in a way that cannot be defined either by what your theoretical and logical approaches pursued to their outermost limits tell you He is or tell you He is not.

This reading of how Maimonides conceives of negative theology and its role in religious thought and practice converges with Wittgenstein's understanding of the relationship of philosophy to the perceptions and judgments of everyday life. In the end, Wittgenstein wants to say that all of the skeptical interrogations that philosophers have mobilized from earliest times in relation to virtually all of the domains of human experience and discourse, from the everyday world to science and mathematics and religion, do not have the effect of dislodging or altering anything. Presumably, one major factor accounting for the inertness of philosophy is that all of the skeptical questioning engaged in by philosophers in order to remain coherent has to foster and sustain a reflexive gesture whereby the questioning is turned inward in relation to itself. Once this reflexive maneuver is enacted, the skeptical critiques of philosophers are unmasked as being vulnerable to the same criticisms as the target areas of knowledge and experience that skepticism was originally invoked to call into question. The engine of criticism in Wittgenstein is deflated to the same level as its targets. As a result, the targets get reassimilated into the domain of the (provisionally) sustainable and the normal.

The nonintersection of the critique with the targets of criticism Wittgenstein christens as the realm or the dimension of the mystical. The skeptical critiques do not work (from Wittgenstein's perspective) not because of a lack or failure of techniques or resources or ingenuity, but because the proper way to view them is as disclosing limits to human understanding and rational appropriation of the world. With skeptical critiques of knowledge for Wittgenstein (just like with negative theological critiques of monotheistic religion for Maimonides), we are trespassing on the border of the mystical where the constitutive condition of silence translates into leaving "everything as it is."[104] The paradoxes affecting both skepticism and negative theology converge upon the result that neither skepticism nor its rebuttals—nor monotheism and its critiques—can be conclusively corroborated or effectively refuted. For Wittgenstein (and by implication also for Maimonides, via the medium of his negative theological critique of monotheistic religion), the everyday world with its paradoxes and contradictions unrelieved constitutes the domain of the mystical. The mystical in the hands of Wittgenstein, Oakeshott, and Maimonides becomes another name for daily reality.

Maimonides thus interprets the term *Yediah* (knowledge)—as in the phrase *Yediat Hashem* (knowledge of God)—negatively hermeneutically. To know for him signifies not to know that there is not (not even to know that knowledge has to be deferred), but this does not translate into knowing that there is in the full-blooded literal sense (or that there is not in the full-blooded literal sense).

4

Political Theory

As we move into a discussion of Oakeshott's political theory, we need to realize that part of the attraction that a liberal society holds for him is that it institutionalizes better than any other form of state the mysticism of everyday life that we have been exploring. In a liberal state with its ongoing, regularized opportunities for reordering priorities and reconfiguring values, the most enduring commitments of the political society are placed on everlasting hold. Just as with "God" in negative theology and "truth" in skeptical theorizing the mystical turn of argument sustains the categories without prejudging their contents, so, too, in liberal political society competing conceptualizations of matters of ultimate value remain in suspended animation, preserving formal notions such as justice and the collective good without precommitting political leaders or average citizens to any particular positive reading of their contents.

The mystical character of the liberal state is also evinced for Oakeshott when one considers the content of the core value that animates it. The ultimate value of liberal society cannot be neutrality—because neutrality itself has to be grounded in some higher conception of the good that identifies the good with neutrality.[1] One strategy for circumventing this difficulty is not to identify the "higher conception" with any substantive declaration of principle, such as neutrality turns out on close scrutiny to be (if, for example, one is a fervent Catholic, then the state's endorsement of a neutral position as between religious belief and nonbelief is theologically and politically offensive—and not in the least neutral), but with something more formal and substantively amorphous: we could call it infinity conceived as horizontal (rather than vertical) transcendence. The normative basis for liberal-democratic politics might be envisioned as a nurturance of time to enable the play of contingency to be redeployed again and again, without succumbing to either premature abstraction or closure or underresponding by failing to notice and capitalize upon the range of possibilities residing within current constellations of forces. From this vantage point, the political within a liberal setting has to do with keeping the prospect of successive presents endlessly available.

Theorizing the liberal understanding of the good in this way constitutes an expression of skepticism, since the substantive content of the good gets endlessly, programmatically deferred. Since (as we have seen) the skepticism associated with this position can be neither affirmed nor denied—it continually and everlastingly neutralizes itself in terms of both its affirmations and its negations—the delineation of the summum bonum of the liberal state as horizontal transcendence constitutes another (an alternative) register for calibrating its mystical character.

Oakeshott's political theory proper in many ways represents a restatement of philosophical liberalism, which was first enunciated and developed in the modern period by Hobbes in *Leviathan*.[2] Oakeshott—just like Hobbes—gives us a metaphysicalized liberalism where the structure and design of political society are crucially responsive to a number of independently argued philosophical imperatives.[3] I take the following imperatives to be among the most salient informing Oakeshott's vision of a liberal society:

As we have seen, in *On Human Conduct* Oakeshott favors those types of states that pattern themselves upon the ideal of *societas*, whose mode of relationship is "formal . . . in terms of rules, not . . . substantive . . . in terms of common action," and is highly critical of modern states that assimilate themselves to the model of "enterprise associations" pursuing the goals of *universitas*, whose principle of association is a "common substantive purpose."[4] This structuring is partially designed to ensure the ongoing primacy of the less self-conscious over the more self-conscious in human personal and collective life. The instrumentalized relationship between the public sphere and the private sphere that Oakeshott advocates in his embrace of *societas* over *universitas* shifts the major focus of human preoccupation from the public sphere (characterized by an intensified self-consciousness) to the private sphere (typified by fragmented self-consciousness, self-consciousness dispersed among a multitude of uncoordinated individuals and groups) and thus serves in a negative but still cogent way as the postmedieval surrogate for tradition in the medieval world.

Another aspect of Oakeshott's metaphysicalized politics has to do with how, once underdetermination is affirmed, this sets the stage for acknowledging the circularity of all arguments. Once one starts with the premise of the underdetermination of words by things (which in a sense is inescapable because if you can entertain it and sustain it even as a thought experiment, then you have already established "underdetermination"), then (as we have seen) contradictory conceptual framings of things are possible. If (as we have also seen) once the first manifestations of contradiction appear then the proliferation of them cannot be blocked, then no possibility can be authoritatively ruled out. If this is so, then circularity becomes the fate of all arguments—inductive as well as deductive. In deductive arguments, the conclusions are already implicit in the premises: the conclusions merely spell out what is already "there" in the premises. In inductive argument as well, given the role of the underdetermination of theory by fact which issues forth in an impossibility of blocking any outcome, the only way that any inductive argument will work (will manage to get off the ground) is by artificially imposing closure on the premises by reading back at least part of what the conclusion is trying to establish into the premises. There is thus an element of deductivism in even the most flamboyantly inductivist argument, thereby ensuring that circularity can never be satisfactorily transcended. The political implication that I think Oakeshott draws from this is that since there is a rational slack attendant to all argument, we need to minimize at least one major locus of coerciveness in society by having the public sphere perform in as sheerly an instrumentalized and subordinate a role as possible.

Another metaphysical motif shaping and influencing the Oakeshottian political vision is the need to fashion a state structured after the image of theory (which is largely negative in character, focused upon what it cannot do) rather than have it function as a servant of a particular ideology. The distinction between theory and ideology is central to the argument of "Rationalism in Politics." All displays of Rationalism in politics conjure up the degeneration of theory into ideology. The modern "practical politician" finds "the intricacy of the world of time and contingency so unmanageable that he is bewitched by the offer of a quick escape into the bogus eternity of an ideology."[5] The only version of eternity sustainable by theory is one that involves endless prolongation and nurturance of an ambiguous present, in which theoretical ideas and understandings prove to be unsusceptible (largely because of their negative, critical force) to immediate abridgement and translation into a practical political program. Rationalist programs of political organization and action are generally not able to reflexively include themselves in the justificatory principles that they enunciate—for example, vulgar Marxism's "theories" of economic determinism and of class resist a reflexive application of their central categories to themselves.[6] To circumvent rationalism in politics—to fashion a state in the image of theory rather than of ideology—means structuring and giving one's allegiance to a political society in which the public sphere remains subordinate to the private sphere and in which the instrumental role of the state (its functioning as a *societas* rather than as a *universitas*) is sealed in a generalized agnosticism.

Oakeshott's precursor (as he acknowledges on multiple occasions) in articulating a vision of metaphysicalized liberalism is Hobbes. By "metaphysicalized liberalism," I also mean a political philosophy liberated from the necessity of "touching down" in the real world. As Oakeshott trenchantly states the point:

> Where in reflection fixed points of reference are demanded as a condition of the profitableness of the reflection, a demand has been made for the arrest of the reflective impulse—a demand which, *ex hypothesi*, political philosophy must refuse. And if we expect from political philosophy conclusions relevant to politics, the result will be either a political philosophy in which the reflective

impulse is hindered and arrested by being made servile to politics, or a political activity in which the reflective impulse, disengaged from the necessary limits of politics, has lost its virtue. Where there is genuine philosophy there can be no guidance; if we seek guidance, we must "hang up philosophy."[7]

Political philosophy, in Oakeshott's classificatory scheme, needs to be distinguished from policy studies, which are "in the service of politics" and are "designed to control political activity."[8] It also needs to be distinguished at a higher level from the formulation of a "political doctrine," which "never loses its character of being an explanation *of* something whose character is already fixed" and is therefore insufficiently radical and subversive to qualify as philosophy.[9] Policy studies and political doctrines can at best be grouped under the rubric of "ideology." They are too encumbered with givens to rank as philosophy. Because of political doctrines' rootedness in the givens of their societies, they inevitably become ideologically distorting as guides to action: "And the degree of subversiveness in the reflective enterprise which terminates in a political doctrine is such as to make the doctrine a necessarily false guide in political activity."[10] Thus, for Oakeshott neither theory nor ideology can serve as a guide to action: theory because it is too subversive, and ideology because it is not subversive enough.

Theory in the end cannot move beyond the parameters of its own reflexive preoccupations: it is about itself and the multiple conditionalities that infect everything that we designate as a "world."

> Institutions and arrangements in the pages of these writers (the philosopher-king of Plato's *Republic*, the monarch of Aquinas, or Hobbes's sovereign) are not recommended

as kings to be established, and therefore properly to be considered in respect of their desirability; they are the emblems of philosophical ideas, and therefore not properly considered in respect of their desirability or their practicability or in respect of any other quality or characteristic of the world of practical politics. Wherever there is genuinely philosophical reflection something is being said, such that if true, things will be as they permanently are—that is, as they are *not* in the world of practical politics. And if this seems to be a severe conclusion, it is at least not wantonly severe; it is a conclusion that springs directly from the character I have attributed to political philosophy.[11]

Hobbes's *Leviathan*—in many respects Oakeshott's major precursor in the formulation of a metaphysicalized liberalism—is about the convergence of negative theology and skepticism in preempting the state from articulating the human good. This convergence provides the major metaphysical impetus for Hobbes to design a state in which the chief role of the public sphere is to facilitate the pursuit of "commodious living" taking place in the private sphere by nurturing a largely legal-formalistic, instrumental role toward it. Hobbes's formulation of the tenets of negative theology is extreme and unyielding: "Therefore the name of God is used, not to make us conceive Him, for He is incomprehensible; and His greatness, and power are unconceivable; but that we may honor Him."[12] Like Moses Maimonides of the twelfth century—and unlike St. Thomas Aquinas in the thirteenth century—Hobbes leaves no escape hatches or alternate routes through which God might be negotiated. The only way that the individual believer and the community of believers can have God is through their acquiescence to be bound by the symbolism He represents. The constitutive formula and metaphysical motif serving as the impetus behind political liberalism are thus both encapsulated in negative theology. The twin notions that "authority is grounded in consent" and "consent is a function of the assertion of will and not of reliance upon certain knowledge" are as definitive of liberalism as they are of negative theology. The theme of deferral (as we have seen) is paramount in both.

Despite Oakeshott's claim in "Rationalism in Politics" concerning the ubiquity of a Rationalist, gnostic character to post-Renaissance politics, clearly the liberal state envisioned by Hobbes and propounded by Oakeshott owes much more of its inspiration to negative theology than it does to gnosticism. I think it is fair to say that Oakeshott would sharply dispute the claim advanced by Eric Voegelin that "the New Science of Politics" advocated by Hobbes and his successors is gnostic.[13] The role of negative theology in helping to shape the thought-world of modern liberalism is indirectly alluded to by Oakeshott in his introduction to *Leviathan* when he talks about the organizing conceptions of modernity deriving their inspiration from Israel and Islam.[14]

For both Hobbes and Oakeshott, there is an additional factor that enters into consideration in the fashioning and design of the liberal state. If reason cannot serve as a source of positive guidance and instruction and all we are left with is tradition, how are we to deal with the fact that in the modern age one cannot simply attach oneself to tradition without it representing a conscious choice—a traditionalistic act? How are we to deal with the fact that traditionalism is the only available modern fate for those hankering after tradition? Hobbes's implicit resolution of this dilemma of tradition versus traditionalism (which Oakeshott shares) is to fashion a political traditionalism, liberalism, which is conceived as a kind of structural traditionalism. Liberalism manages to sustain the phenomenology of tradition: all substantive political matters are converted into questions of a more preliminary sort having to do with conformity to the appropriate processes and procedures for the articulation of the relevant issues. The emphasis on process and procedure within liberalism can be viewed as a phenomenological surrogate for the sanctity of tradition and long-hallowed consensus in the face of the rampant individualism and skepticism of liberalism. Liberal process-oriented politics is intended to re-create tradition on a phenomenological level (with the public life of the society proceeding in a seamless web from what came before) when critical reason has established that there are no traditions (i.e., no unproblematic theoretical starting points from which development can proceed smoothly) but only traditionalisms (self-conscious rehabilitations of the idea of tradition).

There is a tension between Oakeshott's moral philosophy and his political theory proper. In his theorizing of *societas* as a formal, rule-oriented organizational entity, Oakeshott invokes rules affirmatively, while in his "Tower of Babel" essays Oakeshott disparages a rule-centered morality. To reconcile this tension, we need to distinguish (borrowing from John Rawls) two concepts of rules.[15] I remember when I participated in Oakeshott's Seminar in the History of Political Thought at the London School of Economics that Rawls's "Two Concepts of Rules" was on his reading list. I did not quite know what to make of its presence on his syllabus. I realized that Oakeshott shared with Rawls a common revulsion against utilitarianism, but I did not realize what else was at stake. Now I think I can locate more precisely the role of this essay in the Oakeshottian mosaic. The moral rules that Oakeshott criticizes in "The Tower of Babel" essays are substantive and particularistic in character. They purport to tell people what to do in concrete cases. The rules that characterize *societas* are, by contrast, largely "framework rules" that stipulate the salient categories centering around the public-private distinction that typify life in liberal, representative democracies. They outline the disparate sets of practices that attach themselves to these divergent categories without spelling out in any great detail the content of the substantive rules that fall under them. To the extent that there are specifically elaborated rules in *societas*, they are mostly formal in character, relating to the minimization of collision and conflict between people's "external" actions, rather than focusing upon intimate and "internal" movements (of the sort that define moral decisions and actions) that go to the quick of people's self-disclosures and self-enactments.

The way I have envisioned the Oakeshottian liberal state—and its prefiguration in Hobbes—the inspiration for the largely negative character of the state (its instrumentalized, rule-oriented stance vis-à-vis pressures and conflicts emanating from the private sphere) is grounded in metaphysical scruples concerning the limitations of human reason. The skeptical metaphysical ruminations and their intimation of a negatively constituted liberal political order also have an important precursor in Plato's *Theaetetus*. In this dialogue, Plato sets up an ideal typology between two diametrically opposed starting points for Greek philosophy and shows how both terminate in incoherence. Heraclitus and Protagoras had assigned centrality to constant flux and motion, and therefore also to immediate perception, as the source of knowledge. Parmenides had shifted the emphasis to theoretical frameworks (with their extreme heightening in the notion of the One) as enjoying primacy in the generation of knowledge. Much as Oakeshott shows how both theorems and facts are comparably unfinished (that they are both "understandings waiting to be understood"), Plato dramatizes how philosophical thought beginning at either end—the particular and perceived and the general and imposed—is not able to validate its claims. Whether we start with what we see or with what makes sense to us to invoke as the organizing framework for our perceptions, we are not able to bring our analytical apparati into harmony with our judgmental and decision-making practices. The gap between how we reason and how we judge can be closed only by assigning a central role to circularity in reshaping our premises in the light of the directions and ends of action we wish to pursue.[16]

An important implication of the constructive argumentative part (in contrast to the critical, dismantling part) of the *Theaetetus* is how certain limits to knowledge and to truth constrain the assigning of priority to process over substance—how the rhythms of the intellectual life are most in harmony with a continual wrenching away of supremacy from substance and its reallocation to process. This theme is reinforced in the unusual Socratic autobiographical musings that are found in the *Theaetetus*. Socrates tries to fix for Theaetetus the nature and limits of his personality. The supreme metaphor that he adopts (whose ramifications he discusses fully) is that of the midwife.

> SOCRATES: Then do you mean to say that you have never heard about my being the son of a good hefty midwife, Phaenarete?

THEAETETUS: Oh, yes, I've heard that before.

SOCRATES: And haven't you ever been told that I practice the same art myself?

THEAETETUS: No, I certainly haven't.

SOCRATES: But I do, believe me. Only don't give me away to the rest of the world will you? You see, my friend, it is a secret that I have this art. That is not one of the things you hear people saying about me, because they don't know; but they do say that I am a very odd sort of person, always causing people to get into difficulties. You must have heard that surely?

THEAETETUS: Yes, I have.

. . .

SOCRATES: I mean that it is the midwives who can tell better than anyone else whether women are pregnant or not.

. . .

SOCRATES: There's another thing too. Have you noticed this about them, that they are the cleverest of matchmakers, because they are marvelously knowing about the kind of couples whose marriage will produce the best children?

. . .

SOCRATES: So the work of the midwives is a highly important one; but it is not so important as my own performance. And for this reason, that there is not in midwifery the further complication, that the patients are sometimes delivered of phantoms and sometimes of realities and that the two are hard to distinguish. If there were, then the midwife's greatest and noblest function would be to distinguish the true from the false offspring—don't you agree?

THEAETETUS: Yes, I do.

SOCRATES: Now my art of midwifery is like theirs in most respects. The difference is that I attend men and not women, and that I watch over the labor of their souls, not of their bodies. And the most important thing about my art is the ability to apply all possible tests to the offspring, to determine whether the young mind is being delivered of a phantom, that is, an error, or a fertile truth. For one thing which I have in common with the ordinary midwives is that I myself am barren of wisdom. The common reproach against me is that I am always asking questions of other people but never express my own views about anything, because there is no wisdom in me; and that is true enough. And the reason of it is this, that God compels me to attend the travail of others, but has forbidden me to procreate. So that I am not in any sense a wise man; I cannot claim as the child of my own soul any discovery worth the name of wisdom. But with those who associate with me it is different. At first some of them may give the impression of being ignorant and stupid; but as time goes on and our association continues, all whom God permits are seen to make progress—a progress which is amazing both to other people and to themselves. And yet it is clear that this is not due to anything they have learnt from me; it is that they discover within themselves a multitude of beautiful things, which they bring forth into the light. But it is I, with God's help, who deliver them of this offspring. . . . There is another point also in which those who associate with me are like women in childbirth. They suffer the pains of labor, and are filled day and night with distress; indeed they suffer far more than women. And this pain my art is able to bring on, and also to allay.[17]

The intellectual portrait of Socrates juxtaposed to the disclosure of our rational limitations in seeking the foundations of knowledge suggests that given these limitations, the appropriate organization of a human self—and extrapolating from this, the organization of human collective life more generally—consists in a preoccupation with process. The quintessentially human moments are associated with movement, with fashioning the new, with giving birth. The common thread running through Socrates' self-description and self-presentation is that his powers are largely defined in negative terms. He is not able to attain truth, but he can perform the much more humble task of helping his interlocutors to distinguish between "phantoms" and "reality." He can point to logical fallacies and expose the weaknesses of arguments—even if he cannot arrive at truth. Socrates himself is "barren of wisdom." He can only nudge others on to deeper levels of critical awareness and more refined and self-aware reformulations of their positions. The progress some of his dialogue-partners make "is not due to anything they have learnt from" him. He merely gets them to see more clearly who they are—what is already within them. Intellectual growth is defined negatively in terms of the losses it exacts from those devoted to it—as 'labor,' rather than in terms of the fulfillment of some positive goal. The cultivation of "midwifery" is a function of the "tongue-tiedness" of thought. The "tongue-tiedness" of thought in turn (as the overall argument of the *Theaetetus* makes clear) is a function of certain logical-linguistic constraints and is not just a matter of Socrates's verbal aggression against his interlocutors.

After the beginning—the articulation of new possibilities—there are endless deflections, distractions, reconsiderations, and reformulations that restore us to some point in the middle (poised for a new beginning) instead of the end glimpsed in the first crystallization of the beginning. Since the return to beginnings is everlasting, the appropriate—the defining—philosophical emotion becomes wonder: "This is where philosophy begins and nowhere else."[18] Wonder is preeminently the emotion that defines our attitude toward beginnings. To be in a position to initiate things again and again is a primal source of human wonder.[19]

5

Philosophy of Conversation and Philosophy of Personal Identity

OAKESHOTT'S PHILOSOPHY OF CONVERSATION, which denigrates the possibility of achieving moments of such triumphant incandescence that they bring conversation itself to a close, clearly belongs to the same family of terms as "diminished self-consciousness," "skepticism," and "generalized agnosticism" that I have discussed so far in this essay.[1] There is also a subterranean linkage between conversation and mysticism. For the mystic, the great achievement is to be able to say something—to say anything at all, to be able to wrest some verbal quarry from the overwhelming, ineffable silence. Conversation connotes the breakthrough into speech—mobilizing the capacity to break the spell of the silence. At the same time, conversation, with its pauses and "disconnects" and its relatively arbitrary pattern of interconnection, becomes the verbal analogue to silence. In conversation, discourse is periodically overwhelmed by silence, as the participants regroup and refocus in order to revitalize their verbal interaction with each other. The starting points in conversation always evoke other possible starting points stretching back to an infinitely concentrated moment of silence where all these possibilities conjured up a unity that can only be negotiated through conversational fragments.

One primary sense of the term "conversation" for Oakeshott is as an ideologically neutral metatheoretical category for capturing the perpetually evolving and unfinished character of philosophical inquiry and reflection. Oakeshott had articulated such a view of philosophy in *Experience and Its Modes* in 1933, where it was steeped in idealist vocabulary and patterns of argument. With the eclipse of idealism in Anglo-American philosophy in the intervening years between *Experience and Its Modes* and *Rationalism in Politics* (first edition, 1962), Oakeshott apparently sought the least philosophically encumbered way to restate his idealist position. He opted for the term "conversation" as the least philosophically intrusive way of stating the thesis of the perpetually unfinished character of philosophical deliberation, which in turn, at least partially, is grounded in the skeptical idealist thesis of the priority of theory over fact. If, generally speaking, facts are subsumable under a variety of (even contradictory) theoretical rubrics, then our theories are underdetermined by so-called facts, and conversation can perpetually continue concerning what the world is like and what the appropriate categories are for denominating what occurs (and what lies) within it.

Oakeshott's notion of conversation—both his use of it as a metaphilosophical category to indicate the interminable character of philosophical reflection and his invocation of it to theorize a premier mode of human interaction—gives us a handle on one of the most vexing issues in the interpretation of his thought: his defiance of traditional categories of ideological classification. Oakeshott has generally been viewed both in his native England and in the United States as a champion of political conservatism. Richard Rorty, making Oakeshott's philosophy of conversation central to his reading, sees him as a patron saint of postmodernism.[2] Recent literature stemming from the mid-1980s has identified Oakeshott as a liberal.[3] To get Oakeshott into proper focus, we need to realize that given his understanding of the partially ungrounded character of all thinking—"Everything is permitted that can get itself accepted into the flow of speculation"[4]—thought (at least to some extent) needs to be viewed as a species of action. As Oakeshott sharply states it: "He [a person] is a philosopher not in respect to something he achieves at the end, but in respect of his predisposition towards the ascent."[5] Philosophy is thus conceived as a kind of doing. The contingent character of thought-constructs suggests that (at least partially) they are made, fashioned. This is a primary connotation of the term "conversation": the continual transposition of necessity into contingency—so that most of our thoughts and actions turn out to be collapsible into further words and thoughts and actions without any firm negotiation of any "reality" beyond themselves.

Another major connotation of the term "conversation" places a severe limitation on the concept of action. "Conversation" often involves the "pursuit of the intimations" of other speakers' thoughts and verbal expressions—as well as of one's own. "Action" understood from the perspective of this connotation of the term "conversation" always involves (at least partially) retrieval. One might describe Oakeshott as a metaphysical radical and a metaphysical conservative—and one would be describing the same phenomenon from two different points of view. The reduction of thought and speech to action is radical since it places a tremendous stress on human voluntarism and constructivism. But, according to Oakeshott, action involves simultaneously retrieval, since to act is always to be moving among the traces—in the interstices—of what has been said and done before. The same factor that militates against a straightforward construal of thought as thought—the ultimate groundlessness of our thinking that converts thinking and the use of words into a species of action—also leads us to notice the primary role of retrieval in the deployment of language. If our statements are not autonomously grounded in what is indubitably out there in the world, then there are elements of retracing and retrieving what has already been articulated on some level that contribute to engendering and enabling us to say what we want to say. The theorist responsive to the erosion of necessity and the vast play and scope of human contingency must also dutifully acknowledge the self-limiting aspect of human contingency: how contingencies insinuate patterns of their own that limit the directions in which they can be teased. In search of a metaphysicalized Machiavellian necessità as our guide, we confront contingent, provisional verbal formulations that shape individual and collective worlds—and, within their own limits as verbal constructions, post limits to what we as individuals and societies can experience and articulate.

In describing the nature of philosophical activity per se, Oakeshott deploys an idiom of analysis that complements the one I have utilized in making sense of his notion of "conversation." He tries to metatheoretically capture how philosophy manages at one and the same time to ascend from and incorporate its multiple beginnings:

A philosophical enterprise remains attached to the experience from which it sprang, not because of a fettering allegiance to what it left behind, but on account of what may be described as a continuous voyage. A reflective enterprise which, though relieved of the necessity of conforming itself at every moment to its starting-place, is nevertheless hindered by no hiatus, is an enterprise at once free from the spell which the already perceived casts upon present perceptions and one which retains a connection with the experience from which it sprang, a connection which continues to determine its character. In philosophy, reflection does not mount on wings, careless of the stages of ascent; it must be able constantly to rehearse the steps by which it rises and it must be at home on every level. Political philosophy, then, may be said to be the genuine, unhindered impulse of reflection, setting out from a political experience, and keeping faith with the original experience, not by continuous conformity to it, but by reason of an unbroken descent [sic]. This, I believe, is the principle of the One and the Many in all forms of philosophical reflection.[6]

Oakeshott's philosophy of action—and the ensuing difficulties of classification—bears strong affinities to the thought of Hannah Arendt. According to Arendt, to act is to begin. "To act, in its most general sense, means to take an initiative, to begin (as the Greek word *archein*, 'to begin,' 'to lead,' and eventually 'to rule,' indicates), to set something into motion (which is the original meaning of the Latin *agere*)."[7] If we are always engaging in new beginnings, this suggests that none of our old beginnings has satisfactorily worked—has ever moved us beyond the beginning. Action, therefore, for Arendt is simultaneously retrieval—a reconnection with the energies that expired before an adequate translation of the possibilities that resided in them could be

realized. This reading of Arendt is borne out by her construal of the Western intellectual tradition as consisting in a
series of unending "reversibility maneuvers":

> Whoever reads the Cave allegory in Plato's *Republic* in the
> light of Greek history will soon be aware that the *peria-*
> *goge*, the turning point that Plato demands of the philoso-
> pher, actually amounts to a reversal of the Homeric world
> order. Not life after death, as in the Homeric Hades, but
> ordinary life on earth, is located in a "cave," in an under-
> world; the soul is not the shadow of the body, but the
> body the shadow of the soul; and the senseless, ghost-like
> motion ascribed by Homer to the lifeless existence of the
> soul after death in Hades is now ascribed to the sense-
> less doings of men who do not leave the cave of human
> existence to behold the eternal ideas visible in the sky.
> Once Plato had succeeded in making these structural ele-
> ments and concepts reversible, reversals within the course
> of intellectual history no longer needed more than purely
> intellectual experience, an experience within the frame-
> work of conceptual thinking itself. These reversals already
> began with the philosophical schools in late antiquity and
> have remained part of the Western tradition. It is still the
> same tradition, the same intellectual game with paired
> antitheses that rules, to an extent, the famous modern
> reversals of spiritual hierarchies, such as Marx's turning
> Hegelian dialectic upside down or Nietzsche's revaluation
> of the sensual and natural as against the supersensual and
> supernatural.[8]

For Arendt, Plato's postulation of the primacy of thought
over any objective order of reality subsisting independently
in the world becomes a self-fulfilling vision of human beings'
location in the world. Once thought can be conceived as

unmoored from external reality, there is no turning back to extratheoretical fulcra of necessity. Arendt's "reversibility maneuvers" forms a correlative notion to Oakeshott's theorizing human action as simultaneously involving retrieval—an idea that Arendt formulates more directly in her concept of action as consisting in new beginnings. For both Oakeshott and Arendt, the triumph of human contingency condemns men and women to endlessly inhabit a metaphysical "square one" whose contents they ceaselessly retrieve and ceaselessly reverse. Oakeshott and Arendt add a new dimension to the context in which to appreciate Walter Benjamin's famous statement: "Only for the sake of those without hope have we been given hope."[9]

In addition to serving as a metaphilosophical category that helps to clarify the ontological status that philosophical inquiry has for Oakeshott—and as a category that captures the most pervasive and fruitful mode of human interaction—Oakeshott's conception of conversation can also be related to his political theory proper in ways that are evocative of Rawls, Ackerman, and Hobbes.[10] The notion of conversation enables us to reconstruct the terms under which members of a political society can be appropriately understood as relinquishing a part of their freedom for the sake of establishing government. Oakeshott's conceptions of conversation and the just society are symmetrical. They match each other perfectly. "Conversation" for Oakeshott does not yield a content either locally or globally—either in terms of individual statements whose content (meaning and reference) have been stably pinned down or in terms of the larger systematic import (or drift) of the individual statements themselves. "Deconstruction" is part of the activity of conversation itself and affects equally the individual components and the overall structure and tendencies of a conversation. For Oakeshott, the emptiness and absence on the level of conversation get duplicated in the emptiness and absence that characterize the liberal state. The rule-governed *societas* (which Oakeshott favors) that steadfastly refuses transformation into an enterprise association follows the pattern of "conversation" in modeling endless deferral of its ultimate substantive identity and commitments.

Terms and categories such as "conversation," "civil association," and "*societas*," which are placeholders in Oakeshott's argument registering emptiness and absence (in Oakeshott's marvelous formulation, "The irony of all theorizing is its propensity to generate, not an understanding, but a not-yet-understood"[11]), get transformed through their built-in metaphoric momentum into visions and justifications of their own, which have the tendency to deflect the theorist himself away from the austere minimalism of his constructions. Oakeshott sometimes sounds as if he were saying that the epistemologically vacant liberal state is itself a form of society—and the most optimal one at that. If in Oakeshott's conception liberal society is suffused with skepticism, then it, too, marks time (or marks a passage) without being able to sustain a hypostatization into something more concrete and specific. If liberalism institutionalizes deferral (our lack of secure knowledge), then it does not precommit its advocates to favoring representative over more participatory forms of political organization. Neither does it eternally prejudge the question of the extent to which economic issues have to be kept off the political agenda because of the possible taint of the ground rules of civil association by the ground rules of enterprise association. Philosophical uncontamination (on political philosophical grounds, we cannot move beyond the emptiness presaged by a generalized agnosticism) should not preclude the liberal state intervening on pragmatic

grounds that are sheerly interim and instrumental in character to ameliorate flagrant economic and social inequali-
ties. In Oakeshott's own striking formulation: "Political philosophy can provide no principles to be 'followed,' no rules
of political conduct to be observed, no ideals of policy or
arrangement to be pursued."[12] To further invoke an Oakeshottian vocabulary against Oakeshott, not-knowing has to
be enacted on this side of a "shadow line"[13] that prevents
its degeneration into a spurious and unsustainable form of
knowledge.

There is an astounding passage in the middle of *On
Human Conduct* that elegantly captures the thrust and parry
of my mobilization of Oakeshott against Oakeshott. He
says that "Authority is the only conceivable attribute it [a
respublica] could be indisputably acknowledged to have. In
short the only understanding of *respublica* capable of evoking the acceptance of all *cives* without exception, and thus
eligible to be recognized as the terms of civil association,
is *respublica* understood in respect of its authority."[14] In this
passage, Oakeshott gives us something resembling a negative theological reconstruction of authority. What lies at the
basis of *respublica* is authority simply because it cannot be
anything else. Reason or Revelation will not do; so authority
will (have to) do. Authority can be pragmatically, provisionally annexed to all kinds of political programs—including
economically interventionist, politically participatory ones.

A strong parallelism emerges between Oakeshott's conception of a just, well-ordered society and his understanding
of the self. The optimal self for Oakeshott is one characterized by a reduced self-consciousness that allows for the
play of different impulses and an ongoing process of self-
discovery. In his philosophy of history, Oakeshott asks us to
"consider a biography. It may announce itself as 'the life and

times' of John Smith, but the biographer will not (unless he is the victim of a theory) present it as the fortunes of its subject, its subject being an unaltered John Smith from birth to death. Indeed, he will know it to be his business to display John Smith himself as a continuity of differences and be puzzled to put his finger upon the identity he is using to do so. The formal identity of a name will not serve his purpose, nor will John Smith's gene structure nor his soul."[15]

Oakeshott's theorizing of human individuality as consisting of endless dynamism and volatility has mystical roots and overtones. For example, Nicholas of Cusa says that "The end of desire, therefore, is infinite. Thus Thou, O God, art very infinity, for which alone I yearn in every desire, but to the knowledge of which infinity I cannot approach more nearly than that I know it to be infinite. Wherefore, the more I understand that Thou, my God, are not to be understood, by so much the more I attain Thee, because the more I attain the end of my desire."[16] Negative theology, which (as we have seen) both Nicholas of Cusa and Oakeshott subscribe to in different ways, cannot literally encode the view that God is unknown and unknowable. If that were the case, human beings would be in possession of an extremely valuable datum about God that would undermine the premise of God's supreme transcendence and overwhelming metaphysical distance from things human. From a negative theological perspective, we must, therefore, treat "Divine unknowability" as a metaphor that constitutes a disguised description of the human condition, which in no way prejudices how we are to conceive of God. In liberal moral psychology and political theory, the unknowability of man goes hand in hand with the ongoing unknowability of the world. Liberal individuality—a self constituted by its "continuity of differences"—requires an unknown—and unknowable—

universe to explore and to appropriate. We attain, appropriate, and improve the world the more it is "not to be understood." The more the universe is postulated as known—and knowable—the less hospitable an environment it becomes for liberal individuality to flourish.

Oakeshott's conception of personal identity, which sees it as largely fictive in character (since the self is in many respects discontinuous between infancy and old age), gives rise to the paradox that Hume addresses in an oblique way in the appendix to the *Treatise*. Hume famously points to

> two principles which I cannot render consistent; nor is it in my power to renounce either of them, viz. *that all our distinct perceptions are distinct existences*, and *that the mind never perceives any real connexion among distinct existences*. Did our perceptions either inhere in something simple and individual, or did the mind perceive some real connexion among them, there would be no difficulty in the case. For my part, I must plead the privilege of a sceptic, and confess, that this difficulty is too hard for my understanding. I pretend not, however, to pronounce it absolutely insuperable. Others, perhaps, or myself, upon more mature reflection, may discover some hypothesis, that will reconcile those contradictions.[17]

Hume's formulation of his dilemma is itself problematic. I will argue that the resolution of this prior problematic restores coherence to the issue that Hume himself raises. There is something more than reflexively fishy in Hume's dilemma. If the self consists only in "a bundle of perceptions" that are taken to be distinct existences and there are no necessary connections between those distinct existences, where does Hume the philosopher stand in relation to his diagnosis of the inadequacy of our notions of personal identity? He has to have transcended his own analysis in order to be able to offer it in the first place. An analogous problematic also confronts Oakeshott. Hume and Oakeshott themselves as theorists must have a more coherent sense of personal identity than what they attribute to humankind overall in order to be able to notice how largely severed the self is.

Perhaps the most economical way to proceed is to acknowledge that the self as a limiting concept (which registers a central limit to human discourse) highlights the extent to which a normative dimension is integral to even what look like our most commonsensical descriptive statements. Given Oakeshott's subscription to the principle of the underdetermination of theory by fact (of words by things), one needs to postulate an irreducibly normative dimension in even our most determinedly descriptive statements. On a sheerly descriptive, factual basis, we cannot conceptually or categorically resolve how to verbally refer to things without postulating a normative element in our verbal "descriptions" and affirmations. This normative dimension links Hume's and Oakeshott's verbal usage that incorporates their referring to themselves as persons with the more general use of the concept of personal identity, which rests upon a presumptive ascent from a tissue "of differences." The circular encoding of the concept of a self (we normatively embrace the concept of a self and are therefore able to stipulatively, descriptively define it) constitutes our response in particular and general terms to the logical incompleteness of the vocabulary of description.

A universe in which the shape of the "is" is determined by the trajectory of the "ought" is, of course, a mystically saturated universe. The world is kept permanently at bay as we go about in the theoretical and practical pathways and byways of our lives projecting different configurations of possibility. The possibilities are not cashable or translatable into certainties but merely beget further possibilities. The world persistently eludes us, even as we theoretically and practically embrace it. The ontological priority of the normative over the descriptive is already being indirectly communicated to us in Hume's *Treatise* itself. When one turns to the locus classicus of the is–ought distinction in Hume, one discovers that Hume himself flagrantly violates its strictures in an equally famous passage that precedes the is–ought paragraph by fifty-four pages in the *Treatise*. I will cite the two passages side by side:

> I cannot forbear adding to these reasonings an observation, which may, perhaps, be found of some importance. In every system of morality, which I have hitherto met with, I have always remarked, that the author proceeds for some time in the ordinary way of reasoning, and establishes the being of a God, or makes observations concerning human affairs; when of a sudden I am surprised to find, that instead of the usual copulations of propositions, is, and is not, I meet with no proposition that is not connected with an ought, or an ought not. This change is imperceptible; but is, however, of the last consequence. For as this ought, or ought not, expresses some new relation or affirmation, 'tis necessary that it should be observed and explained; and at the same time that a reason should be given, for what seems altogether inconceivable, how this new relation can be a deduction from others, which are entirely different from it. But as authors do not commonly use this precaution, I shall presume to recommend it to the readers; and am persuaded, that this small attention would subvert all the vulgar systems of morality, and let us see, that the dis-

tinction of vice and virtue is not founded merely on the relations of objects, nor is perceived by reason.[18]

Thus it appears, that the principle, which opposes our passion, cannot be the same with reason, and is only called so in an improper sense. We speak not strictly and philosophically when we talk of the combat of passion and of reason. Reason is, and ought only to be the slave of the passions, and can never pretend to any other office than to serve and obey them.[19]

The abrupt and "imperceptible" transition between "is" and "ought," which is the ostensible target of Hume's attack in the is–ought paragraph, is precisely enacted by him when he says that "Reason is, and ought only to be the slave of the passions." Is not Hume contradicting his own strictures concerning the logical impassability between "is" and "ought" in formulating the relationship between reason and the passions in the manner that he does? In his defiance and rejection of the claims of positive reason, is not Hume transgressing against the limits posted by negative, critical reason about how to mount a case against positive reason?

One way to reconcile these two key passages in Hume is to notice how, in accordance with Hume's skepticism formulated much earlier in the *Treatise* than the two passages I have just cited, the very distinction between "is" and "ought" has already been undermined. The pivot of Hume's empiricist epistemology is the centrality he assigns to sense impressions as the source of our knowledge.[20] Hume's concept of sense-impressions, however, is problematic when one juxtaposes to it his nominalism as developed in book 1, part 1, section 7 of the *Treatise*. Hume answers the question of how particular words get attached to particular ideas by invoking his familiar mechanism of "customary association." This is to say that Hume is aware that assigning primacy to sense impressions in his epistemology does not by itself resolve the problem of knowledge. Even if sense impressions are theorized as the original stuff that both generates and supports our knowledge statements and claims, there is still a yawning metaphysical gap between what we might call the brute sense impression and what we take it to signify in our structures of belief and justification. How is this gap to be closed?

It is very important to note that Hume does not retreat from or dilute his skepticism at this point but if anything deepens and expands it. He says: "If ideas be particular in their nature, and at the same time finite in their number, 'tis only by custom they can become general in their representation, and contain an infinite number of other ideas under them."[21] In other words, in order to close the gap between the availability at any given moment in time of only a finite number of words and an infinitely evolving prospect of "things" or experiences in and of the world, we must have recourse to mechanisms of custom. Custom "arbitrarily" seals off infinite possibilities of association and linkage. Apparently, "brute" sense impressions and their attendant ideas taken by themselves are compatible with multiple— and perhaps even conflicting—linguistic constructions. The verbal designations of ideas and impressions are in the end underdetermined by the ideas and impressions they ostensibly refer to. It is only customary association that confers practical closure where otherwise unbridled theoretical openness might run amok.

David Macnabb's skeptical reading of Hume's nominalism-in-conjuction-with-his-empiricism (utilizing a central distinction from the philosophy of Gilbert Ryle[22]) seems entirely appropriate:

> To know what "cat" means is not to be aware of some metaphysical or intellectual archetype and know that "cat" is its name, and that "to be a cat" is to conform to or partake in it. It is more a "knowing how to" than a "knowing that," like knowing how to drive a car. It is knowing how to use the word, what to apply it to and what not to apply it to. And just as a man knows how to drive a car if he has acquired certain habits, so a man knows how to use a word if he has acquired certain habits.[23]

Given "the infinite number of other ideas" which our conceptual terminology will demarcate as falling under its multiple banners—the unforeseen (and unforeseeable) heterogeneity of circumstances with their unplanned concatenations and combinations of ideas that will still be retrievable under the old verbal rubrics—one can only theorize the generalizability of the names that we attach to our ideas as arising out of the operations of "custom." The proliferation of borderline and ambiguous cases that might in theory generate uncertainty concerning the continuing applicability of the ideas with their attendant names in our repertoire of identifications—but which, in practice, give us no trouble at all in mapping the "reality" around us—is suggestive for Hume of the imperious role of custom in diluting and overcoming the residua of arbitrariness in our verbal identifications and designations. On sheerly theoretical grounds, one has to supplement the role of sense data in Hume's validational structure by invoking the irrationalist operation of custom.

Hume's adherence to the thesis of the underdetermination of words by things (of verbalizations by ideas and

impressions) in the form that I have just summarized is suggestive of the radical impurity of the whole category of the
"is" statement. Apparently, from Hume's perspective there
is no string of words that transparently and unproblemati-
cally reflects a state of affairs—a "going-on"[24]—in the world.
Given the fact that words are future-oriented, licenses for
further use—and impressions and ideas are grounded in the
past and in the present—all of our verbal usages (including
what look like our purely descriptive ones) involve a prescriptive leap concerning how we want to (or how we choose
to) continue using our words.

The upshot of Hume's "is–ought paragraph" from this
interpretive perspective is to implicitly call attention to the
ideal character—the empirical unavailability—of the category of the pure is-statement. Hume's ostensibly insuperable difficulty of logically mapping the transition between
"is" and "ought" is circumvented from the perspective of his
own philosophizing because in an important sense we are
always only on the level of the "ought," which is to say that
once the contrast between "is" and "ought" has been undermined, it becomes arbitrary which term to use. The point
of the "is–ought paragraph" is to rhetorically highlight the
problematic that would ensue if the collapse of "is" statements onto "ought" statements (the blurring or obliteration
of the distinction) had not already been analytically negotiated by Hume. Oakeshott's concept of "tradition," which
straddles the divide between "is" and "ought," is thus a post-
Humean category.[25]

In the light of this reading, Hume is being utterly consistent when he says that "Reason is and ought only to be
the slave of the passions." If all "is" statements are disguised
"ought" statements (and this is the import of the "is–ought
paragraph"), then saying that reason ought only to be the

slave of the passions is merely an analytically refined translation of the sentence that "Reason is the slave of the passions."

When we consider one of Oakeshott's major sources of inspiration, Hume, we find the Oakeshottian theme of the inevitability of circularity rearing its head in a very powerful way. Our universes of description, according to Hume, are wagers and posits concerning the future shape of reality. The disguised prescriptiveness of our descriptions suggests that we collectively inhabit and fashion a world in which premise, inference, and conclusion feed into each other in a way that works to ensure that the prescriptive lurch of our stock of descriptions is realized and sustained.

The moral psychology implicit in Hume's delineation of the relationship between reason and the passions is again evocative of circularity. This is the way Stuart Hampshire phrases the point:

> Gradually, . . . I have come to weigh and to appreciate the full force of Hume's dictum—"Reason both is, and ought to be, the slave of the passions."[26] Translated into the linguistic idiom of contemporary philosophy, this dictum becomes—"In moral and political philosophy one is looking for adequate premises from which to infer conclusions already and independently accepted because of one's feelings and sympathies." It is difficult to acknowledge the bare contingency of personal feeling as the final stopping-point when one is arguing with oneself, or with others, about the ultimate requirements of social justice. But I am now fairly sure that this is the true stopping-point.[27]

Just as Oakeshott's theorizing of personal identity coheres perfectly with his understanding of how words are underdetermined by things, so, too, Hume's theorizing of the relationship between reason and the passions is all of a piece with his empiricism—and of the problematic relationship that it bears to his nominalism that I have just discussed. His logico-linguistic mapping of descriptive sentences, which leads him to notice an unfathomable gap between the sensory base of our descriptions and their application to untold circumstances, predisposes him to becoming more fully aware of the circular character of the human stance in the world generally: how our envisionings of where we want to go (as grounded in our passions) has an impact upon and works to configure how we deploy our reason generally (in an instrumental, calculating way). Hume's delineation of the relationship between reason and the passions represents the encoding in the register of a theory of human nature of an insight concerning the relationship between reason and the irrational that is logically linguistically encoded in his theorizing of the relationship between nominalism and empiricism and in the "is–ought" paragraph. Our logico-linguistic grammar turns out to be symmetrical with our moral psychology.

Hobbes serves as a significant precursor for Oakeshott and Hume both in his moral psychology and in the way in which his nominalism and empiricism fuse together to yield primacy to prescription over description. In sketching the relationship between reason and the passions, Hobbes says: "For the thoughts are to the desires, as scouts, and spies, to range abroad, and find the way to the things desired."[28] The instrumentalized relationship between reason and the passions that both Hobbes and Hume envisage—and whose counterpart in Oakeshott is the arbitrary character assigned to personal identity, so that the self is all continuing instrumentalization, and does not represent a stable outcome—is evocative of the circular motion of human life, where the reasons generated by reason are largely concerned with clarifying the ends to which our passions are driving us and figuring out the most expeditious means for getting there, rather than in any objective sense validating the ends themselves. Each one of our mini-projects in life—each building block within our artificially imposed personal identity—is reflective of movement within a charmed circle of our own creation.

Hobbes's theory of nominalism is in sharp overt tension with his theory of truth—and a most persuasive strategy for reconciling that tension situates us for noticing the primacy of the prescriptive over the descriptive in Hobbes. In his formulation of the theory of nominalism, Hobbes says that "There [is] nothing in the world universal but names; for the things named are every one of them individual and singular."[29] This definition suggests that whereas universal terms are only names, with regard to particular names there is a straightforward correlation between the things named and the words that name them. This expectation is exploded two pages later when Hobbes offers us his understanding of truth: "Truth consisteth in the right ordering of names in our affirmations."[30] In his theory of truth, Hobbes does not distinguish between the truth of particular terms and sentences (which would seem to be a matter of correspondence) and the truth of universals. He seems to apply a uniform test for truth—whether we are dealing with the truth of particulars or of universals. This test seems to be an internal one of coherence—of the "right ordering of names in our affirmations"—rather than an external one reflecting some extralinguistic order. For Hobbes, what there is—particular or universal—depends in a crucial sense on our naming of it. Prior to our naming of things, there exists only an indeterminate flux of experience. There is, strictly speaking, no objective, external world in terms of which individual statements about experience can be either verified or falsified until this "objective world" is constituted by us in acts of speech, of naming.

How does one account for the transition—the implicit reversal—between Hobbes's nominalistic theory and his theory of truth? I would argue that a plausible candidate for the relevant factor accounting for this shift is what Hume alludes to at the start of the *Treatise* in setting forth his own theory of nominalism—which can now be read as an intertextual gloss on a problematic passage in Hobbes's *Leviathan*. One cannot logically or rationally account for the extrapolatory gesture that is encapsulated in the imposition of words even upon discrete particulars. For Hobbes, the gap between the word for the finite particular and its projected usage to refer to "an infinite number of other ideas" that in unforeseen ways will be seen to be related to this particular word can only be closed by acknowledging that all words (all names)—even those officially designating particulars—constitute low-level universals (that is to say, encode a rationally and logically unsealable gap). Once this logical structure concerning words and their relationship to things is uncovered, we are in a position to see how descriptive statements function as disguised prescriptives and the extent to which circularity pervades ordinary human discourse.

Hobbes's theorizing of nominalism sets the stage (just as in Hume) concerning how one is to make sense of his empiricism. When Hobbes says that "there is no conception in a man's mind, which hath not at first, totally, or by parts, been begotten upon the organs of sense. The rest are derived from that original,"[31] I think we are intended to read this passage in the light of his nominalism. Particular sense impressions exert their constraints upon the body of statements that we regard as correct only within the context of a prior naming process that has led us to divide up the world and identify discrete particulars in such a manner that allows the discrepancies to arise between our statements about sense data and our other statements.

Hobbes's theorizing of reason as a "scout" of the passions represents (just as in Hume) a transposition to a theory of human nature of insights concerning the predominance of the prescriptive over the descriptive in human discourse and the consequent inevitability of circularity that are already developed in his epistemology and metaphysics.

Oakeshott helps us to see that skepticism itself needs to be viewed as a normative category. Since, as a descriptive-analytic account of the state of our knowledge of the world, skepticism, just like literal affirmation of what we take to be "out there," is, in the first instance, too vulnerable to questioning and, in the second instance, too riddled with paradox and contradiction to hold up, we must acknowledge the presence and even predominance of a normative dimension within skepticism itself. Contrasting Oakeshott with Martin Heidegger highlights what this normative dimension signifies. Heidegger's thought registers what hangs in the balance—what we lose—when we renounce skepticism. Oakeshott very systematically and assertively takes his stand on the other side of Heidegger.

Hobbesian and Humean skepticism (and of the social contract tradition as a whole, as developed since the seventeenth century) sets nineteenth- and twentieth-century political thought on its course. With Nietzsche, this propulsion—and this direction (with political theorizing conceived as a series of responses to skepticism)—gets called into question. In Nietzsche's interrogation of truth, he is also simultaneously devaluing skepticism, which as a denial of truth is also in its own way a theory of truth.[32] With Heidegger, we have a philosophical swerve that completes the process of the displacement of truth as what hangs in the balance in philosophical discourse.[33] In Oakeshott's embrace of skepticism, we have a normative reclamation of truth as the value around which Western philosophical inquiry and Western political theoretical construction center. Skepticism, from Oakeshott's perspective, gives us our best handle on the issue of truth.

I would like to flesh out this historiographical scheme in somewhat more detail: the epistemological and metaphysical challenge posed by British empiricist thought from Hobbes to Hume contributes importantly, if not decisively, to reshaping the agenda of political theorizing as it is insinuated to us in the writings of nineteenth- and twentieth-century political philosophers. The British empiricist investigative program, by seeking to ground even our most abstract categories and knowledge claims in sense-data, ends up rendering problematic some of the key categories of Western self-reflection: personal identity; an external world; material objects; causality; induction; historical knowledge; and ethical and political theorizing more generally. A major displacement that follows from the convulsions introduced by British empiricism is the politicization of the map of knowledge as a whole. This is the direction largely pursued by Marx and his successors. If empiricism places the right constraints on the project of validating knowledge—and one branch of knowledge after another is exposed as failing to meet them—then perhaps the structuring and organizing of power has more to do with the generation and maintenance of fields of knowledge than more objective factors pertaining to the contents of those fields themselves. Literature, philosophy, religion, and politics—and other artifacts of culture—could then be more authentically analyzed as "superstructural epiphenomena" masking the true distributions and exertions of power operating beneath them.

The Marxist response to the erosion of epistemological certainty is just one major stance of nineteenth- and twentieth-century political thought. Many variations are conceivable—and were actualized—in response to the empiricist challenge. It could be argued that empiricism did not have the intellectual tools to thoroughly discredit an external world. What debarred it from validating it would simultaneously debar from fully invalidating it. Empiricism creates the space in which to notice the mind (categorical) dependence of the world. It is not able to guarantee the dispensability of the world. So Hegel, for example, could argue (in accordance with some readings of him[34]) that mind and the world on an ongoing basis create (or re-create) mind and the world. The political world just constitutes one dimension in which this process of joint creation takes place.

The not-fully-grounded character of our conceptual schemata emphasized by Hobbes, Locke, and Hume in somewhat different but still largely overlapping and mutually reinforcing ways nurtures among nineteenth- and twentieth-century theorists an expanded awareness of the role of irrational factors beyond power—such as community, tradition, and a romantically envisioned self—in accounting for the shape, structure, and dynamics of political relationships and political outcomes. The great political thinkers of the nineteenth century extending into the first two decades of the twentieth century—Bentham, Hegel, Marx, John Stuart Mill, Durkheim, and Weber—all theorize in the interstices of the not-fully-worked-out relationship between the claims of reason and assertions of individual and collective power, offering new mappings (usually involving the interpolation of new categories) for how to conceive their relationship.

The sustaining of the viability and legitimacy of skepticism transmitted to nineteenth- and twentieth-century political thought via the medium of liberal social contract theorizing means that there is always an opening wedge for broaching and/or maintaining the prospects of a liberal-democratic society. Liberal democracy both presupposes and institutionalizes the staving off of a final point of equilibrium between competing visions of truth and competing structurings of power. If the value of truth were ever displaced as the overarching value of philosophical inquiry, the fortunes of liberal democracy would be correspondingly dimmed.

In contrast to the received traditions of nineteenth-century political thought culminating in Nietzsche's interrogation of truth, "The great novelty of Heidegger's thought (which did not elude the most attentive observers at Davos, such as Franz Rosenzweig and Emmanuel Levinas)," Giorgio Agamben writes,

> was that it resolutely took root in facticity. As the publication of the lecture courses from the early 1920s has by now shown, ontology appears in Heidegger from the very beginning as a hermeneutics of factual life. The circular structure by which Dasein is an issue for itself in its ways of being is nothing but a formalization of the essential experience of factical life, in which it is impossible to distinguish between life and its actual situation, Being and its ways of Being, and for which all the distinctions of traditional anthropology (such as those between spirit and body, sensation and consciousness, I and world, subject and properties) are abolished.[35]

Heidegger is pursuing and expanding upon the phenomenological program he takes over from his teacher Edmund Husserl. However, one could argue that in order for Husserl to make his case for phenomenology and against skepticism, he has to already presuppose skepticism. The empiricists that Husserl is attacking as the enemies of certitude take for granted a triad of entities—a perceiver, an object that one claims to be perceiving, and a process whereby the perception that one is noticing or encountering an object takes place, and the scrutiny of which can serve to validate or invalidate the perception. Because of the various skeptical conundrums surrounding this triad of entities and their patterns of interrelationship, the late-nineteenth-century empiricists Ernst Mach and Richard Avenarius stripped this triad down to two: they assimilated the meaning of a judgment to the act of judging, so that the numerous pitfalls associated with tracing the veracity of the process of generalizing from the experiencing of sense impressions to the existence of physical objects could be circumvented.[36] According to Mach and Avenarius, all that becomes relevant for the epistemologist in assessing the meaning of a judgment is the act of judging. The process that presumably connects the person judging to his object can be jettisoned as irrelevant for determining the signification of the judgment.

The lingering dyadism pertaining to objects of judgment in Mach's and Avenarius's accounts of knowledge is rejected by Husserl as he theorizes the epistemological project as being fundamentally monadic. He introduces "a change of perspective which makes no use of the judgment concerning existence, but only of the absolute being of the modality of consciousness which makes such judgments."[37] As a result, the "correlates of intentional acts"[38] become primary reality to the exclusion of selves and world and their patterns of perplexing interrelationship.

The important thing to notice about this whole progression of argument to guarantee and circumscribe certainty is that at every step of the way in his putative overcoming of skepticism, Husserl is presupposing it. If the constitutive postulate of philosophical skepticism is the underdetermination of words by things, then Husserl's whole method of argument is pivoted around skepticism. How is Husserl able (from his point of view) to effectively displace the earlier empiricist readings of human beings' relationship to the world and to make room for his own phenomenological reading? By assuming that all three readings in some vital sense refer to the same set of phenomena. They are seeking to describe and philosophically account for the same thing. They can do this only because our descriptions of our relationship to the world are underdetermined by our relationship to the world. This is why Husserl can even begin to mount his case against earlier waves of empiricism and to try to substitute his phenomenology for empiricism. If the shunning of skepticism is what drives his critique of empiricism, in order to have a common identifiable target to attack in the empiricists he rejects, he cannot even begin to make his case without presupposing the truth of skepticism.

Oakeshott's reading notes on Heidegger's *Being and Time* found in his Nachlass[39] provide us with a very illuminating point of entry for appreciating the momentous issues that are at stake in Oakeshott's confrontation with Husserl's rebellious disciple, Heidegger, and their contrasting reception of Nietzsche: Oakeshott implicitly suggesting that the Nietzschean denial of truth constitutes an alternative path within the theory of truth itself rather than a transcendence of it, and Heidegger further extending the project initiated by Husserl of rendering questions of truth phenomenologically unformulable. The correlates of consciousness have an unassailable certainty that has the effect of making issues of skepticism and truth beside the point. This is the way Oake-shott summarizes Heidegger's critique of Husserl: "Man's experience of the world *is* his immediate response to it. In criticism of Husserl—(1) Consciousness is not distinct from the thing-in-the-world but is already in-the-world. (2) The act of consciousness is not unique and 'subjective.' " Hei-degger thinks that Husserl did not go far enough in over-coming skepticism and subjectivity. Consciousness is not distinct from the world but is already in the world. With this postulate, Heidegger (trying to outdo Husserl) believes that the whole basis for philosophical skepticism has been circumvented. Oakeshott's paraphrase of the Heideggerian subversion of skepticism might be construed as containing an undertone relating to how the subversion itself can be subverted: "Consciousness is not a receiver and interpreter of data. It does not posit, presuppose or postulate a correlative 'thing in the real world.' The 'tree' and the consciousness are both components of one world." By way of the implicit Oakeshottian critique of Heidegger, one could say that the postulation of the "one-world" thesis governing conscious-ness and its objects already both presupposes and encodes the daunting metaphysical distance between consciousness and the objects of consciousness that the Heideggerian for-mulation is attempting to remedy and reconfigure.

Oakeshott then goes on to subtly reformulate Heideg-gerian phenomenology in a way that makes it more compat-ible with his own skeptical position: "Consciousness is not a relation between a *knowing* 'subject' and a *known* object. Everything is at once 'inside' and 'outside.' Meaning." Hei-degger's embedding of consciousness in the world is so far correct that the contrast between a knowing subject and a known object is unsustainable. The unity of subject and object for Oakeshott (unlike Heidegger) is achieved under a common skeptical set of auspices: our knowledge and affirmation of the knowing subject is as problematic as the object that he or she claims to know. The idea of a coherent, continuous subject is as epistemologically insupportable as the idea of a coherent, unified, self-subsistent object. Whereas for Heidegger it is the unproblematic and unquestioned certainty of subject and object that makes them part of the seamless, undifferentiated content of a common world, for Oakeshott it is the comparably ontologically uncertain status of subject and object that situates them as part of the common world of the problematic reflective subject who persistently inquires after and interrogates their respective status as autonomous but interrelated entities.

Since neither the subject nor the object of knowledge is in an epistemologically superior position vis-à-vis the other, there is no firm basis for designating one "inside" and the other "outside." "Inside" and "outside" are honorific terms that we supply to paper over our (their) uncertain status. From an Oakeshottian skeptical perspective, we are left with a world of unanchored, endlessly revisable meanings encompassing both subjects and objects.

Oakeshott then continues his summary of Heidegger as follows:

> Human existence is Dasein. Being in the world. Knowing is not a relationship between a subject and an object: It is being in the world. The world displays its meanings to us. Human subjectivity is not an ego uniquely related to a world outside itself. It is already in the world. I exist in the world prior to my description of it. I exist in the world in the mode of concern. The presupposition of all knowing is a man active in the world, already related to it in

action. Something that is recognized to be ready-to-hand is already "understood"—understood in the mode of concern. Any further understanding of it is an understanding of *it*.

Both Oakeshott and Heidegger subscribe to the view that "I exist in the world prior to my description of it." For Heidegger, this is just a manifestation of the certainty that the phenomenological project renders possible. Consciousness and its objects are irrevocably in the world—specifiable elements of Dasein. Skepticism just rests upon a needless invocation of distinctive categories when a simple awareness of "thereness" would do. For Oakeshott, on the other hand, "I exist in the world prior to my description of it" is indicative of the pervasiveness and insurmountability of skepticism. Description of self and object is always after the fact of my being "active in the world, already related to it in action." The mere fact that I need to withdraw from the throes of my ongoing experience in order to describe it already introduces a distorting element that can never be adequately compensated for in terms of being able to confirm that I have provided an independently veracious account of my experience. In the passage quoted, Oakeshott utilizes the Heideggerian phenomenological principle of "thereness" to support his own skeptical inferences and conclusions.

In Oakeshott's summary, Heidegger focuses upon "the voice which calls the self out of its dissipation in actions and calls it to authentic activity. Conscientious life is authentic and acquaints the self with its destiny—its relationship to Time = Destiny. In relation to time—to the life span of a self—the self begins in future." If consciousness is in the world (together with its objects), then it is a project of world transformation that liberates consciousness. However, if consciousness remains sequestered in a self that looms as continually problematic to itself and is vexed on an ongoing basis about its relationship to its objects, then the preliminary work of setting the self in order and maximizing the coherence of the units that are to be managed and orchestrated into larger wholes always preempts the space that one might otherwise be tempted to assign to projects of world transformation. The Oakeshottian skeptic can always appropriately say, "We are not there yet"—whereas the Heideggerian phenomenologist would assert that the "there" is where we have always been, waiting to be summoned and galvanized into revolutionary ecstasy. In Oakeshott's idiom of paraphrase: For Heidegger, "the distracting and disturbing cares of everyday life [need to be overcome]. The 'central task' is side-tracked." Whereas for Oakeshott himself, "There is no 'central task.' "

There is another subtle, but crucial, difference between Heidegger and Oakeshott. In Oakeshott's summary of Heidegger, "Dasein is always a 'not-yet' of what it will be—futurity." Consciousness and its objects being situated in the world, it is always only a question of what their future actualizations and consummations are going to be. For Oakeshott, by contrast, we might say that Dasein is always a "not-yet" of what it is—of what it is all about. The Oakeshottian skeptical self is haunted wherever it turns by unbridgeable metaphysical distances (the gap between consciousness and itself is as impassable as the gap between consciousness and its regular array of objects), so that the future is never able to settle its account sufficiently with the past to become a Heideggerian future. In an Oakeshottian universe, we are too much preoccupied with the paltry materials of the present to be moving toward any well-defined and readily negotiable future. The future consists in a set of contingencies that have been (in terms of "past futures") imperfectly harnessed and imperfectly realized.

In conscious opposition to his teacher's—Edmund Husserl's—central category of facticity as *Zufälligkeit*, contingency, Heidegger theorizes facticity as *Verfallenheit*, fallenness, "which characterizes a being that is and has to be its own ways of Being."[40] The jettisoning of contingency and the assigning of priority to fallenness in its stead already bespeaks (in accordance with a well-known biblical dictum in Deuteronomy) an embrace of death and a rejection of life. The Bible in Deuteronomy 30:19 says, "And therefore choose life." The juxtaposition of the two terms "choice" and "life" suggests that from a biblical perspective life is bound up with the continual exercise of choice. There is no aspect of our lives that falls outside of the parameters of choice. Contingency infiltrates and haunts the basic categories that we invoke to structure and make sense of our lives as well as the more ephemeral and secondary choices that we make in the course of daily living. Life is celebrated and extended when we persevere with our romance of contingency.

Heidegger's commitment to a facticity that is gnostically conceived as fallenness rather than negatively theologically projected as contingency lies in the immediate background of his famous nightmare of our not only "forgetting Being" but also "forgetting the forgetting." For Heidegger, the central problem is "how to respond to Nietzsche—how to respond, not to the possibility that we may never know the truth, but to the possibility that we may no longer know what to make of our desire for truth, and thus how to think a 'form of life' constructed neither around true principles nor about the absence or impossibility of true principles, without finding ourselves in the world of normative technology or sheer will to power."[41]

Heidegger affirms the facticity of those strands of post-modernist sensibility and culture that posit themselves as being beyond skepticism without sufficiently taking into account how the normative issue of reflexivity (of consistency) can be raised with regard to this facticity, thereby rendering it more precarious and unstable than it would be without this normative hookup. A postskeptical facticity raises the specter of a skepticism so complete that it has lost track of itself as skepticism. Nevertheless, the traces of the older vocabulary that form perhaps the deepest strata in the new terminology connoting supersession provide a haunting link with the unarticulated question concerning the consistency of this position: how can one be skeptical of everything without also being skeptical of skepticism? Skepticism in the consistent form that I call a generalized agnosticism constitutes the best set of countermoves for staving off the Heideggerian nightmare of "forgetting the forgetting." Skepticism, by emphasizing the lack of secure foundations for our beliefs and utterances, enhances our responsibility for our choices of epistemological and meta-physical categories. Encoded in the generalized agnosticism (a conception of evolving time in which the returns pertinent to any domain of inquiry are never fully in) to which Oakeshott subscribes is an ethic of remembering: maybe the past will return—perhaps tradition (in particular and general senses) will be reconstituted—perhaps being will be rendered whole. There is a lurking issue of reflexivity in Heidegger's formulation: if you need to theorize the forgetting of the forgetting, then neither you nor your audience has properly forgotten. This residual issue of reflexivity suggests that Heidegger is still caught up in the dynamic of the Western past—including its skeptical past.

The acknowledgment of the unavoidability of circularity in Oakeshott creates an extraordinary philosophical space for the cultivation and nurturance of the idea of liberal democracy—which, of course, is much more prominent in Oakeshott than it is in Hobbes or Hume. If the implicit motion conjured up by the whole spectrum of statements that we make, from our everyday descriptive statements to the articulation and pursuit of our most fundamental political premises and principles, is circular, then at least on the level of rhetorical affinity liberal democracy seems to be the form of government that is most closely congruent with our limitations and aspirations—or our limitations-in-the-context-of-our-aspirations (as these aspirations themselves are disclosed through the distorted medium of our limitations). Nothing is given in our individual and collective lives—from our perceptions and judgments concerning what the world is like and what is going on within it to the ends of action that we are pursuing. Descriptions are disguisedly prescriptive and prescriptions are openly prescriptive, so we spend our lives moving among a kingdom of uncertain ends on all levels of discourse and analysis. The liberal-democratic state becomes the collective engine for negotiating our plural kingdoms of uncertain ends.

In liberal democracy, the openness and persistent flux of our metaphysical condition is replicated in the openness and persistent flux of our political categories and institutions. Democracy can be theorized as a political counterpart to the fact that our arguments do not transcend circularity. This undercuts the claims of particular individuals or groups to superior knowledge, and from a negative standpoint (no one can put forward an incontrovertibly grounded positive claim) it justifies the inclusion of as many people as possible in public decision making. At the same time, because the results reached through majority rule cannot claim an unreserved epistemological sanction, liberalism introduces a series of braking mechanisms that allow existing democratic outcomes to be reconsidered and revised. Liberalism as a preoccupation with process facilitates a continual adjustment and replenishment of democratic content. In liberal democracy, no public verdict on any issue can be conceived or recognized as final. Majority rule is counterbalanced by minority rights, and the content of "rights" in turn is subject to majority interpretation and redefinition.

Linking together Oakeshott the metaphysician and philosopher of religion with Oakeshott the political theorist, we can say that for him liberal society in its proceduralism, openness, and deferral of questions of ultimate value instead of epitomizing secularism represents a monotheistic world outlook pushed to extreme—that is, an institutionalized political translation of a mystical sensibility. All possibilities (of interpretation, translation, and continuation) hover over the edges of all events and phenomena. No reading is exhaustive—and no identity (identification) is final. Encapsulated in all moments of liberal culture and political time are all other moments, stretching forward to infinity.

Neutrality has to be perceived from this liberal perspective as a persistent theoretical interrogation of the truth claims of different policy positions rather than as an exercise of moral self-restraint—or, rather, as the second growing out of and building upon the first. Neutrality is first and foremost an intellectual virtue that clears the path for a mystical engagement of reality—before it can be conceived of and practiced as a moral virtue.

In keeping with our discussion of the fusion of the normative and the descriptive in Oakeshott, it is important to note

that for him human ideals and purposes are inductive extrap-
olations that only after the fact are codified as a set of moral
dicta that sanctify the actions that fall under them. To act in
good faith given the limitations of human reason and the
consequent untrustworthiness of our emotional responses
requires us to invert our understanding of the relationship
between "ideals" and "purposes" and "activities"—between
human reason and human will:

> It is a favorite theory of mine that what people call "ideals"
> and "purposes" are never themselves the source of human
> activity; they are shorthand expressions for the real spring
> of conduct, which is a disposition to do certain things and
> a knowledge of how to do them. Human beings do not
> start from rest and spring into activity only when attracted
> by a purpose to be achieved. To be alive is to be perpetu-
> ally active. The purposes we attribute to particular kinds
> of activity are only abridgements of our knowledge of how
> to engage in this or that activity.[42]

Keeping the level of self-consciousness low is what
enables the Oakeshottian inversion between "purposes" or
"ideals" and "activities" to take place. Purposes and ideals
take a backseat to abilities because the center of gravity for
the self is located in what it does, and not in how it makes
sense of what it does. Making sense of the self is always
derivative and after the fact—an enhancement and embellishment of the conceptual shell surrounding the original
doing. For Oakeshott, as for classical Rabbinic sensibility,
"doing" precedes "knowing."[43]

In Oakeshott's depictions of the optimal human self, it is
very hard to distinguish the descriptive from the normative
dimensions. On the one hand, a self characterized by maximum
freedom whose purposes and ideals represent ex post facto

congealments out of previously undertaken actions seems to follow as straightforward inference and conclusion from Oakeshott's premises concerning the pervasiveness of skepticism. On the other hand, though, Oakeshott clearly writes with great moral fervor about the human being who cherishes freedom above all other values. This sort of self (aspiring to it; enacting it) constitutes a norm and is not just a descriptive outcome from some premises concerning the limitations of human reason. How do we make sense of Oakeshott at this point?

As I have already suggested, I believe that the most coherent approach to take is to notice that for Oakeshott with regard to all statements that we make, there is a coalescence of the descriptive and the normative. Underdetermination of theory by fact, which we have seen is central to Oakeshott's metaphysics and epistemology, suggests that there is no purely descriptive reading of any situation or event. The ontological gap between words and things or events is closed by acknowledging that there is an ineradicably normative dimension in every "descriptive" formulation. Our "description" attains closure through our normalizing one particular reading of an event or an action in relation to its possible alternatives. "Descriptive statement" and "normative statement" do not constitute two contrasting categories. Properly analyzed from an Oakeshottian perspective of "underdetermination," the descriptive is already the normative in order to be able to follow through on its project of being "descriptive."

Oakeshott's descriptions of the emergence of the individual (and of the opposition and threats to individuality) in modern Europe in his essay "The Masses in Representative Democracy" need to be read in the light of this fusion of the descriptive with the normative.[44] In the story that Oakeshott has to tell in this essay, during the course of the fourteenth and fifteenth centuries in Western Europe "the new opportunities of escape from communal ties gradually generated a new idiom of human character."[45] The new idiom consisted in "the emergence of individuals," whom Oakeshott defines as "persons accustomed to making choices for themselves."[46]

What is arresting in Oakeshott's narrative is not his account of the process of transition from premodernity to modernity, which has been told many times before utilizing the plotline of the legal theorist and historian, Sir Henry Maine, who sees the story of modernity as a movement "from status to contract." In Oakeshott's idiom, modernity comes to the foreground with the dissolution of "communal ties" and "the emergence of individuals." What is unusual in Oakeshott's account is the normative pitch and resonance he strikes in offering his description of the new individual: "A new image of human nature appeared—not Adam, not Prometheus, but Proteus—a character distinguished from all others on account of his multiplicity and of his endless power of self-transformation."[47] This vision of the new individual ties in well with Oakeshott's generalized agnosticism, which suggests that we are bereft of all orientating markers when it comes to determining not only the means but also the ends of life. Even skepticism fails us in this regard because a generalized agnosticism imposes upon us the requirement to be skeptical of skepticism. A generalized agnosticism restores us to an everlasting succession of human presents in which each present is hostage to future presents in terms of filling in with more perspicuous content (without, however, attaining certainty) statements and events stemming from the current present. An attractive option for a self that is metaphysically vexed and challenged by a generalized agnosticism is the cultivation of the protean character that

In Oakeshott's Kantian vision, the state is debarred from behaving paternalistically in promoting particular substantive visions of the good amongst its citizens. The most it can do is to foster and protect the freedom that enables individual citizens to make substantive choices for themselves. To the charge that in serving as the custodian and guarantor of neutrality the state is de facto promoting one particular substantive vision of the good that favors neutrality and is already implicitly combating alternative visions of the good that on religious, moral, or philosophical grounds oppose neutrality, I think that the best Oakeshottian response is to affirm a generalized agnostic reading of skepticism and neutrality. The liberal state seeks to cultivate a neutral stance vis-à-vis proponents of antagonistic policy positions not because it knows that neutrality is true but because it does not know where truth resides in any given policy controversy. Its policy of neutrality, which is effectuated by its limiting its role to the formal legal interventions enshrined in the notion of *societas*, is a means of putting both the contradictory policy options of any current controversy and *its own policy of neutrality* on hold, awaiting resolution in some unknown future. The liberal state's countenancing its calling itself into question alongside alternatives to itself suggests that its ultimate allegiance is not to liberalism as a narrow, sectarian political ideology but to pluralism as an expression of philosophical liberalism which puts liberalism to the same tests of truth and consistency that it seeks to uphold in relation to liberalism's competitors.[49]

The same processes of economic and social dislocation that facilitated the emergence of the individual also gave rise to the individual's opposite numbers in the form of the "individual manque," the "anti-individual," and "mass-man."

"This individual manqué," Oakeshott says, "was not a relic of a past age; he was a 'modern' character, the product of the same dissolution of communal ties as had generated the modern European individual."[50] The individual manqué was not a "leftover" from a previous historical age who persisted in clinging to older ways of doing things after the world had moved beyond him. He was not a simple follower of tradition, but rather a traditionalist who, in response to the same constellation of pressures that led to the emergence of the modern individual, self-consciously affirmed tradition with its particular blend of satisfactions and rewards. Traditionalism in this case represented a perversion of individuality— an individualistic assertion for the sake of shedding (or not fully assuming) one's individuality. The anti-individuals who proliferated in modern European societies required a sense of gnostic connectedness or embeddedness in order to be at home in the world. This was in contrast to the individuals who harbored a "negative theological" attitude toward the self and who consequently were able to live (relished living) with unsealable distances.

Two organizational styles were fashioned with regard to these two personality types: one associated with "rulership" and the other linked to "leadership." Rulership was the appropriate organizational mode for regulating relations between individuals whose projects in life were autonomously generated and who required the state mainly to stake out and protect the space wherein such pursuits could occur and to adjudicate conflicts between individuals when they emerged. For the anti-individual, rulership was too nugatory to meet his needs. What he required was a leader who would outfit him with thoughts, desires, and projects that would then serve as a source of empowerment. Whereas the individual could empower himself through his own choices (power itself accruing from the assertion of power by choosing), the anti-individual through his very inability to make independent choices deprived himself of the prime opportunity for the generation of power. The alchemy of power is such that one has to claim it and assert it before it can germinate. The sources of power in the world are mysterious and intractable, requiring human intervention and appropriation before they can be known and realized. To achieve gnostic embeddedness, the anti-individual renounces the power of the self for the sake of the power of the group. To actualize power in the first setting, the individual needs to choose. To experience it in the second setting, one can camouflage the need for choice. As Oakeshott says, "The masses must be regarded as the invention of their leaders."[51] The leaders are the only ones who choose in the political setting of the mass-man.

The political morality associated with Oakeshott's *societas* centers around a set of moral-metaphysical virtues, rather than social and economic ones: namely, liberty and self-determination.[52] By contrast, the political morality of *universitas* reflects the largely social and economic goals pursued by the anti-individual. These goals Oakeshott denominates as security, equality, solidarity, and salvation[53]—and they too, of course, have their moral-metaphysical resonances and overtones. The security the anti-individual needs entails "a genuine equality of circumstances imposed upon all. The condition he sought was one in which he would meet in others only a replica of himself: what he was, everybody must become."[54] Oakeshott's mode of social analysis is consonant with his generalized agnosticism. Given the absence of a substantive termination point to rational argument, paraphrase and substitution become the standard currency of human social analysis and discourse. Economic and social inequality have often become the stand-ins for liberty and self-determination for the individual; and economic and social equality and solidarity have often been the stand-ins for the annihilation of individuality and the fostering of a sense of embeddedness for the anti-individual. Salvation for the mass-man consists in a "release from the burden of making choices."[55]

The politics of the mass-man is shot through with Nietzschean *ressentiment* from start to finish. Making choices would mean acknowledging and confronting other choosers. It would mean accepting responsibility for tensions, conflicts, and rivalries with others. The *ressentiment* of the mass-man expresses itself in his refusal to accept that the scope of individuation extends this far. He would rather have a collective stunting of the individuating capacities of all people than endure the guilt and anxiety associated with being an individual. Salvation for the mass-man becomes political deliverance from the need to choose. The institutionalization of such a form of government (what Oakeshott calls "popular government" in contrast to "parliamentary government"[56]) becomes a masking of the original masking mechanisms endemic to *ressentiment* that is so complete that the mass-man feels at last free.

There is very little overt discussion of substantive ethical principles in Oakeshott's work. The specific, detailed norms that are supposed to regulate relations between human beings receive scant attention in his writings. Aside from the "The Tower of Babel" essays, one of the major textual sites for Oakeshott's discussion of ethics is in *On Human Conduct*, where he distinguishes between self-disclosure and self-enactment.[57] This distinction revolves around "the differences which distinguish conduct in respect of its being an agent seeking what he wants from conduct in respect of its being an agent thinking as he chooses to think and enacting or re-enacting himself as he chooses to be."[58] Oakeshott calls the first type of conduct "self-disclosure"—and the second type he denominates as "self-enactment." Both types of conduct evince a bias in favor of the Same—or self. "Self-disclosure" is geared toward trying to evoke from others a response that we want to elicit from them. Oakeshott says about it that "It is a hazardous adventure; it is immersed in contingency, it is interminable, and it is liable to frustration, disappointment, and defeat."[59] In "self-enactment," by contrast, "the consideration in doing is not what is intended to be achieved but the sentiment in which it is done, conduct is released from its character as a response to a contingent situation and is emancipated from liability to the frustration of adverse circumstances."[60] From the terminology that is used, it is apparent that Oakeshott ranks self-enactment as subsisting on a higher ethical level than self-disclosure. Looked at in the way that ethics is traditionally conceived, this ranking appears quite dismaying. In self-disclosure, there is at least some kind of consequentialist link to the other. We initiate action toward the other in order to achieve some favorable result for ourselves. In self-enactment, on the other hand, it is fidelity to one's own sense of being that is the hallmark of ethical behavior. In self-enactment, we are revolving almost completely within the orbit of the self. In what ways can a self moving within its own orbit enact, authorize, and validate its stance as an ethical being?

Apparently, we need to supplement Oakeshott's distinctive ethical theorizing by his more systematic theorizing of human nature elsewhere in his writings in order to glean how he would make sense of what is supposed to guide and inspire us in working out our relationships with other people. How he interprets Hobbes's moral psychology would also be a fertile source of clues concerning how he conceives of human responsibility toward other human beings. Not surprisingly, I believe that the most cogent reading of Oakeshott on ethics is that he derives the salient categories and obligations subsumed under the term "ethics" from an unreconstructedly skeptical reading of human nature. It is the self circumscribed by its myriad limitations, including those surrounding its being able to sustain itself as a coherent, unified self, that paradoxically contributes to fostering its nurturing an altruistic, benevolent stance in relation to the other. I would first like to trace this model of ethical theorizing in Maimonides and then show how Oakeshott implicitly follows it (without having given any overt indication that he read Maimonides) in his reading of Hobbes's ethics.

For Maimonidean negative theology, arbitrariness emerges as the fundamental epistemological category. Given the premises of negative theology (which state that we can only say what God is not, but not what He is) and the dilemma to which it gives rise (that we have no entity to deprive of literal import, if all we are doing by way of definition of this entity is depriving it of literal import), all descriptions of Divine attributes misfire: they are equally epistemologically arbitrary. Since the infinite distance separating us from God debars us from being able to declare with finality that our conventional, literal images of God do not apply to Him, we need to transpose the arbitrariness surrounding our philosophical quest for God to a human domain. For Maimonides, the ethical correlative to epistemological arbitrariness is ḥesed (loving-kindness or benevolence or generosity). Maimonides identifies ḥesed with "practicing beneficence toward one who has no right at all to claim this from you."[61] It is a form of unstinting, uncalculated, utterly gallant generosity. The lack of a basis for a knowledge statement signifies arbitrariness; the lack of a basis in worldly factors and considerations for behaving kindly toward others constitutes generosity. Generosity serves to render active the passivity, the helplessness engendered by epistemological arbitrariness. By converting the lack of a basis for action into itself a principle of action, one achieves generosity. Ethics redeems epistemology; principles of action render pliable and humanly usable irrefragable principles of thought.

The form that the transmutation of arbitrariness into generosity takes in Maimonides's thought follows a Platonic trajectory:

> It is clear that the perfection of man that may truly be gloried in is the one acquired by him who has achieved, in a measure corresponding to his capacity, apprehension of Him, may He be exalted, and who knows His providence extending over His creatures as manifested in the act of bringing them into being and in their governance as it is. The way of life of such an individual, after he has achieved this apprehension, will always have in view loving-kindness, righteousness, and judgment, through assimilation to His actions, may He be exalted, just as we have explained several times in this Treatise.[62]

We find in this passage a duplication of a Platonic motif. Maimonides emphasizes that after the supreme intellectual insights concerning human rational limitation have been achieved, one must return to the cave—to the realm of shadows—and imitate the divine attributes of loving-kindness, righteousness, and judgment through one's sustained interaction with the world. There is no secure basis to our knowledge statements and claims—knowledge about God and the world is without foundations[63]—so that what gets denominated as intellect really consists in the crystallizations of energies of will. All knowing is a form of doing, of directly intervening in the world to discover and fashion what is. Such actions involve risk taking. Behaving generously in an ethical sense fills in a central gap in Maimonides's epistemology because "generosity" (an "overflow" of the self that enables us to take risks) is the nonfoundational material that constitutes a "foundation" for our knowledge claims.

We can even go further and say that for Maimonides, given how monotheistic religion remains rationally unchartable, participating in it (practicing its rituals; assuming its obligations) constitutes a gigantically gratuitous, overwhelmingly generous act. In this extremely important sense, religion not only provides us with a series of very important incentives to do *ḥesed* (to engage in acts of *ḥesed*), but practicing it is itself *ḥesed*. Religion comes into being—and is sustained—through unremitting human acts of *ḥesed*. The sets of beliefs and practices surrounding the entity that we call the Necessarily Existent represent on a Maimonidean level of analysis the epitome of antinecessity.

There is an analogous circuit in Hobbes connecting his skepticism, nominalism, and contractarian theorizing to the pragmatic circuit that links Maimonides's epistemology to his ethics and political theory. The whole game-theoretic outlook, which facilitates the triumph of the institutional status quo over the state of nature and lone defiance in Hobbes's delineation of the social contract,[64] presupposes an environment where coordinated social interaction is possible and the consequences of deviating from societally approved schemes of preference are palpable to all. However, Hobbes's problem, both historically (in writing during a time when the traditional political order had become deranged and some competitors for political power were relishing the need for periodic disorder) and theoretically (in providing a justification for political authority from the ground up, engaging in an intellectual *creatio ex nihilo* that takes nothing for granted) is also to be able to account plausibly for the establishment of his vision of a properly ordered society. In terms of the aspirations of his political theory, it is at least as important for him to provide a satisfactory resolution of the problem of the first generation, of institution, as it is to account for his image of a just society and the mechanisms that perpetuate it.

As Oakeshott has pointed out, Hobbes is as much concerned with cultivating a personality type concerned with honor as he is with those devoted to the ends of survival or prosperity.[65] Hobbes says, "That which gives to human actions the relish of justice is a certain nobleness or gallantness of courage, rarely found, by which a man scorns to be beholden for the contentment of his life to fraud, or breach of promise. This justice of the manners is that which is meant, where justice is called a virtue; and injustice a vice."[66] Hobbes refers to two emotions that can counteract the inherent weakness of covenants, which rely on "the force of words": "a fear of the consequence of breaking their word," and "a glory, or pride in appearing not to need to break it."[67] Hobbes identifies magnanimity with the just conduct that springs from a "contempt" of injustice, and he recognizes that men are sometimes prepared to lose their lives rather than suffer some sorts of shame.[68] He also says that "magnanimity is a sign of power."[69]

How does Hobbes account for the first steps in a society's transition from a state of nature to a social contract society? The answer implicit in the quotations above is that at least some members of the original society have to be of a sufficiently magnanimous temperament—in Maimonidean terms, sufficiently adept in manifesting *ḥesed*—that they are willing to take unprecedented risks for the benefit of all, even though the mechanisms of mutual calculation and restraint designed to limit the scope of those risks are not yet in place. The mechanism of calculation is institutionalized only when the social contract is established. Before that, it is only in accordance with such motivational factors as "honor" and "magnanimity," the Hobbesian counterparts to Maimonidean *ḥesed*, that one breaks into this circle, begins to act on the basis of the new prudential principles, and thereby fosters the creation of the new society.

Machiavelli—as astounding as it might appear—perpetuates and extends the Platonic-Maimonidean motif we have been exploring. In *The Prince*, Machiavelli insinuates to us the ontological equivalence or interchangeability between receiving and giving. A prince is better able to induce a stable display of indebtedness to him on the part of his subjects, so that they will remain loyal to him and fight on his behalf when foreign powers threaten his regime, by getting his subjects accustomed to doing things for him during times of peace than by showering benefits upon them and expecting them to show gratitude when he needs their help. Machiavelli says that "The nature of man is such that people consider themselves put under an obligation as much by the benefits they confer as by those they receive."[70] The ethical import of Machiavelli's insight into the ontological interchangeability of giving and receiving is that giving embeds us as much in an interpersonal network of mutual obligation, acknowledgment of the Other, and reciprocity as receiving does. In terms of its impact on the self and fostering a sense of obligation toward others, giving accomplishes the same results as receiving. Both when we receive a benefit from others and when we confer benefits upon them, we feel under an obligation (an inner compulsion) to do more—to protect and nurture our gift and investment. Doing in the context of doing something for others resembles doing in other spheres of human interaction with the world in the sense that it begets further doing—further involvements and assertions on our part to amplify, define, redefine, and secure a greater sense of mastery over our initial action. The great difference between doing and receiving is that receiving is dependent upon others, whereas doing is within our control to engage in or not. Generalizing Machiavelli's insight concerning the ontological equivalence between giving and receiving for ethics as a whole, we might say that his implicit and recurring principle of economy (to achieve the most maximal effect with the most minimal investment[71]) would counsel us to do and to give as often as we can rather than to wait and receive. Giving is within our power; receiving makes us subject to the initiatives of others. A principle of economy would advise us to give (of ourselves, from ourselves) as often as we can in order at the very least to sustain the self in sane and stable equilibrium with others without being subject to the vicissitudes and capriciousness associated with dependence on (waiting for) others. A self that is merely solicitous toward itself (pursuing an ethic of self-care) can without direct and continuous self-conscious engagement of the Other create a world of mutually resplendent goodness.

From an Oakeshottian vantage point, we also need to notice how skepticism itself can serve as an inhibiting factor toward giving expression to some of the worst ethical vices, such as anger. From the perspective of the solitary, theoretically insecure individual that is paradigmatic and normative for the skeptic, we can identify as a root cause of anger our inability to live with and tolerate theoretical insufficiency. We are angry because we want to pierce limits and fortify and expand our sense of mastery. In this sense, anger and pride are correlative vices. Haughtiness and pride are a function of our claiming as our own (in terms of knowledge—and other kinds of resources) that which lies beyond our grasp—and anger results when one despairs of the prospect of remedying the inadequacies and deficiencies in one's intellectual and other resources. Pride is a gleefully and externally directed denial of limits—and anger is a despondently and inwardly directed chafing against limits. Pride that is not able to muster the panache to deny that which defies and inhibits it becomes anger. Anger is self-lacerated pride—which takes out upon the self and others its inability to set up a confidence game to indiscriminately deceive itself and others.

From this perspective, cultivating the metaphysical terrain of the Same—learning to be at home in a skeptical mode of discourse and analysis—is not just a prolegomenon to ethics, but is itself ethics. One way to at least partially accommodate the dilemma that if skepticism truly resists certainty then it needs to shed the mantle of being one more theory of knowledge (as a critique of the possibility of knowledge, it stands poised to becoming one more spurious variety of that which it rejects) is to envision skepticism itself as a form of ethical doing. In conformity with his or her own premises, the skeptic does not claim to know that there is no truth—but only perpetually dramatizes for himself or herself and others what the condition of not knowing with certainty consists in. This dramatization—this form of doing—the series of persistent Oakeshottian self-enactments that we abridge under the rubric of skepticism very importantly includes an acclimation to limits and a delineation of a life of limits as part of the content of what its own skeptical quest is about. In this way we can begin to theorize ethics as a vision of human life generated from the perspective of the Same—

and its status as First Philosophy is sealed by the same fate that dooms us to be swirling endlessly within the ambit of skepticism.

The ethics implicit in Oakeshott's theorizing of skepticism as I have sketched it here is evocative of mysticism. A self that is not fully transparent to itself and is constantly evolving so that its grip on continuity can also be called into question seeks to elaborate a set of organizing principles for regulating its behavior with others whose status as autonomous, self-contained individuals is as problematic as its own. The questioning of the knowability and durability of self and other both derive to an important extent from the underdetermination of the categories invoked to make sense of them by the "facts" surrounding their existence. This skepticism, in order to render itself consistent, must tolerate—and even invite—a skeptical interrogation of itself, leading to a full-scale rehabilitation of those entities that were impugned by the first go-around of skeptical questioning. Ethical principles and guidelines not being able to presume upon a stable world—or a stable self—or stable others need to be very parsimoniously pitched as a function of the mystical oscillation that defines the world in the broadest sense in which they have to be applied. An ethics generated from the perspective of the Same would have to be a mystical ethics.

The Talmudic sage Hillel's Mishnah[72] in *Pirkei Avot* (the Ethics of the Fathers) serves as a famous precursor-text to Oakeshott's ethics fashioned out of the materials of the Same. This Mishnah at Avot 1, 14 states: "He used to say: If I am not for myself who will be for me? And if I am for myself, what am I? And if not now, when?"[73] As we shall see, the third clause of Hillel's Mishnah illuminates the ontological priority he assigns to the Same over the Other in his theorizing of ethics. Ethics—a concern for and involvement with the Other—has to grow out of a recognition of the precariousness of the Same. The conceptual tools for theorizing and sustaining a viable, consistent identity for the Same are limited and impoverished. Skepticism aborts all attempts to project a consistent "container" (a homogeneous and readily inferrable and identifiable self) upon all of our thoughts, feelings, and actions. The data of human living moment-to-moment are compatible with the notion of a single, unified self as well as with the idea of pluralistic, successive selves, and with the possibility of there not being a self at all but only continuing miraculous interventions that engender a sense of successive crystallizations of selfhood, with only incomplete somatic or psychological evidence to back this claim up. So when Hillel says, "If I am not for myself who will be for me," one way of comprehending him is that he is pointing to the absence of an objective order of being that will underwrite my sense of selfhood. The self, at best, is a skeptical posit—and the crucial question becomes what, aside from pragmatic considerations, can be conceived as motivating the posit?

One way of reconstructing Hillel's response to this implicit question is to say that the provisional disarming of skepticism that a proper appreciation of the logic of skepticism discloses enables us to reclaim the plausibility of the concept of selfhood. In order for the teaching of skepticism to be consistent, it must incorporate a reflexive gesture of skeptical self-interrogation, which immediately transforms it into a generalized agnosticism, whereby skepticism itself becomes one of the targets of skepticism. However, as we have seen, there are at least two possible interpretations of what a skeptical questioning of skepticism involves. In accordance with one reading, a generalized agnosticism issues forth in the formulation of a tepid "maybe" to all of the objects of human thought and experience—including skepticism. A second reading of the doctrine of a generalized agnosticism would argue that if skepticism cannot be sustained because of an issue of consistency inherent in skepticism itself, then this becomes the occasion for rehabilitating in their full force all of the objects that skepticism had previously questioned. This means that the idea of a self can always rebound due to the fragility of the critical mechanism that devastated it. But the idea of a self can always be critically dismantled again by reinvoking the critical skeptical apparatus, which is neither less cogent—nor more cogent—than the counterthrust of rehabilitation. Neither move—of critical destruction or reconstruction—can overpower the other.

In the second clause of Hillel's Mishnah, the self generously posits the Other—and the need to behave kindly and generously toward the Other. The buoyancy, playfulness, and open-ended character of the positing of the self serves as a goad and inspiration for the positing of other selves. The idea of the Other that is not governed by logical or empirical necessity (the Other as a contingent extension of a contingently understood self) represents an act of generosity. Behaving generously and benevolently toward the Other consists in the superimposition of generosity upon generosity—protecting our first investment in generosity by a second and a third, indefinitely. The reality of the Other is as precarious as the reality of the self. The Other can be skeptically interrogated—and skeptically rehabilitated endlessly. The "unitary selves" that I encounter in my dealings in the world are a shadow—rationalist fictions—concocted out of a past skeptical interrogation of the reality of other selves and a future skeptical rehabilitation of their reality that remains permanently oscillating between these two sets of possibilities.

The third clause of Hillel's Mishnah—"And if not now, when?"—can be read as encapsulating in relation to time the skeptical approaches to self and other reflected in the first two clauses of his Mishnah. It may very well be that the model of how Hillel relates to time guides him in delineating his approach to self and other.[74] A central paradox surrounding time is that we can never point to any present moment. The moment of specification of any present is already the moment of its supersession by another present—so that in our calibration and demarcation of time all we have is past and future, but no present. Hillel's approach to this paradox is contained in his rhetorical question—"And if not now, when?" Under the prism of the paradox surrounding time, there is never a delimitable "now," but only an unquenchable "when?" The "now" is a "when" that has by sheer will and fiat been transformed into a "now." The irresolvability of the "now" gets translated into the incompleteness of the past and the open-endedness of the future. The "before" and the "after" absorb the ontological space of the "now"—and there is never a "now" to compare them with. This becomes the paradigm in terms of which Hillel configures the self and the Other. When skepticism has run its full gamut between questioning and self-questioning, the objects of its interrogation oscillate perpetually between a critique that can never be completed and a restoration that can never fully restore. The mental objects that skepticism questions that it cannot demolish or restore are never fully in view. Endless displacement becomes definitive of the human condition—and the world that we are in is the world that was not and the world that is not yet.

Oakeshott's ethics emerges as being in dramatic contrast with that of Emmanuel Levinas.[75] Levinas argues in *Otherwise than Being* for the phenomenological priority of the

Other over the self, so that all phases of self-development and all facets of philosophical inquiry take place with this priority in view. Levinas inverts the modern philosophical tradition that generally treated other minds as being more philosophically questionable than self-affirmation by making the self primordially indebted to the multiple selves that inhabit the planet, thereby rendering it more derivative and more ontologically dependent than it was heretofore. This strategy for ensuring the primacy of ethics contravenes the approach also suggested by Levinas in parts of his writings that argue negatively that the unsustainability of skepticism restores a new legitimacy upon the targets that skepticism had formerly impugned—including God and the other.[76] In any event, just as Oakeshott's ethical stance is evocative of Hobbes, Levinas's phenomenological engagement of ethics conjures up Rousseau. I would like to briefly flesh out this juxtaposition.

The unusual way that Levinas "parcels-up" sensibility—linking its earliest, most primordial manifestations with passivity, incarnation, and substitution for the other[77]—is not a function of something brutely given in experience but is rather the result of the application of a particular conceptual framework. It is thoroughly contestable whether this earliest of the early phases of human psychosocial development subsists independently of the theoretical framework that Levinas provides for it. It is not clear whether there are neurophysiological correlates to Levinas's phenomenological descriptions, so that a genuine research program can be undertaken to corroborate Levinas's formulations. Even if this turned out to be the case (which is doubtful), it is by no means apparent that Levinas's vocabulary is the only psychological vocabulary that matches or correlates with the neurophysiological states and movements under consideration.

If there is more than one vocabulary that can plausibly hook-up with ostensibly relevant neurophysiological data, then Levinas's theoretical formulations are underdetermined by the facts, and one can interrogate those formulations on grounds of their ethical and theological filiations and resonances since they are not directly constrained by the facts. If, as seems more likely, Levinas is providing us with a phenomenological description that makes no claims of uniquely illuminating a scientifically distinctive slice/sector of neurophysiological experience—if his description is a contribution to philosophical anthropology that in no way purports to intersect with work in more narrowly scientific domains—then the issue of underdetermination of theory by fact rears its head even more forcefully. If Levinas wants us to imaginatively project human sensibility as primordially harboring the gestalt that he attributes to it—while tacitly acknowledging in advance that other pictures of human relatedness can equally well square with the best-attested facts of human experience—then he is responsible for the ethical, theological, and metaphysical import of the picture he advances. If underdetermination is assumed, then the ethical and theological ramifications of Levinas's picture come to the foreground and assume center stage.

Levinas, without directly noticing it, seems to be haunted by the model of Rousseau. Levinas wants to arrive at a description of a stage of development of human consciousness that is so early and formative that what occurs later has to be viewed as distorting and deflecting human beings away from their original orientation and promise. The problematic that Levinas confronts in theorizing this original stage is analogous to the problematic that bedevils Rousseau. To qualify as supremely primary, this stage of development of human consciousness has to be virtually out of view of everybody except the theorist. On the other hand, however, the indirect evidence for this stage has to come from a common awareness of the degenerate condition of humanity, which makes people receptive to a projection of an early version of humanity that circumvented the current pitfalls. Both Rousseau and Levinas are democrats of different varieties who make the case for democracy in an authoritarian manner (because they are the only ones privy to the ontological picture supremely justifying it) by invoking the earliest phases of human psychosocial development they are capable of theorizing as a touchstone for condemning current antidemocratic and not properly ethical arrangements.

There is a means-end tension in both Rousseau and Levinas. The end of equal respect for persons is validated through the invocation of a picture of how humankind started out on its common adventure to which only the theorist is privy. What Rousseau and Levinas overlook is that the only way to make the means of democratic theorizing commensurate with its end is to steadfastly display before the reader mounting evidence of the pervasiveness of skepticism: how wherever we turn in our examination of human experience and the sustainability of our knowledge claims we encounter limitations and conditionalities that call into question our ability to achieve certainty. The theorist is already engulfed by conditions of equality before he or she begins to theorize. Democratic political institutions as being grounded in the collective decision making of equals achieve their greatest force when that equality is grounded in an equality of ignorance when confronting the challenges of theoretical justification. Acknowledging that we all labor under a cloud of such ignorance means that we have only each other to rely on in fashioning and sustaining a fabric of collective living.

The continuity between Levinas and Rousseau almost pertains to the content of their theorizing and not just to its form. Rousseau depicts the earliest stages of the state of nature as consisting in a state of such radical independence of one human being from the next—the ego mechanisms that constantly goad us to compare ourselves with and incessantly compete with our neighbors have not yet had an opportunity to develop[78]—that it almost makes equal sense to reverse the description and say that we have all achieved effective substitutions of the Other for ourselves. In an animal-like stage of underdeveloped self-consciousness, where other human beings are simply brutely there as part of the landscape and the only social cement (as with animals) is the outpouring of natural pity, the degree of detachment and isolation that characterizes the scene of "human interaction" can be described with equal plausibility in a contradictory vein: human beings are either hopelessly unaware of each other except on those occasions where (as with animals) circumstance evokes from them the outpourings of natural pity or their identification with and substitution for each other are so complete (like two cats huddling together) that the social dynamics of self-differentiation and competition are nowhere in evidence. In crucial respects, Levinas gives us an alternative, contradictory vocabulary to capture the Rousseauean picture of the earliest phases of the state of nature. The basis for critique in both cases is authoritatively conjured up by the theorist and bears almost no relation to the anthropological profile of the human beings and the social dynamics (with its staging of human relationships) it is intended to criticize.

What Levinas as a liberal political theorist (and, more ambivalently, Rousseau, whose overriding commitment is to republican communitarianism rather than to liberalism) is not sufficiently taking into account is that in order to emerge with a maximally coherent liberal political theory, the stages that lead to the affirmation of a liberal political state (or—to switch metaphors—the conceptual materials out of which it is constructed) have to match the fully developed liberal state and not be out of sync with it. The beauty and persuasive force of Hobbes's state of nature reside in the fact that it represents an unbridled microcosm of all that is artificially and instrumentally controlled in the full-blown civil state itself. There is no marked discontinuity in Hobbes's account between the motivational apparatuses and the limits to knowledge affecting the people who populate the state of nature and the motivational mechanisms and the limits to knowledge characteristic of members of the social-contract society. The major difference between the two phases of individual and social development for Hobbes and for social contract theory generally is the creative transmutation of these joint limits to goodness and to knowledge into a set of constitutive factors shaping a new political order called liberalism. The limits to knowledge and to goodness can be mobilized against the limits—so that we end up in a metaphysical location that we can classify as a generalized agnosticism. Manifesting limited goodness also suggests that political order has to be fashioned out of appeals to self-interest. In addition, limited knowledge nurtures the vision of a state committed to procedural rules and safeguards that on a transient and ongoing basis generate different configurations of political substance. The theorist in the end is on a par with the human beings he theorizes about and is the first citizen of the ideal republic to submit to the imperative of equality.

The ideal self of representative democracy posited by Oakeshott in his essay on "The Masses in Representative

Democracy"—a generalized agnostic self that is able to take full responsibility for its interim insights and allegiances—evokes Nietzsche's description of the ideal self in *Beyond Good and Evil* as being capable of sustaining itself without any "crutches." Nietzsche's generalized agnostic conception of the human person invests with only provisional credence every commitment, enthusiasm, and achievement of the self:

> Not to remain stuck to a person—not even the most loved—every person is a prison, also a nook. Not to remain stuck to a fatherland—not even if it suffers most and needs help most—it is less difficult to sever one's heart from a victorious fatherland. Not to remain stuck to some pity—not even for higher men into whose rare torture and helplessness some accident allowed us to look. Not to remain stuck to a science—even if it should lure us with the most precious finds that seem to have been saved up precisely for us. Not to remain stuck to one's own detachment, to that voluptuous remoteness and strangeness of the bird who flees ever higher to see ever more below him—the danger of the flier. Not to remain stuck to our own virtues and become as a whole the victim of some detail in us, such as our hospitality, which is the danger of dangers for superior and rich souls who spend themselves lavishly, almost indifferently, and exaggerate the virtue of generosity into a vice. One must know how *to conserve oneself*: the hardest test of independence.[79]

The contingency of human becoming—the rejection of being in the sense of a final, quintessential human end—is also underscored in *Twilight of the Idols*:

> The fatality of his [man's] essence is not to be disentangled from the fatality of all that has been and will be. Man is not the effect of some special purpose, of a will, and

end; nor is he the object of an attempt to attain an "ideal of humanity" nor an "ideal of happiness" or an "ideal of morality." It is absurd to wish to devolve one's essence on some end or other. We have invented the concept of "end": in reality there is no end.[80]

Nietzsche's formulations articulate a point of equilibrium for the self that runs strikingly parallel to that envisioned by Hobbes and Oakeshott for society as a whole. Virtually unlimited openness for Hobbes and Oakeshott (the subordination of the public to the private sphere) is the conceptual and institutional guarantee of societal stability. In Nietzsche, as well, not becoming "stuck to ourselves"—remaining perpetually open to the instrumentalized, masklike function[81] of every aspect and pose of the self we have cultivated and assumed (acknowledging the possibility of an infinity of interpretations residing in all of our actions)—is our only route toward conserving ourselves, maintaining ourselves on an even keel.

6

Philosophy of Law and Philosophy of History

OAKESHOTT'S PHILOSOPHIES of law and history also exemplify the generalized agnosticism that is the philosophical doctrinal equivalent to the diminished self-consciousness integral to Oakeshott's conception of a well-ordered morality and political state. Oakeshott is rigorously consistent in his application of the principle of the underdetermination of theory by fact—in the cases at hand the principle is best denoted by the formulation, "the underdetermination of meaning by text"—to the subject matter of law and history. With regard to law, Oakeshott says:

> Now, the expressions "theory," "explanation" and "interpretation," even when it is clear that they are to be applied to "the nature of law" and not to any particular law, body of laws or system of laws, are liable to be misleading. They are apt to suggest . . . that we have two things to deal with, (i) law, and (ii) the theory, explanation or interpretation of law; whereas, in truth, there is only one thing: law. The "nature of law," and a theory, explanation or interpretation of the nature of law are the same thing. Any reading of

law is an explanation of law; the difference between explanations is one of degree and relative comprehensiveness. What is true of interpretation of a text is true universally of interpretation; the text and interpretation are one and inseparable. It is true that we appear to begin with one thing, the text, and proceed to a second thing, the interpretation; but what we call "the text" is itself an interpretation, a meaning, for which (in interpretation) we substitute another, different or more extended, interpretation or meaning.[1]

In relation to the philosophy of history, Oakeshott expresses a comparable view: "Evidence" is a rarely used word in Oakeshott's vocabulary; "inference" from "sources" that are themselves the results of "inference" becomes the key understanding:

This product of historical enquiry and imagination is not like the resolution of a jigsaw puzzle, what is on the table being made to correspond to the picture on the lid of the box. There is no such picture and there are no such firm shapes to be picked up and put into their predestined places one at a time. What an historian has are shapes of his own manufacture, more like ambiguous echoes which wind in and out, touch and modify one another; and what he composes is something more like a tune (which may be carried away by the wind) than a neatly fitted together, solid structure.[2]

With regard to the domains of law and history, Oakeshott collapses the dualities of interpretation and text and inference and source into the unities of interpretation and inference. A text just is how it is interpreted—and a piece of historical source material just is the inferences that are derived from it, and the inferences from which it is derived. We have here the same open embrace of contradiction that we have discerned throughout all of Oakeshott's philosophy. The interpretation and inference are at the same time (at least for heuristic purposes) something other than the text and the source—and are the text and the source. How are we able to account for that patch of intelligible and coherent exposition (so vital and integral to the argument) that sustains the distinctness of "interpretation" and "text" and "inference" and "source" at the same time that it unreservedly ontologically affirms that they are one? On what basis can Oakeshott have it both ways? We must therefore say (as he says about himself) that he is a skeptic. As a skeptic who questions both the self-evident and the empirically supportable character of the relationship between the words that we use and the things which they name, he opens himself up immediately to the specter of contradiction—of contradictory words being able to coherently frame a homogeneous stream of "things." Once contradiction has been normalized in this fashion, there is no humanly conceived entity or category that can legitimately be excluded from the train of speculation—and from efforts at translation into practice. The world of human endeavor becomes a mystically saturated realm, where the price of internal coherence seems to be metaphysical severance and inconsequence. We confront again the mysticism of everyday life: keeping the reality of the world at arm's distance, as the world hovers on an endless brink of possibility.

For Oakeshott, all that exists are interpretations—human consensual readings—with regard to God (negative theology); the furniture of the world (both theories and facts are "understanding[s] waiting to be understood"[3]); science ("Without the categories and the method [of science], there is no matter; without the instruments of measurement, nothing to measure"[4]); politics (the utterly subordinate, formal legalistic role that the public sphere plays in relation to the private sphere—maximizing the freedom and opportunity for private readings all the way down from ends to means); and now texts in general. A world of appearances in which there is no certain reality to back them up restores us to the mysticism of everyday life in which this-worldly existence in all of its dimensions and ramifications can be conceived as a yawn in the face of eternity.

The mystical penumbra surrounding Oakeshott's philosophy of history is reinforced when we consider that the contexts in terms of which we seek to comprehend the multidimensional texts that have survived from the past themselves consist of tissues of texts. The very factors doing the elucidating are subject to the same quandaries as their objects. The only resolution for the problem of pinning down the meaning of a text is to replicate the problem with regard to more and more texts. Ontologically speaking, there is no movement: only a frozen moment of incomplete incomprehension. We are at a beginning that is not even able to validate itself as a beginning. We are enacting (and find no way of exiting) the mystical moment par excellence.

The genre of philosophical jurisprudence to which Oakeshott is contributing ("philosophical" in the sense that it seeks to expose presuppositions and thereby, at least in relation to the subject matter it is immediately discussing, positions itself beyond them) is analytical jurisprudence. Oakeshott says that "What distinguishes it [analytical jurisprudence] from all other explanations is not the exclusion of both ethical and historical considerations (indeed, it does not belong to its character to exclude these altogether and absolutely), but its presupposition that law is a body of interrelated principles. It is distinguished, that is, by the philosophy of identity which it assumes."[5] The character of a society governed by "the rule of law" is fixed for Oakeshott by the postulates of analytical jurisprudence. "It distinguishes between *jus* and *lex*, it recognizes a kind of moral discourse appropriate to the deliberation of *jus* and *injus*, but it is a self-sustained mode of relationship in terms of the ascertainable authenticity of *lex*."[6]

The emphasis on formalism in this conception ties in very neatly with Oakeshott's preference for *societas* over *universitas*. The proceduralist emphasis of "the rule of law" is paramount. It consists of "non-instrumental rules prescribing conditions to be observed in performing self-chosen actions."[7] It is not surprising that Oakeshott points to some of the same factors that have obstructed the career of *societas* in the modern world as also having undermined the prospect of "the rule of law." One common target of attack is political parties: "Political 'parties' have rarely escaped the character of organizations of interests, not necessarily the interests of their electoral supporters but interests of some sort which they regard themselves as committed to promote if they are returned to office. And, of course, this runs counter to the rule of law which is not concerned either to promote or to obstruct the pursuit of interests."[8] A second common target of criticism is the engagement in public policymaking beyond promotion of the rule of law: "In general, the character of a state as an association in terms of the rule of law is qualified when upon the authority and the engagement to deliberate and to make law is superimposed the authority and the engagement to deliberate and to make 'policy,' and upon the authority and engagement to adjudicate is superimposed that of pursuing and administering a 'policy.' . . . To pursue 'policy' and to exercise authority to make such subventions imposes upon the associates the *persona* of members of a co-operative undertaking, upon a state the character of an enterprise association and upon government the character of estate management."[9] Oakeshott is also averse to both a Bill of Rights and judicial review as constitutive of a substantive, interest-balancing liberalism rather than a proceduralist, rule-centered liberalism: the rule of law "has no room for . . . either a so-called Bill of Rights (that is, alleged unconditional principles of *jus* masquerading as themselves law), or an independent office and apparatus charged with considering the *jus* of a law and authorized to declare a law to be inauthentic if it were found to be 'unjust.' Such considerations and institutions may perhaps have an appropriate place where association is in terms of *interests* and *jus* is no more than an equitable accommodation of interests to one another, but they have no place whatever in association in terms of the rule of law."[10]

Given the heavily formalistic and proceduralist emphasis in Oakeshott's philosophy of law, it becomes understandable that issues of underdetermination, indeterminacy, and circularity become crucial for making sense of his position. What (as we have seen) is true globally for Oakeshott in relation to the text of the law that "text and interpretation are one and inseparable"[11] is true locally for him in relation to each particular case that comes up for adjudication. "Laws are unavoidably indeterminate prescriptions of general adverbial obligations. They subsist in advance and in necessary ignorance of the future contingent situations to which they may be found to relate. And even if these prescriptions were 'certain' (that is, as free as may be from ambiguity and conflict with each other) they could not themselves declare their meaning in respect of any circumstantial situation."[12] Oakeshott's commitment to underdetermination and indeterminacy deepens for him the problem of circularity. If the rule of law is marked by the radical formalism we have described, authentication becomes the supreme metasystemic norm guiding one through the system of rules. If law forms a thoroughly self-contained system, then the major question to resolve in studying and applying the system is whether a particular law is authentically mandated or not. What is the status of this rule of authentication? Oakeshott's response to this question seems deceptively straightforward: "The expression 'the rule of law' denotes a self-sustained, notionally self-consistent, mode of human association in terms of the recognition of the authority or authenticity of enacted laws and the obligations they prescribe in which the considerations in terms of which the authenticity of a law may be confirmed or rebutted are themselves enacted law; in which the jurisdiction of the law is itself a matter of law."[13] Oakeshott's formulation provokes an immediate question: even if the rule of authentication is part of the system, since consultation of historical and sociological circumstance is blocked by the presuppositions of an analytical jurisprudence, does not the rule of authentication need to be authenticated in turn by a further rule of authentication and so on ad infinitum so that "the rule of law" never gets off the ground? Its formal purity seems to render it thoroughly "deoperational" as a legal system.

Oakeshott's implicit response to this objection is contained in his tantalizing note 5 to page 151 of "The Rule of Law." He says, "That 'law regulates its own creation' is not a paradox but a truism." For Oakeshott, law regulating its own creation—the irrevocably circular character of law—is not unique to law but pervades all of our conceptualizations and verbalizations. Given the principle of the underdetermination of theory by fact (of words by things) to which Oakeshott subscribes, no noncircular formulation of argument or systematic presentation of views can be floated since, given the radical, contradictory openness of the terms that we use and the conceptually dependent character of the phenomena that our words inscribe, unless we seal off the openness of words and things by reading back into our premises and the constituent parts of our system what our conclusions and systems as a whole are arguing for, we have no arguments and no systems altogether. Oakeshott makes this point very emphatically in "The Concept of a Philosophical Jurisprudence": "There is, of course, no such thing as a 'purely inductive enquiry'; and least of all is such an enquiry characteristic of 'science.' Induction, I suppose, means keeping your eye on the facts; but it does not tell you what facts, and until we have some means of identifying our facts there is no such thing as an enquiry: 'pure induction' is pure nonsense."[14] Apparently, according to Oakeshott, in order to know what we are looking for—and also what we are saying—certain things have to be posited and not merely inferred.

There is an instructive contrast to be drawn between Oakeshott's philosophy of law and that of Carl Schmitt since they both acknowledge a very strong debt to Hobbes as being among their most significant precursors.[15] Building upon the rigidly formalistic and analytically rigorous principles we have discussed, Schmitt's philosophy of law eventuates not in a truism (as it does for Oakeshott) but in a paradox—what he calls the Paradox of Sovereignty. This paradox (in Giorgio Agamben's paraphrase) goes as follows: "I, the sovereign, who am outside the law, declare that there is nothing outside the law."[16] Schmitt's paradox refers to the moment of institution of sovereignty where the sovereign's (whether it be a single person or a group) relationship to his or her handiwork (how the simultaneous inside-outside relationship between the sovereign and sovereignty can be sustained) defies coherent expression. The sovereign has to be configured as being outside the system of law in order to be able to institute it—but at the very moment of institution the sovereign also comes within its purview. Agamben utilizes the Paradox of Sovereignty as a point of entry for theorizing the phenomenon of Nazism. He makes central to his interpretation of the Holocaust the Nazis' obsessive preoccupation with bare life—or what he calls, following Michel Foucault, biopolitics. Through their organization of the various Jewish ghettoes around Europe, the Nazis pushed masses of people to this level. In their lavish and ghastly medical experiments upon humans, they seemed to be driven by a desire to arrive at an objective biochemical translation of what constitutes bare life. In the monumentally destructive apparatuses of the extermination camps, they were simultaneously riveted upon scientifically isolating, destroying, and mocking bare life. Schmitt's paradox seems to register a significant limit to our logico-linguistic capacities to transparently reflect reality. From Agamben's perspective, the Nazis' overwhelmingly destructive riveting upon bare life represented an attempt to escape "the prisonhouse of language"[17] and to be in contact with the indubitably real.

It is worth noting (a point Agamben does not develop) that the Paradox of Sovereignty is symptomatic of five other paradoxes that are important in the history of Western consciousness (some of which we have been considering in the course of this essay): the paradox surrounding negative theology; the paradox affecting skepticism; the Liar Paradox; Russell's Paradox; and Mannheim's Paradox. I would like to say something about each of these in turn to illustrate a common thread with the Paradox of Sovereignty.

Negative theology's codification of the tenets of monotheism exhibits a similar intramural tension between its various components as we found in the case of the Paradox of
Sovereignty. Negative theology wants to limit our comprehension of God to a disowning of the literal import of the
attributes ascribed to Him—it wants desperately to preclude
our rationally relating to God in any other sense—and yet
on some level that deeply challenges analytical plotting God
has to be postulated in more than a negative sense because
otherwise there is nothing to disown. Just like the sovereign
in relation to sovereignty, God in more than a negative sense
is both presupposed and undermined by the tenets of negative theology.

Analogously, in the case of skepticism our definition
boomerangs at the point where it fails to acknowledge and
incorporate how being skeptical of everything challenges
our ability to adhere even to skepticism. Skepticism—just
like the sovereign, and God—both falls inside and remains
obdurately outside its respective definition.

The Liar Paradox stems from Epimenides the Cretan,
who said that all Cretans were liars. "If he spoke the truth,
he was a liar."[18] Epimenides himself is thus both inside and
outside his formulation about "all Cretans."

In *The Principles of Mathematics*, Bertrand Russell points to
a paradox surrounding the notion of "a class of all classes."[19]
A graphic illustration of Russell's Paradox would be: "If
the barber of Seville shaves all the men of Seville who do
not shave themselves, does he shave himself? If he does, he
doesn't, and if he doesn't, he does."[20] The barber of Seville—
like Epimenides the Cretan—paradoxically falls both inside
and outside the ostensibly inclusive statement that either is
made about him or that he makes himself.

According to Karl Mannheim, the "total conception of ideology" refers to "the ideology of an age or of a concrete historico-social group, e.g., of a class, when we are concerned with the characteristics and composition of the total structure of the mind of this epoch or of this group."[21] Total ideology gives rise to what Clifford Geertz has called "Mannheim's Paradox."[22] From the perspective of Mannheim's concept of ideology, his theorizing of total ideology is itself a function and expression of the ideological pretensions of an age, and the question becomes how it can lay claim to being a neutral assessment of the epistemological and ontological status of the primary concepts and categories regnant in a particular society at a particular time. The concept of total ideology is both inside and outside the definition of total ideology.

Situating Schmitt's paradox in comparative relation to these other kindred paradoxes confers greater depth on Agamben's interpretive perspective on the Holocaust. It clues us into how conjoined to a rebellion against the limits of logic and language reflected in the Nazis' cataclysmic outbursts was a possible subliminal awareness of the convergence and continuity between monotheistic religion and Western skepticism—of how paradoxical and futile the Western "progression" from religion to modernity is. The Nazi obsession with bare life was their way of rebelling against the inextricability of the situation I have just described by destructively locating "bare life" as the secure focal point of their interventions beyond the endless meanderings and paraphrases of language.[23]

If Agamben is right in locating what I would call a perversion of the idea of necessity (the "unavoidable paradoxes" I have just enumerated) as constituting a metaphysical root of fascism and Nazism, then the Oakeshottian idea of the pervasiveness of contingency and its partnered notion of the underdetermination of theory by fact and of words by things should have a correspondingly liberating effect. It could be argued that just as the embrace of these paradoxes leads to a gnostic politics focused on individual and collective deliverance, so, too, the circumvention of these paradoxes is conducive to the expansion of metaphysical space for the reception of political liberalism. In finding a way around these paradoxes, one is renouncing a yearning for contact with ultimate reality by disenchanting a new embodiment of a "Myth of the Given."[24] The affirmation of a paradox where it is deconstructible is also symptomatic of being captive of a "Myth of the Given."

In heeding Oakeshott's imperative of "underdetermination" (which, as I have argued, along with the key terms in the Oakeshottian vocabulary, has normative as well as descriptive import), I think it is possible to reconfigure the conceptual material entering into these six paradoxes so that they do not eventuate in paradox. I would like to review these six paradoxes in turn to show how the paradoxes can be dispelled.

1. Schmitt's Paradox of Sovereignty occurs on the level of language—as you seek to delimit in words how it is that the real-world institution of the political ruler (the sovereign) can be conceived as falling both inside (for purposes of evoking his compliance) and outside (for purposes of warding off an infinite regress in accounting for how sovereignty came to be established) the institution the ruler sets up. The paradox is not immediately "given" or generated by the notion of sovereignty but results from an act of conceptual "slicing" geared in a certain way. If you enlarge the framework of analysis, a paradox does not have to result. If you consider both the institution of sovereignty and its effects, then "institution" requires or presupposes an

instituter, and the effects that become apparent later in time than the moment of institution can encompass the instituter as well as the other members of society. If you enlarge the horizon of analysis to include how sovereignty operates once it is established as well as the process of establishment itself, then there is nothing inconsistent in noting that the sovereign has to precede sovereignty at the moment of institution while coming under its rubric once it is established. Schmitt's paradox emerges only if you "cut" the horizon of analysis much more narrowly. If you focus exclusively on the moment of institution, then it looks like the sovereign is both "inside" and "outside" sovereignty—that the sovereign's situation is paradoxical.

However, what is crucial to notice here is that a choice or decision is present not only where Schmitt and Agamben say it is in order to arrest the infinite regress associated with the concept of sovereignty, but in delineating the infinite regress and its impact that gives rise to the paradox. If you conceptually "cut" the topic at a later stage in its unfolding, there is no paradox. If you "cut" sovereignty at the moment of institution, then you confront the paradox. There has to be a decision in order to have a problem in the first place—and not just to devise a solution for it.

2. With regard to the paradox surrounding the formulation of the tenets of negative theology, that paradox, too, emerges only when you restrict the focus of space-time to concentrate on the moment of formulation itself. But if you expand the spatial/temporal horizon to encompass postulation of and belief in an utterly transcendent deity as well as a description of the antiliteralist character of this belief, then you can plausibly adhere to your postulation of an inscrutable God and a specification of the ways (expressed in your

theorizing of the tenets of negative theology) in which His inscrutability becomes evident.

3. Analogously, with regard to the paradox surrounding the formulation of the tenets of skepticism, if you expand your spatial/temporal horizon beyond the moment of formulation of these tenets to encompass the completed statement itself and the intellectual context in which it is situated, then the not-inconsistent outcome that emerges is that the furthest we can go in the direction of skepticism—of doubting everything—is in not being skeptical about skepticism, in not doubting the validity of doubt. To emerge with a paradox one would have to restrict the conceptual slicing to the moment of formulation and cut oneself off from awareness of a broader slice that would enable one to integrate the consequences of the formulation into the formulation itself. Again, therefore, to have the paradox is the result of an antecedent choice or decision about where to conceptually "cut" one's focus.

Eliminating Schmitt's Paradox (or the other analogous paradoxes that we are considering) does not diminish the scope of skepticism but rather augments it. The fact that there is a choice involved in order to situate a problem to begin with suggests that the language of problem identification (and not just the vocabulary involved in the spinning of a resolution) is metaphoric. It does not transparently reflect a situation that exists independently of our formulations. So even though in accordance with our second way of "slicing" the "paradox" of skepticism, a generalized agnosticism appears to be rejected (since we can now make sense of how it is possible to be skeptical of everything but skepticism itself), skepticism in its more encompassing sense where it eventuates in a generalized agnosticism supervenes once we become aware of how dealing with the paradox surrounding skepticism more conservatively by expanding the spatio-temporal horizon of inquiry leads to a problematizing of the problem and therefore to an augmentation of skepticism.

4, 5, and 6. The pattern of analysis developed in relation to the Paradox of Sovereignty and the paradoxes surrounding formulations of the tenets of negative theology and of skepticism is equally relevant with regard to the Liar Paradox, Russell's Paradox, and Mannheim's Paradox. If you conceptually restrict your focus to the raw formulation in each case, then the paradoxes emerge. But if you expand your spatio/temporal horizons to encompass the context as well as the content of the statement, then the paradoxes get dissipated. Epimenides as speaker clearly wants to exempt himself from the statement that "All Cretans are liars." He wants to consider his statement about the behavior of Cretans in general as true. Once we expand the spatio-temporal horizons of our analysis, we realize that his statement needs to be read as shorthand for the longer, more circuitous statement that "All Cretans are liars except Epimenides the Cretan when reporting on the behavior of his fellow Cretans." Similarly, we need to expand the statement about the barber of Seville to read that "Aside from himself, the barber of Seville shaves all the men of Seville who do not shave themselves."

A similar approach seems persuasive with regard to Mannheim's Paradox. If you enlarge the spatio-temporal framework of the analysis, then Mannheim (probably serving as a stand-in for an enlightened intellectual class) wants to claim himself (and them) as exceptions to the theory of total ideology. Mannheim's statement is more complexly and elaborately about how a group of intellectuals has the capacity to pierce through the claims of others while preserving the moral autonomy and the epistemological self-discipline to refrain from such class-taintedness themselves. In order for Mannheim's Paradox to emerge, as well, there has to be a decision in place to "slice" what he is saying at the moment of formulation instead of expanding one's horizon to include the broader context in which the formulation takes place.

The combustibility of these six paradoxes, which Oakeshott indirectly endorses by his statement that with regard to the Paradox of Sovereignty "that 'law regulates its own creation' is not a paradox but a truism," is evocative of Oakeshott's "feel" for the mystical character of human life as a whole. The "unreality" of human life is extended so far as to encompass the question whether the designation of it as "unreal" achieved through the medium of posting the various paradoxes that we have discussed is itself real or unreal. The questioning encoded in the formulation of the paradoxes is itself as vulnerable to questioning as the original states of affairs in each case that served as the occasion for the raising of the paradoxes. The dispelling of the paradoxes is a function of a "conceptual slicing" maneuver that we engage in and is not intrinsic to the circumstances of each particular case. From the perspective of our analysis of Oakeshott, reality is kept at an irretrievable arm's length—mystically conjured up and remaining mystically elusive on an ongoing basis.

Oakeshott's philosophy of history reencodes the same skeptical motifs we have been considering throughout this essay. The historian inhabits a doubly veiled world. He or she has access to the past only through certain enactments that he or she engages in in the present—and the content of the present independently of the aim to use some portion of it as an occasion for retrieving some aspect of the past comes under the sway of the principle of "underdetermination."

"Survivals [items and objects that have survived from the past]," Oakeshott says, "constitute an historian's present and are the only past upon which he can lay his hands, although even here his knowledge is not direct or immediate; but they provide nothing he seeks. For what he seeks—an historically understood past—is of a wholly different character: it is a past which has not itself survived. Indeed, it is a past which could not have survived because, not being composed of bygone utterances and artefacts, it was never itself present. It can neither be found nor dug up, nor retrieved, nor recollected, but only inferred."[25] Oakeshott also says that "What we ordinarily perceive rarely . . . has . . . absence of ambiguity: it is a much more messy affair in which we come and go somewhat inconsequentially between a variety of universes of discourse."[26] "Underdetermination" thus impairs the possibility of securely negotiating the furniture of our world even when it consists of items that securely relate to our present. To try and move in the direction of more extreme immediacy for Oakeshott (just like for Nietzsche, as we saw earlier) only exacerbates the problem. "Although an object of 'immediate perception' (a mere 'this,' a 'here,' and a 'now') may perhaps be said to be unconditional, it escapes conditionality only on account of its extreme abstraction, insignificance and exiguity."[27] To redeem "immediate perception" of its "extreme abstraction, insignificance, and exiguity," one needs to destroy its immediacy—and thereby rob it of its potential as a validating source for our modes of identification and classification of items in our experience.

Since even with regard to present items (not "survivals") that populate our environments there is no stable substratum but only inference, the process becomes immensely more complicated (even though qualitatively speaking it is still on the same ontological plane) when we are confronted by "survivals" and are attempting to piece together an image of some portion or sector of the past. The historian engages in "inference" without a stable historical record to infer from. If "text and interpretation are one and inseparable,"[28] then both the person concerned to relate to his or her current experience and the historian preoccupied with deciphering "survivals" from the past are drawing inferences from inferences in an unceasing chain that finds no resting place anywhere. The historian's work is all "inference"—and no "text"—which suggests (in order to redeem this position from an extreme skepticism that is self-refuting) that "inference" has to be interpreted in a generalized agnostic fashion as endlessly deferring itself and keeping all possibilities (including the possibility of a stable text that would minimize the role of inference) open. The same sort of generalized agnostic reading is of course applicable to the ordinary perceiver of the present concerned to make sense of his world to one degree or another. This reading should also be extended to Oakeshott's valorization of the present—where he says that invocations of the past and future are inextricably conceptually linked to the present. Since given Oakeshott's own critical strictures this present is not an immediate present but a theorized present—that is, it is a skeptical construction out of what defies direct sensory and conceptual access by us—in order not to engulf itself as an expression of extreme skepticism it has to be understood in a generalized agnostic way. This means that it leaves the door open to all possibilities—which would encompass a realistic reading of all temporal dimensions, including the present.

This reading suggests that Oakeshott's vision of historical understanding—just like his analysis of how we comprehend the present—is mystical in character. Contradictory possibilities are enduringly harbored that establish a permanent

If the historical past is "inferred" and "constructed"—in relation to what is it inferred and constructed? What motivates or drives the inference and construction? Oakeshott's answer to this question is straightforward and compelling— and merges with that propounded by Hans-Georg Gadamer in his philosophy of hermeneutics:[29] "A past composed of passages of related historical events (that is, happenings, not actions or utterances, understood as outcomes of antecedent happenings similarly understood) [is] assembled as . . . answers to questions about the past formulated by an historian."[30] Visions of the past projected by historians thus bespeak "contingency" on a number of interrelated levels: First, there is the aspect of identifying the "survival" that one is talking about, which is itself a tissue of interpretations—and nothing more hard-core than that. Second, there is the factor that one is not able to control which survivals will enter the historian's present and be identified as a survival. The identification of an artifact as a "survival" is itself partially at least a contingent matter. Third, there are the questions posed by historians to "survivals," which vary contingently from one generation to the next—and from one historian to the next.

"Historical understanding is nothing so remote of possible achievement as a seamless web of related events, nor anything so simple as events truly inferred from surviving record, and it has nothing to do with origins. It is the gift of an opportunity to understand a passage of the past in terms of hitherto unrecognized conjunctions, convergences and relationships of events and thus to imagine it more distinctly and perspicuously."[31] Historical understanding for Oakeshott thus conjures up an ever-expanding middle in which ever-changing patterns of relationship between events are disclosed in relation to the changing menus of questions that historians pose to the past. The incompleteness of understanding insinuated by Oakeshott's theory of historical understanding is evocative of a generalized agnosticism in which human presents succeed one other without producing undeniable intellectual progress or yielding theoretical certainty.

There is an important affinity between the generalized agnosticism suggested by Oakeshott's theory of historical understanding and his political theory, whose formalism and instrumentalism (the public sphere situated in an instrumental and subordinate relation to the private sphere) can also be construed as an expression of a generalized agnosticism. The state remains subservient to the initiatives undertaken in the private sphere at least partially because it lacks the rational wherewithal to arrive at and impose a more comprehensive plan of its own. The formal role of the state is to help ensure the institutionalization of a series of successive presents whose intellectual understandings and moral visions and intuitions are theoretically irresolvable to some more primary level of insight beyond what is contingently, historically articulated in any given political generation. Oakeshott's philosophy of history reinstalls the normative vision of his political theory in a backward-looking direction. The same endless succession of metaphysically interchangeable moments (coming from nowhere, leading nowhere) characterizes both the history and the political theory.

Oakeshott's depiction of historical analysis can be understood as a normative vision of human life and not just as a description of the activity of being an historian. The historian's reading of any given set of historical events is also a normative reading, and not just a purely descriptive one. Underdetermination of theories by facts and of words by things leads Oakeshott to emphasize the inferential character of historical understanding. Assigning centrality to "inference" in a context that questions the availability of "texts" is manifested in his avoidance (for the most part) of the term "evidence," his emphasis on events rather than motives or intentions,[32] his strictures about situating events in relation to interlocking networks of other events, and his expatiating on the role of the historian in discerning and fashioning new patterns of interrelationship between events. Oakeshott's rejection of the search for causes of events as the proper focus of historical inquiry can also be traced to the same source. He says that "There is no *explanans* of a different character from an *explanandum*: a 'law,' a 'cause' or a propensity. Historical events are themselves circumstantial convergencies of antecedent historical events; what they are is how they came to be woven."[33] Part of the reason, at least, why the categories of "law" and "cause" are expunged from the historical vocabulary is to dispel the illusion that there is some stable external conceptual "fulcrum" (something approximating to a theory) that can make sense of the "facts" or events that are integral to the historian's account. In all of the ways that I have enumerated, then, Oakeshott is depriving the historian's inference of any stable text or conceptual counters in relation to which inference can occur.

"Inference" without a stable text is evocative of "underdetermination." "Underdetermination," in turn (as we have seen), suggests that there is no purely descriptive reading of any situation or event. The ontological gap between words and things or events is closed by acknowledging that there is an inescapably normative dimension in every "descriptive" formulation. This insight can be applied both to Oakeshott's role as a philosopher of history and to the works produced by practicing historians. Oakeshott's description of historical

inquiry as involving the discovery/construction of ever-
expanding networks of interconnection between events in
which to situate the event under historical scrutiny can also
appropriately be viewed as a normative vision concerning
the shape, location, and promise of human life. As I suggested earlier, Oakeshott's political theory proper can be
viewed as a restatement in a forward-moving temporal direction of the philosophical vision enunciated in a backward-
looking direction in his theory of historical understanding.
In both cases, you have severed, unmoored events sustained
in their severed status in the case of the political theory
by the instrumental, deferential role played by the public
sphere in relation to the private sphere, and in the case of
the theory of historical understanding, by detaching historical events from such theoretical props as "historical causes"
and "historical laws," so that the chief vocation of the historian emerges as weaving ever-new patterns of interrelationship between the events themselves, which never receive a
conclusive confirmation or corroboration.

Analogously, the "survivals" that serve as the basis for the
picture of the historical past invoked by individual historians
give rise to inexpugnably normative pictures of particular
events and episodes of the historical past. To make sense
philosophically of how the ontological gap between "survivals" theoretically pointing in a multiplicity of directions and
"inference," which constructs out of the "survivals" a coherent, unified historical picture, gets closed, the normative
strata in the historical picture need to be highlighted.

The nonnegotiability—the ineffability—of the whole in
Oakeshott's political theory and philosophy of history (the
successive series of contingently concatenated political presents that typify political time; the kaleidoscopically reshifted
patterns of relationship between events that are articulated

by historians without benefit of invocation of either historical laws or causal laws) is evocative of the subterranean mystical tendencies of his thought. Visions of the whole are placed on infinite hold in Oakeshott's philosophy. One can gesture toward them—note them by their absence—without ever tangibly intersecting with them. The silent, displaced partner of Oakeshott's skepticism is a mystical wholeness that can only be conjured up by what persistently interrogates it and calls it into question.

Oakeshott begins *On History* with an elaborately mounted effort to delineate and defend the distinction between the "practical past" and the "historical past." Oakeshott defines the "practical past" as a "'living' past which may be said to 'teach by example,' or more generally to afford us a current vocabulary of self-understanding and self-expression."[34] The "historical past," by contrast, is also anchored in the present, but it is a present "exclusively composed of objects recognized as survivals from past."[35] In relating to the past in a practical vein, we are immediately concerned to extrapolate from past events and occurrences to address our problems and quandaries in the present. We are not concerned to understand the past qua past, but to use it to ameliorate our condition in the present. A classic example for Oakeshott of a practical relationship to the past is Machiavelli in *The Prince* and *The Discourses*, who turns to Roman history for guidance for remedying the rampant instability of Italian politics.[36] The "historical past" tries to abstract out of immediate practical concerns and to recover (to the extent possible) aspects of what was, independently of the ways in which they fit in (or fail to fit in) in relation to our needs and designs in the present.

Given our discussion of Oakeshott's philosophy of history until this point, we can already begin to appreciate how counterproductive (and unreflective of the larger tendencies of his thought) the distinction between the historical past and the practical past turns out to be. Most of his arguments in support of the distinction end up downgrading and eroding it. In the end, the distinction can be sustained only by acknowledging that both the "practical past" and the "historical past" are invented pasts fabricated in one's present— except that the "historical past" is an invented view of the "pastness" of the past and the "practical past" is an invented view of how the past might be coopted for use in our present. For Oakeshott, of course, "invention"—as a key term in his skeptical vocabulary—has to be construed in a generalized agnostic fashion. It cannot rule out the possibility that what it takes to be invented is real. If the "historical past" referred to a real past, then the Nietzschean point that I am about to make concerning how the "practical past" interpenetrates the "historical past" would not be applicable. Oakeshott's keeping this possibility in "suspended animation," however, gives me the space to make the point.

The following are some arguments telling against a "thick" construction of Oakeshott's distinction between the "historical past" and the "practical past":

1. Oakeshott advances what amounts to a coherence theory of historical interpretation: "The present in historical enquiry is, then, composed of performances which have survived, and the first engagement of such an enquiry is to distinguish and understand these performances in terms of their connections with others to which they may be circumstantially related. The principle of this enquiry is that everything is what it is in respect of such relationship; and its procedure is one in which recorded exploits are made to interpret and criticize one another. There is no independent criterion of their historical authenticity."[37] In accordance

with the coherence view that Oakeshott advances in this passage, the procedure for unearthing the "historical past" is no different from the one used to unearth the "practical past." In both cases we are merely using "recorded exploits . . . to interpret and criticize one another." It is just that how we choose to classify—and what we derive from—our juxtapositions of such "exploits" that differs. In the end, the categories of the "historical" and the "practical" "past" become distinctions in mode of stipulation that cannot be corroborated or validated by any materials outside of themselves.

2. The argument of the preceding paragraph is intensified when you consider it in the light of Oakeshott's understanding that the historian creates his own sources: "No small part of this [i.e., historical] enquiry is properly devoted to finding better reasons for accepting a current interpretation or good reasons for modifying it. It is in this manner that an historian himself creates his present, his so-called 'sources,' and endows them, not with 'authority,' but with 'authenticity.'"[38] The materials (artifacts and texts) out of which coherence is generated acquire their character as relevant materials from the antecedent judgments of the historian and are in no way independently, transpersonally confirmed.

3. Oakeshott's theory of historical identity and continuity reinforces the previous argument: "Every historical event is a difference recognized in terms of the difference it made in the constitution of the not yet understood character of a subsequent event, itself a difference. The identity which constitutes a passage of historical change must be itself a difference or a composition of differences, and every such difference must be an historical event. . . . Such a passage of antecedent differences related to a subsequent difference does not lie, already identified, somewhere in the past, waiting to be picked up; it does not exist until it is assembled

by an historian in search of clues to the character of a not-yet-understood historical event."[39] We have proceeded now to what we might call the "third plateau." It is not just "concrete sources" that the historian needs to juxtapose to one another in order to generate the "historical past." The historian must also authenticate and thereby establish his sources—and in addition he must determine through his identification of relevant differences what constitutes the subject matter of history (where the outer perimeters of his historical inquiry lie with regard to each piece of "evidence" that he mobilizes in defense of his reading). The historian must thus demarcate out of his own intellectual resources the version of history he is telling, the sources out of which he is telling it, and the boundaries of relevance and interconnection within which his historical inquiry proceeds. I think that at this point it becomes purely a matter of arbitrary designation whether to call such inclusive manifestations of the "taint of self" examples of the "historical past" or of the "practical past."

I think that Nietzsche would have conceded all of Oakeshott's analytical points about how to theoretically distinguish the "historical past" from the "practical past" but still would have claimed that Oakeshott's analytically distinguished "historical past" comes in crucial respects under the rubric of the "practical past." What would make it conform to the "practical past" for Nietzsche is Oakeshott's persistent acknowledgment (as we have seen throughout) concerning the unavoidability of interpretation (the pervasiveness of "underdetermination"). For Nietzsche, acknowledging "interpretation" to this extent affirms life because it resists the urge to "mummification"[40]—to recover pristine, uncontaminated specimens of the past—that inspired many nineteenth-century German historians. To mummify the past, for

Nietzsche, means to renounce life generally because at least one historical tributary feeding in from the past (the one under scrutiny by the historian) has been shut off as fully, authentically recaptured and therefore (by implication) disposable. To acknowledge the centrality of interpretation—and thereby to be supremely invoking the "practical past"—is to affirm life. The following is the way Nietzsche negatively draws the equation between interpretation and life:

> That general renunciation of all interpretation (of forcing, adjusting, abbreviating, omitting, padding, inventing, falsifying, and whatever else is of the *essence* of interpreting)—all this expresses, broadly speaking, as much ascetic virtue as any denial of sensuality (it is at bottom only a particular mode of this denial). That which *constrains* these men, however, this unconditional will to truth, is *faith in the ascetic ideal itself*, even if as an unconscious imperative—don't be deceived about that—it is the faith in a *metaphysical* value, the absolute value of *truth*, sanctioned and guaranteed by this ideal alone (it stands or falls with this ideal).[41]

We are finally in the position to resolve the question with which this essay began: how does one make sense of the stylistic paradox that Oakeshott does systematic philosophy in the compressed essay form? I think that we are able to appreciate at this point in my exposition of Oakeshott's thought that he does not believe, in terms of what they deliver, that the treatise-writers get any further than what is communicable in the essay form. Or, alternatively: given the mystical strains in Oakeshott's thought, we can say that for him the philosophical treatise that represents completion is not a humanly attainable goal. Properly understood, the philosophical-treatise writers who think they are going beyond the metaphysical middle in their explorations only end up affirming the interminableness of the middle. The etymological linkage of the term "essay" to the word "assay," which means to try or to attempt, suggests that the knowledge value of an essay is not necessarily achieved after its composition and represents something accessed by the essay but subsisting outside it. Rather, the implicit ontological claim of the essay form might be that its truth consists only in the process of its writing—its provisional and necessarily arbitrary attempt to "get" at something beyond itself.[42] In the interstices of this gesturing outward while analytically only prolonging the "middle" of preoccupation with what might lie beyond itself, we have encoded the space wherein the mysticism of everyday life might flourish. In his metaphysics and epistemology, philosophy of religion, philosophy of science, political theory, philosophies of conversation and of personal identity, philosophy of law, and philosophy of history, Oakeshott persistently theorizes the unexitability of the middle. His preferred form of literary expression— the essay—symbolically registers an implicit critique and commentary on all those who aspire to anything more.

Notes

Chapter One. Introduction: Epistemological Backdrop

1. Paul Franco, *The Political Philosophy of Michael Oakeshott* (New Haven: Yale University Press, 1990), 207; Paul Franco, *Michael Oakeshott: An Introduction* (New Haven: Yale University Press, 2004), 29; Terry Nardin, *The Philosophy of Michael Oakeshott* (University Park: Pennsylvania State University Press, 2001), 5–6; Stuart Isaacs, *The Politics and Philosophy of Michael Oakeshott* (London: Routledge, 2006), 13–50.

2. Isaacs, *Politics and Philosophy of Oakeshott*, 63.

3. Michael Oakeshott, *What Is History? and Other Essays*, ed. Luke O'Sullivan (Exeter: Imprint Academic, 2004), 193.

4. Ibid., 194.

5. The locus classicus for the justification and elaboration of the theory of tacit knowledge is Plato's dialogue *Phaedrus*. Also see the discussion in Michael Polanyi, *Personal Knowledge: Towards a Post-Critical Philosophy* (Chicago: University of Chicago Press, 1958); Michael Polanyi, *The Tacit Dimension* (Garden City, NY: Doubleday, 1966; Anchor, 1967); Aryeh Botwinick, *Skepticism and Political Participation* (Philadelphia: Temple University Press, 1990), 61–117.

6. Isaacs, *Politics and Philosophy of Oakeshott*, 2; John Gray, *Liberalisms: Essays in Political Philosophy* (London: Routledge, 1989), 199–216; John Gray, *Post-Liberalism: Studies in Political Thought* (London: Routledge, 1993), 40–46; John Kekes, *A Case for Conservatism* (Ithaca: Cornell University Press, 1998), 112–13.

7. Michael Oakeshott, *Rationalism in Politics and Other Essays*, new and exp. ed. (Indianapolis: Liberty Press, 1991), 221–94.

8. Isaacs, *Politics and Philosophy of Oakeshott*, 8; Franco, *Oakeshott: An Introduction*, 149–52.

9. Benjamin Barber, *The Conquest of Politics: Liberal Philosophy in Democratic Times* (Princeton: Princeton University Press, 1988), 152–76; Isaacs, *Politics and Philosophy of Oakeshott*, 8.

10. Robert Devigne, *Recasting Conservatism: Oakeshott, Strauss, and the Response to Postmodernism* (New Haven: Yale University Press, 1994), 12; Isaacs, *Politics and Philosophy of Oakeshott*, 53.

11. Compare Oakeshott on conversation: "It has a dialectic of its own; circular, without beginning or end." Oakeshott, *What Is History?*, 187.

12. John Gray, *Liberalism: Second Edition* (Minneapolis: University of Minnesota Press, 1995), 63; Wendell John Coats, Jr., *The Activity of Politics and Related Essays* (Selinsgrove, PA: Susquehanna University Press, 1989), 42–57; Isaacs, *Philosophy and Politics of Oakeshott*, 75.

13. Franco, *Political Philosophy of Oakeshott*, 216–17; Nardin, *Philosophy of Oakeshott*, 212–13; Franco, *Oakeshott: An Introduction*, 175–76.

14. Isaacs, *Politics and Philosophy of Oakeshott*, 171. The works by Laclau relevant for the discussion in the text are Ernesto Laclau and Chantal Mouffe, *Hegemony and Socialist Strategy: Towards a Radical Democratic Politics*, trans. Winston Moore and Paul Cammack (London: Verso, 1985); Ernesto Laclau, *New Reflections on the Revolution of Our Time* (London: Verso, 1990); Ernesto Laclau, *Emancipation(s)* (London: Verso, 1996); Ernesto Laclau, *The Populist Reason* (London: Verso, 2005).

15. Isaacs, *Politics and Philosophy of Oakeshott*, 173.

16. The idea of infinite freedom linked with infinite responsibility is one of the themes encapsulated in Plato's Myth of Er. See Francis MacDonald Cornford, ed., *The Republic of Plato* (Oxford: Oxford University Press, 1975), X.618 (356). For a good discussion of Oakeshott's relationship to Plato, see Debra Candreva, *The Enemies of Perfection: Oakeshott, Plato, and the Critique of Rationalism* (Lanham, MD: Lexington Books, 2005).

17. W. H. Greenleaf, *Oakeshott's Philosophical Politics* (London: Longmans, 1966), 92; Preston King and B. C. Parekh, eds., *Politics and Experience: Essays Presented to Michael Oakeshott* (Cambridge: Cambridge University Press, 1968), 93–124; Franco, *Political Philosophy of Oakeshott*, 104; Jesse Norman, ed., *The Achievement of Michael Oakeshott* (London: Duckworth, 1993), 96; Nardin, *Philosophy of Oakeshott*, 18, 26, 232; Roy Tseng, *The Sceptical Idealist: Michael Oakeshott as a Critic of the Enlightenment* (Exeter: Imprint Academic, 2003), 116; Efraim Podoksik, *In Defence of Modernity: Vision and Philosophy in Michael Oakeshott* (Exeter: Imprint Academic, 2003), 38; Franco, *Michael Oakeshott: Introduction*, 60, 113–14; Kenneth B. McIntyre, *The Limits of Political Theory: Oakeshott's Philosophy of Civil Association* (Exeter: Imprint Academic, 2004), 63–66; Glenn Worthington, *Religious and Poetic Experience in the Thought of Michael*

Oakeshott (Exeter: Imprint Academic, 2005), 72; Suvi Soininen, *From a 'Necessary Evil' to the Art of Contingency: Michael Oakeshott's Conception of Political Activity* (Exeter: Imprint Academic, 2005), 58; Isaacs, *Politics and Philosophy of Oakeshott*, 164–76.

18. Isaacs, *Politics and Philosophy of Oakeshott*, 166.

19. See Karl R. Popper, *Conjectures and Refutations: The Growth of Scientific Knowledge* (London: Routledge and Kegan Paul, 1963; 2nd rev. ed., 1965), 312–35 (and especially 317), and the literature cited in this essay.

20. Ludwig Wittgenstein, *Tractatus Logico-Philosophicus*, trans. D. F. Pears and B. F. McGuinness (London: Routledge and Kegan Paul, 1961), propositions 6.54 and 7 (151). See my discussion of Wittgenstein in my book *Skepticism and Political Participation*, 43–60.

21. This paraphrase of Wittgenstein comes from James C. Edwards, *Ethics without Philosophy* (Tampa: University Presses of Florida, 1982), 14.

22. See the discussion of this paradox in my book *Skepticism, Belief, and the Modern: Maimonides to Nietzsche* (Ithaca: Cornell University Press, 1997), 15.

23. "An Essay on the Relations of Philosophy, Poetry and Reality," in Oakeshott, *What Is History?*, 67–115.

24. Letter from Oakeshott to Patrick Riley, quoted in Patrick Riley, "Michael Oakeshott, Philosopher of Individuality," *Review of Politics* 54 (1992): 664. This article is cited in Franco, *Michael Oakeshott: Introduction*, 22–23.

CHAPTER TWO. METAPHYSICS

1. Oakeshott, *Rationalism in Politics*, 5–42, 465–87.

2. Michael Oakeshott, *Experience and Its Modes* (Cambridge: Cambridge University Press, 1933; reprinted 1966), 3, 350.

3. Michael Oakeshott, *On Human Conduct* (Oxford: Clarendon Press, 1975), 2.

4. Michael Oakeshott, *Religion, Politics and the Moral Life*, ed. Timothy Fuller (New Haven: Yale University Press, 1993), 141; italics in original.

5. Oakeshott, *Rationalism in Politics*, 465–87; and Michael Oakeshott, *On History and Other Essays* (Indianapolis: Liberty Fund, 1999), 179–210.

6. Oakeshott, *Rationalism in Politics*, 5–9, 16.

7. Hans Blumenberg, *The Legitimacy of the Modern Age*, trans. Robert M. Wallace (Cambridge: MIT Press, 1983), parts 1 and 2.

8. First Kings 19:11–12. This constitutes an account of Elijah's private reception of Revelation at the scene of the original Revelation on

Mount Sinai. In contrast to "wind, earthquake, and fire," Elijah perceives the Revelatory Moment as "a sound of thin silence."

9. Michael Oakeshott, ed., *The Social and Political Doctrines of Contemporary Europe*, 2nd ed. (Cambridge: Cambridge University Press, 1939), xxii.

10. Emmanuel Levinas, *Proper Names*, trans. Michael B. Smith (Stanford: Stanford University Press, 1996), 59.

11. Emmanuel Levinas, *Totality and Infinity*, trans. Alphonso Lingis (Pittsburgh: Duquesne University Press, 1969).

12. Gilles Deleuze, *Difference and Repetition*, trans. Paul Patton (London: Athlone Press, 1994); Gilles Deleuze, *The Logic of Sense*, trans. Mark Lester with Charles Stivale, ed. Constantin V. Bourdas (New York: Columbia University Press, 1989).

13. Michel Foucault, *Language, Counter-Memory, Practice*, ed. Donald F. Bouchard (Ithaca: Cornell University Press, 1977), 182.

14. Ibid., 185.

15. Ibid.

16. Cited in the work of Rav Simcha Zissel's grandson, Eliyahu Eliezer Dessler, *Michtav M'Eliyahu*, vol. 1, ed. Aryeh Carmel and Alter Halpern (Bnei-Brak, Israel: n.p., 1964), 294; my translation.

17. Foucault, *Language, Counter-Memory, Practice*, 187.

18. Oakeshott, *Rationalism in Politics*, 5.

19. Oakeshott, *On Human Conduct*, 201, 204.

20. Oakeshott, *Rationalism in Politics*, 467.

21. Ibid., 472.

22. While Oakeshott says that the plot-line of the story of the Tower of Babel "is to be found among the stories of the Chinese, the Caldeans and the ancient Hebrews, and among the Arab and Slav peoples, and the Aztecs of Peru" and compares its plot-structure to the "fortunes of Faust and the adventures of Don Juan" and to "Arthurian legend," he does acknowledge that "the story is most familiar to us in the version first heard by the ancient Hebrew people, elaborated by Josephus and by the learned authors of the Talmud, and exciting the imagination of some of the early Christian Fathers. There it is the story of the Tower of Babel" (Oakeshott, *On History*, 179–80). Presumably, then, it is the biblical story of the Tower of Babel that Oakeshott is indirectly providing an exegesis of in his two essays.

23. Oakeshott, *Religion, Politics and the Moral Life*, 142–44.

24. Ibid., 142–43.

25. Ibid., 143.

26. Ibid.

27. Ibid., 144.

28. Oakeshott, *On History*, 197.
29. Ibid., 185.
30. Oakeshott, *Rationalism in Politics*, 40.
31. Blumenberg, *Legitimacy of the Modern Age*, part 2.
32. Botwinick, *Skepticism, Belief, and the Modern*, 7–8.

CHAPTER THREE. PHILOSOPHY OF RELIGION AND PHILOSOPHY OF SCIENCE

1. Max Kaddushin, *The Rabbinic Mind* (New York: Bloch, 1972), 301.
2. Oakeshott, *Experience and Its Modes*, 292–93.
3. See the discussion in Botwinick, *Skepticism, Belief, and the Modern*, chap. 4.
4. Oakeshott, *Experience and Its Modes*, 295.
5. I am indebted to Justin Murphy for helping me sharpen the analogy between religion and cooking.
6. Oakeshott, *Rationalism in Politics*, 53.
7. Oakeshott, *Religion, Politics and the Moral Life*, 31.
8. Ibid., 32.
9. Ibid., 33.
10. Ibid., 34.
11. Ibid., 36.
12. Ibid., 37.
13. Ibid.
14. Ibid.
15. Oakeshott, *On Human Conduct*, 85. The only additional dimension this work adds to Oakeshott's previous discussions of religion in "Religion and the World" and *Experience and Its Modes* is the role religion plays in cultivating in us "a reconciliation to the unavoidable dissonances of a human condition," which for Oakeshott does not become "a substitute for remedial effort"—for the persistence in doing—that characterizes the rest of the religious life. (See *On Human Conduct*, 81.)
16. Oakeshott, *Religion, Politics, and the Moral Life*, 38.
17. The phrase "weak messianism" famously comes from Walter Benjamin's "Theses on the Philosophy of History" contained in his book *Illuminations: Essays and Reflections*, trans. Harry Zohn, ed. Hannah Arendt (New York: Schocken Books, 1968), 254.
18. Friedrich Hölderlin, *Sämtliche Werke*, ed. F. Beissner, Stuttgarter Ausgabe vol. 3 (Stuttgart: Kohlhammer, 1957), 81; English translation: W. R. Trask, *Hyperion or the Hermit in Greece* (New York: Ungar, 1965), 93. The quote was cited as chapter epigraph to Robert Bernasconi, "Skepticism in the Face of Philosophy," in *Re-Reading Levinas*, ed. Robert

Bernasconi and Simon Critchley (Bloomington: Indiana University Press, 1991), 149.

19. According to Oakeshott's biographer, Robert Grant, Oakeshott in the course of his two stays in Germany (1923 and 1925) read Hölderlin (as well as Nietzsche). (E-mail from Robert Grant, September 17, 2009.)

20. Oakeshott, *Experience and Its Modes*, 294.

21. Ibid., 308.

22. Ibid.

23. Ibid., 309–10.

24. Ibid., 310.

25. Ibid., 353.

26. Ibid., 350.

27. Ibid., 310–11.

28. Oakeshott, *Rationalism in Politics*, 14, n. 7.

29. Compare the article by James Peterman, "Why Zhuangzi's Real Discovery Is One That Lets Him Stop Doing Philosophy When He Wants to," *Philosophy East and West* 58, 3 (July 2008): 372–94, which also argues for a connection between the skeptical idealism of the Zhuangzi and Wittgenstein's mystically suffused understanding of philosophy as presiding over its own withdrawal. For a reading of Wittgenstein that explores underlying continuities between his later and earlier philosophy, see my chapter on "The Political Implications of Wittgenstein's Skepticism" in Botwinick, *Skepticism and Political Participation*, 43–60.

30. Oakeshott, *Rationalism in Politics*, 417–18.

31. Ibid., n. 2.

32. Oakeshott, *Experience and Its Modes*, 105.

33. Ibid., 315.

34. Oakeshott, *On Human Conduct*, 2.

35. Friedrich Nietzsche, *Beyond Good and Evil*, trans. Walter Kaufmann (New York: Random House/Vintage, 1966), 224.

36. Karl R. Popper, *Conjectures and Refutations: The Growth of Scientific Knowledge* (London: Routledge and Kegan Paul, 1963; 2nd rev. ed., 1965), 317.

37. Oakeshott, *Religion, Politics and the Moral Life*, 139; italics in the original.

38. Ibid., 141–42; italics in original.

39. Popper, *Conjectures and Refutations*, 317.

40. Popper's philosophy of science harbors antirealist elements that are not reflected in the quotations cited in the text. According to Popper, all of the failed disproofs of an experiment do not confirm the hypothesis that served as its basis as belonging to the order of reality. Reality on philosophical grounds remains as distant as ever, even with all the failed

disproofs of theories in the world. The meta-scientific schema of "conjectures and refutations" conceives of science in negative terms. Conceptualizing experimentation as a self-consciously designed effort at refutation (rather than an attempt at corroboration) of a hypothesis means that reality can never be conclusively negotiated. Ibid., 3–65.

41. Oakeshott, *Experience and Its Modes*, 182–83, 191.

42. Wassily Kandinsky, *Circles in a Circle*, is part of the permanent collection of the Philadelphia Museum of Art.

43. Oakeshott, *What Is History?*, 115, n. i.

44. Robert Grant has confirmed for me in a series of e-mails that during the period preceding his writing of his dissertation at Cambridge, Oakeshott had been exposed to an academic cultural atmosphere in Germany that was very hospitable to new philosophical, religious, and mystical currents. Oakeshott studied in Germany during his summer vacations in 1923 and 1925. He attended both Tübingen and Marburg universities, and it is highly likely that he heard both Rudolf Bultmann and Martin Heidegger (who were both in Marburg) lecture. Butlmann's "modernist theology" in all likelihood had an impact on Oakeshott, as my discussion in the text of Oakeshott's philosophy of religion suggests. Heidegger was already an academic "star" when Oakeshott can be presumed to have attended his lectures—and one can easily imagine that as a recent university graduate he was captivated by Heidegger's heady brew of metaphysics coupled with an esoteric hermeneutic that claimed to both decipher and reconfigure the whole Western intellectual past. However, as I argue later in the book, the structure of Oakeshott's skeptical metaphysics taken in conjunction with the ways that he maps its connection with philosophical and political liberalism looms as being in dramatic contrast with Heidegger's phenomenological approach.

Taking a long view on Oakeshott's German academic exposure, one can perhaps say that it came to embody both what attracted him and what repelled him in his intellectual work. The modernist theology sprouted a thousand flowers in Oakeshott's thought—including, preeminently, his willingness to treat skepticism itself as a vehicle for carrying forward his religious aspirations. Heidegger's phenomenology, by contrast, in its futile attempt to overcome skepticism, modeled the pursuit of metaphysical certainty that Oakeshott came to loath—as well as unleashing the pernicious political consequences that he spent much of his career decrying.

Grant also points out that Oakeshott greatly valued the Russian mystics who helped to shape the German cultural milieu when Oakeshott was there in the 1920s. Lev Shestov, Vasily Rozanov, and Nicholas Berdayev were figures he admired. The inner logic of the mysticism that I work out in the text—theorizing its relationship to Oakeshott's skepticism—has its counterparts in the declared preferences and commitments evident in Oakeshott's biography.

45. Oakeshott, *What Is History?*, 115.

46. Spinoza, *Ethics*, I; cited in ibid., 67.

47. Plotinus, *Enneads*, VI.ix.4; cited in Oakeshott, *What Is History?*, 67.

48. Oakeshott, *What Is History?*, 90, n. 64.

49. Ibid., 69; italics in original.

50. Ibid., 104.

51. Ibid., 95.

52. Ibid., 82–83.

53. Ibid., 71.

54. Compare ibid., 87: "All art is mystical."

55. Ibid.

56. Ibid.

57. Ibid., 89, n. 59, and 105.

58. Ibid., 99.

59. Ibid.

60. Ibid., 89.

61. Ibid.

62. Ibid., 95.

63. Ibid., 102, n. 88.

64. Ibid., 74, n. 16.

65. Ibid., 115.

66. Ibid., 67.

67. Nicholas of Cusa, *The Vision of God*, trans. Emma Gurney Salter (New York: Frederick Ungar, 1960), 58–59.

68. Ibid., 59.

69. Anselm, *Basic Writings*, trans. and ed. Thomas Williams (Indianapolis: Hackett, 2007), 76.

70. Ibid., 75.

71. Ibid., 82–83.

72. Ibid., 75.

73. Ibid., 82–83.

74. The *Proslogion* was written in 1077–1078.

75. R. W. Southern, *Saint Anselm: A Portrait in a Landscape* (Cambridge: Cambridge University Press, 1990), 198–202.

76. Ibid., 202–5.

77. Anselm, *Basic Writings*, 237–326; Southern, *Saint Anselm*, 205–27.

78. Cited in Southern, *Saint Anselm*, 210.

79. Anselm, *Basic Writings*, 249.

80. See the discussion of the relationship between negative theology and pantheism in my book *Skepticism, Belief, and the Modern*, 45–46, 48–49.

81. Southern, *Saint Anselm*, 224–25.

82. Nicholas of Cusa, *The Vision of God*, 16–17.

83. Nicholas seems to have adopted (or to have arrived at on his own—or through the influence of more immediate predecessors) the Rabbinic hermeneutical principle encapsulated in the phrase "V'Halachtah B'Drachav." See the discussion below.

84. Ibid., 17.

85. Ibid., 18.

86. Ibid., 24–25.

87. Ibid., 26.

88. See n. 18 above.

89. Nicholas of Cusa, *The Vision of God*, 78.

90. Emmanuel Levinas, *Otherwise than Being or Beyond Essence*, trans. Alphonso Lingis (The Hague: Martinus Nijhoff, 1981), 5. See also Emmanuel Levinas, *Proper Names*, trans. Michael B. Smith. (Stanford: Stanford University Press, 1996), 59.

91. Cited in James C. Edwards, *Ethics without Philosophy* (Tampa: University Presses of Florida, 1982), 11. See the discussion of this passage in Botwinick, *Skepticism and Political Participation*, 50.

92. See my discussion of this topic in "Nowhere to Go but Back, Nowhere to Go but Forward: The Circular Stance of the Law in the Thought of Hans Kelsen," *Telos*, no. 131 (Summer 2005): 132–33.

93. Peter Winch, ed., *Studies in the Philosophy of Wittgenstein* (London: Routledge and Kegan Paul, 1969), 13.

94. Michael Oakeshott, *Hobbes on Civil Association* (Indianapolis: Liberty Fund, 1975), 7–8.

95. M.A.F. Mehren, ed., *Avicenna on Prayer* (Leiden: Brill, 1894), 32–33; cited in Lenn E. Goodman, *Avicenna* (London: Routledge, 1992), 167.

96. See my article "On Avicenna," in *Telos*, no. 139 (Summer 2007): 123–31.

97. Michael Oakeshott, *The Politics of Faith and the Politics of Scepticism*, ed. Timothy Fuller (New Haven: Yale University Press, 1996), 30.

98. Ibid., 31, 37.

99. Ibid., 23–31.

100. Ralph Lerner, *Maimonides' Empire of Light: Popular Enlightenment in an Age of Belief* (Chicago: University of Chicago Press, 2000), 141.

101. Maimonides, "Laws Concerning the Foundations of the Torah," 1:12; Lerner, *Maimonides' Empire of Light*, 143.

102. Deuteronomy 28, 9. The relevant Talmudic and Midrashic sources for the discussion in the text are the following: Babylonian Talmud, Sotah 14a; Ketuboth 111b; Shabbath 133b; Vayikrah Rabbah 25, 3; Sifre, Piska, 49.

103. Deuteronomy 4, 24; 9, 3.

104. Ludwig Wittgenstein, *Philosophical Investigations*, trans. G.E.M. Anscombe, third ed. (New York: Macmillan, 1968), para. 124.

CHAPTER FOUR. POLITICAL THEORY

1. Compare Thomas Nagel, "Review of John Rawls, *A Theory of Justice*," *Philosophical Review* 82 (1973): 227.

2. This is in contrast to practical, ideological liberalism, which stems from Locke.

3. Given Oakeshott's skepticism, which needs to be sustained skeptically rather than dogmatically, the connection between these philosophical imperatives and the structure of liberal society that Oakeshott recommends is merely rhetorical, rather than strictly logical, in character. There are only strong affinities between Oakeshott's philosophical understandings and his vision of the good society. For a thoughtful discussion of Oakeshott's relationship to Hobbes, see Ian Tregenza, *Michael Oakeshott on Hobbes: A Study in the Renewal of Philosophical Ideas* (Exeter: Imprint Academic, 2003).

4. Oakeshott, *On Human Conduct*, 201, 204.

5. Oakeshott, *Rationalism in Politics*, 34.

6. Marx (as one would expect) needs to be dissociated from vulgar Marxism. I attempt to validate this disassociation in my forthcoming book, *Emmanuel Levinas and the Limits to Ethics*.

7. Oakeshott, *Religion, Politics and the Moral Life*, 155.

8. Ibid., 146–47.

9. Ibid., 147–48; italics in original.

10. Ibid., 149.

11. Ibid., 155; italics in original.

12. Thomas Hobbes, *Leviathan*, ed. Michael Oakeshott (Oxford: Basil Blackwell, 1946), chap. 3, p. 17.

13. Eric Voegelin, *The New Science of Politics* (Chicago: University of Chicago Press, 1952); *Science, Politics and Gnosticism* (Chicago: Henry Regnery, 1968). For a good discussion of Oakeshott's and Voegelin's differing views of Hobbes, see Elizabeth Campbell Corey, *Michael Oakeshott on Religion, Aesthetics, and Politics* (Columbia: University of Missouri Press, 2006), 191–210.

14. Oakeshott, *Hobbes on Civil Association*, 7–8.

15. John Rawls, "Two Concepts of Rules," in *Collected Papers*, ed. Samuel Freeman (Cambridge: Harvard University Press, 1999), 20–46.

16. Compare Nelson Goodman, *Fact, Fiction, and Forecast* (Indianapolis: Bobbs-Merrill, 1956), 63–65.

17. Myles Burnyeat, *The Theaetetus of Plato*, trans. M. J. Levett (Indianapolis: Hackett, 1990), 149a–51a, 268–71.

18. Ibid., 155d–e, 277.

19. The connection between "action" and "beginning" is a premier motif in the thought of Hannah Arendt, which I will be discussing shortly in relation to Oakeshott.

CHAPTER FIVE. PHILOSOPHY OF CONVERSATION AND PHILOSOPHY
OF PERSONAL IDENTITY

1. The central texts outlining Oakeshott's philosophy of conversation are "The Voice of Conversation in the Education of Mankind," in *What Is History?*, 187–99, and "The Voice of Poetry in the Conversation of Mankind," in *Rationalism in Politics*, 488–541.

2. Richard Rorty, *Philosophy and the Mirror of Nature* (Princeton: Princeton University Press, 1979), 264, 318, 389–94. Compare also Rorty's later invocations of Oakeshott in his essay "Solidarity or Objectivity?" in his *Objectivity, Relativism and Truth: Philosophical Papers*, vol. 1 (Cambridge: Cambridge University Press, 1991), 21–34, esp. 25.

3. Wendell John Coats, Jr., "Michael Oakeshott as Liberal Theorist," *Canadian Journal of Political Science* 18 (December 1985): 773–87; Paul Franco, "Michael Oakeshott as Liberal Theorist," *Political Theory* 18 (August 1990): 411–36; Paul Franco, *The Political Philosophy of Michael Oakeshott* (New Haven: Yale University Press, 1990).

4. Oakeshott, *Rationalism in Politics*, 490.

5. Oakeshott, *Religion, Politics and the Moral Life*, 144.

6. Ibid., 153.

7. Hannah Arendt, *The Human Condition* (Chicago: University of Chicago Press, 1958), 157.

8. Ibid., 265–66.

9. Cited in Hannah Arendt's introduction to Walter Benjamin, *Illuminations*, trans. Harry Zohn (New York: Schocken Books, 1969), 17. Translation slightly altered.

10. John Rawls, *A Theory of Justice* (Cambridge: Harvard University Press, 1971); Rawls, *Justice as Fairness: A Restatement*, ed. Erin Kelly (Cambridge: Harvard University Press, 2001); Bruce A. Ackerman, *Social Justice in the Liberal State* (New Haven: Yale University Press, 1980).

11. Oakeshott, *On Human Conduct*, 11.

12. Oakeshott, *Religion, Politics and the Moral Life*, 153–54.

13. Oakeshott, *Rationalism in Politics*, 436, citing the novelist Joseph Conrad.

14. Oakeshott, *On Human Conduct*, 154.

15. Oakeshott, *On History*, 108–9.

16. Nicholas of Cusa, *The Vision of God*, 77.

17. David Hume, *A Treatise of Human Nature*, ed. L. A. Selby-Bigge; second ed. ed. P. H. Nidditch (Oxford: Clarendon Press, 1978), 636; italics in original.

18. Ibid., 469–70.

19. Ibid., 415.

20. Ibid., 1–7.

21. Ibid., 24.

22. Gilbert Ryle, *The Concept of Mind* (New York: Barnes and Noble, 1949).

23. D.G.C. Macnabb, *David Hume: His Theory of Knowledge and Morality* (Oxford: Basil Blackwell, 1966), 37.

24. "Going-on" is Michael Oakeshott's terminology in *On Human Conduct* (Oxford: Oxford University Press, 1975).

25. I am indebted to Justin Murphy for pushing this point to the foreground.

26. Hampshire's citation distorts Hume's text, which is quoted accurately in the body of the essay above.

27. Stuart Hampshire, *Justice Is Conflict* (Princeton: Princeton University Press, 2000), xii–xiii.

28. Thomas Hobbes, *Leviathan*, chap. 8, p. 46.

29. Ibid., chap. 4, p. 19.

30. Ibid., 21.

31. Ibid., chap. 1, p. 7.

32. Friedrich Nietzsche, "Truth and Lie in an Extra-Moral Sense," in *The Portable Nietzsche*, trans. and ed. Walter Kaufmann (New York: Penguin Books, 1954), 42–47. The following famous paragraph epitomizes Nietzsche's critique of truth as a value:

> What, then, is truth? A mobile array of metaphors, metonyms, and anthropomorphisms—in short, a sum of human relations, which have been enhanced, transposed, and embellished poetically and rhetorically, and which after long use seems firm, canonical, and obligatory to a people: truths are illusions about which one has forgotten that this is what they are; metaphors which are worn out and without sensuous

power; coins which have lost their pictures and now matter only as metal, no longer as coins. (Ibid., 46–47)

33. Martin Heidegger, *Being and Time*, trans. John Macquarrie and Edward Robinson (New York: Harper and Row, 1962).

34. Hilary Putnam, *Reason, Truth and History* (Cambridge: Cambridge University Press, 1981), xi.

35. Giorgio Agamben, *Homo Sacer: Sovereign Power and Bare Life*, trans. Daniel Heller-Roazen (Stanford: Stanford University Press, 1998), 150.

36. In my reconstruction of phenomenological argument, I am indebted to Leszek Kolakowski, *Husserl and the Search for Certitude* (New Haven: Yale University Press, 1975). As I argue in the text, Kolakowski seems to fit in very well with where Oakeshott stands on the question of phenomenology.

37. Henry Staten, *Wittgenstein and Derrida* (Lincoln: University of Nebraska Press, 1984), 5.

38. Kolakowski, *Husserl and the Search for Certitude*, 23.

39. London School of Economics 3/5. Robert Grant, who was kind enough to make his typed copy of these notes available to me, says that "The folder contains what appear to be three separate sets of notes on Heidegger's *Being and Time*, all undated. They are distinguished in the transcript at Set One, Set Two, and Set Three, in the order in which they were arranged in the folder." No page numbers are listed in the folder. (E-mail from Robert Grant, December 28, 2009.)

40. Agamben, *Homo Sacer*, 150.

41. Frederick Dolan, "Comments on Aryeh Botwinick's *Skepticism, Belief, and the Modern: Maimonides to Nietzsche*," delivered at the "Roundtable on Aryeh Botwinick's *Skepticism, Belief, and the Modern: Maimonides to Nietzsche*," held at the Annual Meeting of the American Political Science Association, Atlanta, Georgia, September 2–5, 1999.

42. Timothy Fuller, ed., *The Voice of Liberal Learning: Michael Oakeshott on Education* (New Haven: Yale University Press, 1989), 95.

43. When Moses initiates the Jewish people into the covenant with God at Mount Sinai (which, in the biblical account, is the scene of original collective Revelation), they respond by saying "We will do and we will listen" (Exodus 24,7). "Listening" is interpreted by the Rabbis as signifying "listening with the inner ear"—which is to say, understanding. The Rabbis comment in the Midrash on this verse that it is wondrous that the Jewish community at Mount Sinai had picked up a secret that was previously reserved only for the angels—namely, that doing precedes understanding.

44. Oakeshott, *Rationalism in Politics*, 363–83.

45. Ibid., 365.
46. Ibid., 364.
47. Ibid., 366.
48. Ibid., 367–68.
49. This reading of Oakeshott suggests a strategy of resolution to a tension that is central to the later writings of Isaiah Berlin. Berlin appears vexed by the ways in which the value-pluralism implicit in liberalism can overwhelm liberalism itself. From the perspective developed in the text that I take to be most faithful to Oakeshott's premises, we can say that a generalized agnostic reading of liberalism renders pluralism (which now encompasses liberalism itself) constitutive of its teaching, rather than adversarial to it. As I have been emphasizing throughout, in Oakeshott we get a metaphysicalized liberalism.
50. Oakeshott, *Rationalism in Politics*, 371.
51. Ibid., 373.
52. Ibid., 374.
53. Ibid., 374, 380.
54. Ibid., 378.
55. Ibid., 380. Economic and social equality can, of course, also be (as I have argued earlier) the considered, rational choices of Oakeshottian individuals who realize that a self-interrogating skepticism increases their menu of choices to include an activist, more egalitarian-inclined state. Oakeshott, I think, is merely arguing that in the twentieth century totalitarian politics has most often been linked with the anti-individualism of the mass-man. This historically valid generalization does not mean that theoretically speaking a participatory, egalitarian politics is not supportable in the light of Oakeshott's skeptical metaphysical postulates. The pursuit of greater political and economic equality can be just as valid an expression of one's freedom as the acceptance of inequality. Philosophy (in accordance with Oakeshott's own premises) cannot resolve this issue. It cannot speak directly to politics.
56. Ibid., 377.
57. Oakeshott, *On Human Conduct*, 70–78.
58. Ibid., 72.
59. Ibid., 73.
60. Ibid.
61. Maimonides, *Guide*, 631.
62. Ibid., 638.
63. Maimonides's nominalism and conventionalism, which are a presupposition and implication, respectively, of his negative theology, serve as additional mediating categories linking his negative theology with his view more generally that our knowledge of the world is "without

foundations." See Botwinick, *Skepticism, Belief and the Modern*, 32–33, 36–39.

64. David Lewis, *Convention: A Philosophical Study* (Cambridge: Harvard University Press, 1969), 88–96.

65. Oakeshott, *Rationalism in Politics*, 344.

66. Hobbes, *Leviathan*, chap. 15, p. 97.

67. Ibid., chap. 14, p. 92.

68. Oakeshott, *Rationalism in Politics*, 340–41.

69. Hobbes, *Leviathan*, chap. 10, p. 60. ⁊

70. Niccolo Machiavelli, *The Prince*, trans. George Bull (New York: Penguin Books, 1961), chap. 10, p. 73.

71. Concerning Machiavelli's "principle of economy," see Sheldon Wolin's classic discussion of it in *Politics and Vision: Continuity and Innovation in Western Political Thought*, expanded ed. (Princeton: Princeton University Press, 2004), 197–200, and my extension of Wolin's interpretive strategy in my book *Skepticism and Political Participation*, 99–103.

72. The Mishnah is the most influential early systematic compilation of the Oral Law of Judaism done by Rabbi Yehudah HaNasi (the Prince) (135–219 C.E.). The phrase "Hillel's Mishnah" refers to a particular statement of Hillel's codified in the Mishnah.

73. The translation comes from *The Complete ArtScroll Siddur*, trans. Nosson Scherman (Brooklyn: Mesorah Publications, 1984), 549.

74. Paradoxes about time are famously associated with St. Augustine. In the *Confessions* (book xi.14), he asks: "What is time? If nobody asks me I know; but if I were desirous to explain it to one that should ask me, plainly I know not." If my reading of Hillel is on target, then Hillel becomes an important precursor for St. Augustine.

75. Oakeshott's politics is utterly congruent with his ethics. Both start out by by assigning priority to the Same—or self—over the Other. Levinas, by contrast, argues in *Totality and Infinity* for an instrumentalized relationship between the public sphere and the private sphere after the manner of classical liberalism, apparently because he believes that it is the role of the state to facilitate maximum fulfillment of individual life programs as these are formulated and pursued in the private sphere. He conceives of ethics, however, as being predicated upon self-immolation in the face of the unlimited demands stemming from the other. The existence of what Levinas calls "the third party"—society—which engenders a whole host of very serious moral dilemmas for his ethical theory because of the radical moral isolation of the self in the face of the imperious demands of the Other, Levinas does not consider in any way as having displaced his ethics. He believes, rather, that it has merely raised the bar on the

strategies of integration between self and Other that ethics will have to mobilize: "The presence of moral dilemmas, ways of characterizing them, and solutions to them—these are not challenges to his [Levinas's] ethical insight but rather part of the process of coping with it and living with our realization of it." Michael L. Morgan, *Discovering Levinas* (Cambridge: Cambridge University Press, 2007), 418.

76. Levinas, *Otherwise than Being*, 5–9; Emmanuel Levinas, *Totality and Infinity: An Essay on Exteriority*, trans. Alphonso Lingis (Pittsburgh: Duquesne University Press, 1969), 33–52. The vocabulary of "infinity" is evocative of reconciliation with categories such as God and the Other whose reality and/or priority reason is able to call into question.

77. "This breakup of identity, this changing of being into signification, that is, into substitution, is the subject's subjectivity, or its subjection to everything, its susceptibility, its vulnerability, that is, its sensibility." Levinas, *Otherwise than Being*, 14.

78. Jean-Jacques Rousseau, *The Second Discourse*, in *The First and Second Discourses*, ed. Roger D. Masters (New York: St. Martin's Press, 1964), 78–228.

79. Friedrich Nietzsche, *Beyond Good and Evil*, trans. Walter Kaufmann (New York: Vintage Books, 1966), 52.

80. Friedrich Nietzsche, *Twilight of the Idols*, in *The Portable Nietzsche*, 500.

81. Compare Nietzsche, *Beyond Good and Evil*, 50: "Whatever is profound loves masks; what is most profound even hates image and parable."

CHAPTER SIX. PHILOSOPHY OF LAW AND PHILOSOPHY OF HISTORY

1. Michael Oakeshott, "The Concept of a Philosophical Jurisprudence," *Politica* 3 (1938): 204.

2. Oakeshott, *On History*, 126–27.

3. Oakeshott, *On Human Conduct*, 2.

4. Oakeshott, *Experience and Its Modes*, 191.

5. Oakeshott, "The Concept of a Philosophical Jurisprudence," 207.

6. Oakeshott, *On History*, 161.

7. Ibid., 164.

8. Ibid., 167.

9. Ibid., 176.

10. Ibid., 156.

11. Oakeshott, "The Concept of a Philosophical Jurisprudence," 204.

12. Oakeshott, *On History*, 156.

13. Ibid., 151.

14. Oakeshott, "The Concept of a Philosophical Jurisprudence," 206.

15. Oakeshott, *On History*, 162–63; Carl Schmitt, *Political Theology: Four Chapters on the Concept of Sovereignty*, trans. George Schwab (Cambridge: MIT Press, 1985).

16. Agamben, *Homo Sacer*, 15.

17. The phrase "the prison-house of language" comes from Nietzsche: "We have to cease to think if we refuse to do it in the prison-house of language; for we cannot reach further than the doubt which asks whether the limit we see is really a limit." This quotation serves as the epigraph for Frederic Jameson, *The Prison-House of Language: A Critical Account of Structuralism and Russian Formalism* (Princeton: Princeton University Press, 1972).

18. W. V. Quine, *The Ways of Paradox and Other Essays* (New York: Random House, 1966), 8.

19. Bertrand Russell, *The Principles of Mathematics* (London: Routledge, 1903), 527–28.

20. Cited in *New York Times*, November 15, 2000, E8.

21. Karl Mannheim, *Ideology and Utopia: An Introduction to the Sociology of Knowledge*, trans. Louis Wirth and Edward Shils (New York: Harcourt, Brace, and World, 1936), 56.

22. Clifford Geertz, *The Interpretation of Cultures* (New York: Basic Books, 1973), 194–96.

23. This is not to gainsay in any way that Nazism constitutes a monstrous pathology even if its inspiring impulses might have included deep-seated metaphysical anxieties.

24. The phrase is Wilfrid Sellars's in his classic essay, "Empiricism and the Philosophy of Mind," in *Minnesota Studies in the Philosophy of Science*, vol. 1: *The Foundations of Science and the Concepts of Psychology and Psychoanalysis*, ed. Herbert Feigl and Michael Scriven (Minneapolis: University of Minnesota Press, 1956), 253–329.

25. Oakeshott, *On History*, 36.

26. Ibid., 25–26, n. 8.

27. Ibid., 24–25.

28. Oakeshott, "The Concept of a Philosophical Jurisprudence," 204.

29. Hans-Georg Gadamer, *Truth and Method*, trans. and ed. Garrett Barden and John Cumming (New York: Seabury Press, 1975).

30. Oakeshott, *On History*, 36.

31. Ibid., 75–76.

32. This emphasis is also in line with that strand in Oakeshott's metaphysics and theory of human nature that assigns primacy to doing over thinking.

33. Ibid., 73.

34. Ibid., 21.
35. Ibid., 31.
36. Ibid., 41–43.
37. Ibid., 54.
38. Ibid., 56.
39. Ibid., 121, 123.
40. Friedrich Nietzsche, *On the Advantage and Disadvantage of History for Life*, trans. Peter Preuss (Indianapolis: Hackett, 1980), 21. "Antiquarian history itself degenerates the moment that the fresh life of the present no longer animates and inspires it." Ibid.
41. Friedrich Nietzsche, *On the Genealogy of Morals and Ecce Homo*, trans. and ed. Walter Kaufmann (New York: Vintage Books, 1967), 151; italics in original.
42. I am indebted to Justin Murphy for sharpening this connection for me.

Index

ethics of, 186–90; and political liberalism, 190–91; on the saying and the said, 100; on totality and infinity, 65; on underdetermination, 188

liberalism: Berlin on, 235-36n49; classical, 237n75; and democracy, 166; and fascism, 42; and generalized agnosticism, 235-36n49; ideological, 232n2; and individualism, 125, 141–42; interest-balancing and rule-oriented, 199; metaphysicalized, 118–19, 121, 124, 235–36n49; modern, 124; and moral psychology, 141; and mysticism, 117–18, 166; and negative theology, 123–24; and neutrality, 117–18, 166, 171; Oakeshott's, 11, 38, 118, 134; and pluralism, 171, 235–36n49; political, 141, 171, 190–91, 205, 229n44; and the political, 118; and political structure, 124, 139; and process-oriented politics, 125, 166; and skepticism, 139; and the social contract theory, 156

liberty. *See* freedom

Lichtenberg, G. C., 32

Locke, John, 155, 232n2

logics, multivalued, 67

Mach, Ernst, 157

Machiavelli, Niccolò, 135, 217; on giving and receiving, 180–81

Macnabb, David, 146–47

Maimonides, Moses, 105, 123; on arbitrariness and generosity, 176–77; and the conceptualization of God in *Hilchot Yesodei HaTorah*, 110–112, 114; ethical theorizing of, 176–80; on negative theology, 112–16, 176, 236n63

Maine, Sir Henry, 169

majority rule and minority rights, 166

Mannheim, Karl, 202, 204, 208–9

Marcion of Sinope, 34, 46

Marx, Karl, 232n6; and economic determinism, 121; and Hegelian

dialectic, 137; and the politicization of knowledge, 154–55

Meno, 74

metaphysical radical, 134

middle, the, 222

Mill, John Stuart, 155

modernity, 15, 31, 33, 36–37, 42, 105, 109–10, 120, 124, 137, 169–70, 172, 187, 198, 204, 229n44

modes of experience, 12–14, 49–52, 56, 58–59

Montaigne, Michel de, 27

morality, 126, 167, 193, 237n75; as custom, habit, and tradition, 15–16, 29–31, 33, 42–43, 45–46, 97; discourse of, 198; and freedom, 170; and ideology, 46; and the individual, 170; and perfection of another, 170; political, 173; rationalism in, 45; rule-centered, 125–26; and self-restraint, 166

Moses, 235n43

mysticism, 21, 65, 229n44; and asceticism, 107–9; and certainty, 96; in the *Chuang Tzu*, 62–63; circular arguments in, 75–76, 78; and conversation, 132; as creation, 76; and the diurnal, 105; on a Divine beginning, 96; and ethics, 183; of everyday life, 8–11, 23, 56, 60, 82–83, 96–97, 103, 105–6, 116–117, 196–97, 208, 212, 222; extraordinary, 108–9; generalized, 51; and generalized agnosticism, 31, 45, 54, 60, 105; and God, 25–26, 51, 80–83, 98–99, 109, 115; and individuality, 141; inner logic of, 229-30n44; on intellect and intuition, 73; and the is-ought distinction, 143–46; and liberalism, 117–18, 166; and the limitations of reason, 108; and logic, 76; and negative theology, 48, 56, 63, 76, 83–84, 94–96, 99; and neutrality, 166; Nicholas of Cusa on, 80–81; in Oakeshott's thought, 78, 105–6, 221–22; in Oakeshott's view of religion,

mysticism (*cont'd*)
51, 57; a performative contradiction of, 104; and philosophical jurisprudence, 197–88; and philosophical and theological arguments, 77; and philosophy, 27; and philosophy of history, 197, 211–12, 217; and poetry, 69, 75–76; of the Rabbis, 49, 104–7; and reality, 22; and the reallocation of God, 79; and redemption, 212; Russian, 229n44; and self-propulsion, 170; and silence, 217; and skepticism, 2–4, 25–26, 31, 83–84, 99–101, 106–7, 183, 196, 217; and tacit knowledge, 10; and tradition, 56; and truth, 79, 96; and wholeness, 217; Wittgenstein on, 24, 26, 96–97, 100–105, 115–16, 228n29
Myth of the Given, 205

Nazism, 36, 202, 204–5, 239n23
necessity, 50, 85, 135–35, 138, 178, 185 204–5
negative theology, 26, 42, 47–48, 60, 65, 196; and agnosticism, 56; Augustine influence on, 46; and authority, 140; Avicenna on, 108; as backdrop to Anselm's ontological argument, 93; and contingency, 163; defined, 33–34; and generalized agnosticism, 112; and Gnosticism, 35; and God's nature, 52–54, 79, 117, 176, 203, 206–7; and Hobbes, 124–25; and the intellectual universe, 44; and liberalism, 123–24; Maimonides on, 112–116, 176, 236n63; and the modern individual, 172; and monotheism, 203; and mysticism, 48, 56, 63, 76, 83–84, 94–96, 99; and Nicholas of Cusa, 141; paradox of, 202–3, 206–7; paradoxes in, 77; and the self, 172; and skeptical idealism, 34; and skepticism, 77, 79, 83–84, 95–96, 99, 107–8, 116, 123; and the Tower of Babel, 46; and weak messianism, 54

neutrality, 204; and generalized agnosticism, 171; and the good, 171; in a liberal society, 117–18, 166, 171; and mysticism, 166; and religion, 118; and truth, 166, 171
Nicholas of Cusa: on eternity and this world, 98; on free will and human relationships with God, 95–96, 98; on God and infinity, 141; on God and mysticism, 80–81, 94, 98–100; on negative theology, 141; on theory and practice, 97; on V'Halachtah B'Drachav, 231n83
Nietzsche, Friedrich, 210, 238n81; and generalized agnosticism, 192; on interpretation and life, 221; on interpretation and mummification, 220–21; and language, 238-39n17; on the natural and the sensual, 137; on the practical and historical past, 218, 220; on *ressentiment*, 174; on the self, 192–93; on subjectivity and objectivity, 65; on truth, 153, 156, 158, 163, 221, 234n32

Old and New Testaments, 88
ontological argument, 84–90
Oral and Written Law, 49

pantheism, 26, 93
paradox, 22–23; regarding access to God, 81–82; affirmation of, 205; of belief in God, 108; of creation and withdraw, 44; of difference, 40; of God's firstness, 110–11; of God's wholeness, 92–93; of law, 200; Liar, 202–3, 208; Mannheim's, 202, 204, 208–9; of the mystical and the diurnal, 105; of the mystical and the normal, 104–5; of negative theology, 77, 202–3, 206–7; in Oakeshott's style, 221–22; in Oakeshott's thought, 14, 29, 60; of reflexivity, 66–67, 83; Russell's, 202–3, 208; of the self, 142–45, 176; skeptical, 3, 9, 116, 153, 157, 202–3, 207; of sover-